THE ULTIMATE GUIDE TO
MUSCLE CARS

THE ULTIMATE GUIDE TO
MUSCLE CARS

Jim Glastonbury

CHARTWELL
BOOKS, INC.

Published in 2010 by
CHARTWELL BOOKS, INC
A division of BOOK SALES, INC.
276 Fifth Avenue Suite 206
New York, NY 10001
USA

ISBN-13: 978-0-7858-2694-1
ISBN-10: 0-7858-2694-7

Printed in China

Photographic acknowledgements for revised
edition.
Page 52: Wikimedia Creative
Commons/Morven.
Page 53: Flickr Creative Commons/Jakob
Montrasio.
Page 92/93: By kind courtesy of Mustang.
Page 120: Flickr Creative Commons/Chad
Kainz.
Page 121: Flickr Creative Commons/Nexeus
Fatale.
Page 192/193: Courtesy kind of Hemi
Engines.
Page 374: Flickr Creative Commons/Flynbyu.
Page 375: Flickr Creative Commons/Chad
Kainz.
Photo credits continued page 441.

CONTENTS

W hat is a muscle car? First of all, let us eliminate what it is not: it is not a piece of Italian exotica, a Ferrari or a Lamborghini, cars which are just too complex and too specialized; nor is it a German Porsche, which is too efficient and too clever by half; nor yet a classic British sports car, a Morgan, TVR or Jaguar, which could never be regarded as fitting the bill. Sports cars, by and large, are not muscle cars, with two notable exceptions: the legendary AC Cobra of the 1960s, and the Dodge Viper of the 1990s. These followed the muscle car creed of back-to-basics raw power.

In effect, muscle cars always were, and always will be, a quintessentially North American phenomenon. The basic concept is something like this: take a mid-sized American sedan, nothing complex, upmarket or fancy, in fact the sort of car one would use to collect the groceries in any American town on any day of the week; add the biggest, raunchiest V8 that it is possible to squeeze under the hood; and there it is.

The muscle car concept really is as simple as that. Moreover, the young men who desired these cars, and most of them were young and men, though that would change, were not interested in technical sophistication, nor handling finesse, nor even top speed. Cubic inches, horsepower and acceleration rates were the only figures that

counted. Muscle cars were loud, proud and in your face, and did not pretend to be anything else. They might have been simple, even crude, but for roaring, pumping, tyre-smoking standing starts, they were the business. To an American youth culture raised on drag racing, red-light street racing and hot-rodding, they were irresistible.

The 'Big Three' manufacturers soon woke to this fact, and joined the power race to offer more cubic inches, more horsepower, and fewer seconds over the standing quarter. For a few short years, between 1965 and 1970, it seemed as though the race would never end. The result was often more power than the car (and the driver) could handle safely, but then part of the attraction was making a four-seater sedan go faster than it was ever intended.

But the situation could not last. The combination of high horsepower in the hands of young drivers saw accident rates soar, and insurance premiums followed suit. Moreover, the climate of the times was changing, with a whole raft of safety and emissions legislation coming into force in the late 1960s and early 1970s. So even before the first oil crisis made itself felt, the first-generation muscle cars were already on their way out. By the 1980s, however, they were beginning to creep back, first with turbocharged fours, then V8s; by the 1990s, muscle cars were back with a vengeance: more 'high-tech' than before, even sophisticated, with ABS, electronic fuel injection and multi-valve engines. Manufacturers were by now talking virtuously about catalytic converters and air bags, but the truth was that performance was selling once again. Anti-social? Yes. Irresponsible? Of course. But one thing was certain, the muscle car was back.

LEFT
The AC Cobra, the English muscle car.

OPPOSITE
A Dodge Viper, the modern muscle car.

7

Chapter One
FORERUNNERS:
The Pre-Muscle Cars

Conventional wisdom has it that the Pontiac GTO was the first true muscle car. And it was, in the sense that it used a relatively large V8 engine crammed into an intermediate bodyshell, with performance the prime aim. But there had been plenty of high-performance V8s well before the GTO came along. They did not come into the same big engine/small car category, but performance was certainly part of their appeal. As to when such vehicles emerged from the primeval slime of automotive development, it is a case of how far back one is prepared to go.

Take the Ford flathead V8 of 1932. It may have been small, slow and feeble by the standards of the 1960s, but for its time it also offered good performance at a low price. It formed the backbone of the U.S.A.'s early drag-racing movement, and a whole generation of hot-rodders grew up with it, coaxing ever higher speeds from Ford's first V8, which after all, is what defines a muscle car.

Then there was the Oldsmobile 88 of 17 years later. Once peace had been restored following World War II, most manufacturers made do with rehashes of early 1940s models, but the 'Rocket V8' was the first of

a new generation. The name alone indicated where Olds was heading: performance had by now become a key selling point, and the Rocket made an Oldsmobile the hottest American car of the early 1950s. With overhead valves, the Rocket could rev harder and faster than any flathead, and was so successful that Olds dropped its other engines and sold nothing but V8s until 1964.

Other manufacturers took note and swiftly introduced their own overhead-valve V8s, each attempting to outdo the other on sheer horsepower. Chevrolet's small-block motor, nicknamed 'the hot one', was produced in a 265-cu in (4.34-litre) 'Power Pack' version in 1955, with a four-barrel carburettor, dual exhaust and 180hp (134kW). That same year, Pontiac unveiled its own new V8, overhead-valve, of course, and in 1957 introduced the famous 'Tri-Power' option: three two-barrel carburettors. Some Bonnevilles were given fuel injection

in 1958 and the famous Super Duty parts began to appear the year after that.

Oldsmobile had no intention of being left behind, and added a triple-carburettor set-up to the Rocket V8 in 1957, coaxing 300hp (224kW) from the 371-cu in (6.08-litre) J2 version. Chrysler had already beaten many of them to it with the 1951 'Firepower' V8, the first Hemi. Even with 180hp (134kW), its style was cramped by the heavy Saratoga into which Chrysler chose to fit it, but the Hemi's day would come. A foretaste of that appeared with the Dodge 'Red Ram' Hemi in 1955, with 193hp (144kW) from 270 cu in (4.42 litres) and the D-500 (more cubes, more horsepower) in the following year. Ford, apart from offering supercharged Thunderbirds for a while, seemed somewhat left out, which is rather ironic when one remembers that it was Ford's original flathead that started the

whole thing off. It was not until go-ahead Lee Iacocca took over as general manager that Ford regained its performance image.

But Ford (and AMC) was the exception. A power race had already begun long before the muscle car boom of the mid/late-1960s. By 1964, when the GTO was unveiled, muscular V8s of over 400 cu in (6.55 litres) were commonplace. Perhaps we should take a look at some of these 'pre-muscle' muscle cars.

ABOVE
Big but brawny, the Ford Galaxie.

LEFT
The ancestor of the muscle car, the Ford V8 Coupé.

OPPOSITE
Pontiac GTO, 'The Judge'.

The 442 – Oldsmobile's response to the GTO – was a hot Cutlass. The numbers stood for four-barrel carburation, four-on-the-floor transmission and two dual exhausts. For many they became as evocative as 'Z28' or even 'GTO'. This is a 1968 example, when the 442 dropped its Cutlass badge and became a model in its own right.

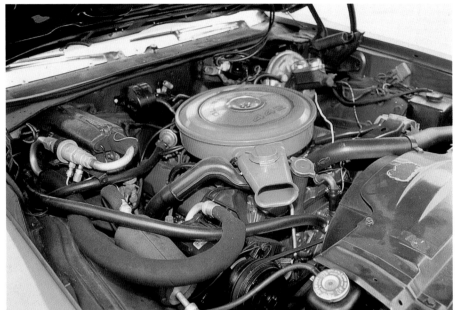

GENERAL MOTORS

Take Chevrolet's Impala, a prime candidate for a muscular beef-up, having been downsized in 1961; this was a case of less weight equalling more performance, particularly with a big V8 under the bonnet. The 1970s are usually remembered as the U.S.A.'s downsizing era, when cars became smaller and milder to suit an age of expensive gas. But the same thing had happened a decade and a half earlier, with big cars losing some of their surplus size and poundage, plus new U.S.-built compacts like the Ford Falcon and Chevrolet's own Nova appearing on the scene.

The 1961 downsized Impala was therefore a classic example, still available with large and decidedly meaty V8s, as long as one was prepared to lay down the extra dollars. There were two of them: the 348-cu in (5.7-litre) Turbo Thrust came in hot 340-hp or hotter 360-hp (single four-barrel or three two-barrel carburettors respectively). If that was not quick enough, there was the legendary 409 Turbo-Fire, the V8 so revered by young drivers that the Beach Boys wrote a song about it. This came with 360-hp (268.4-kW) single four-barrel, 380-hp (283-kW) three two-barrel or full 409-hp (305-kW) twin four-barrel versions, the most powerful of which would bump the price up by around $500. All had a high 11.25:1 compression, but a close-ratio four-speed transmission cost another $188. Even with the base 360-hp 409, the Impala two-door hardtop was convincingly quick, achieving 60mph (96.5km/h) in 7.8 seconds and turning in a quarter-mile time of 15.8 seconds. With the full-power 409, a Bel Air coupé made that 12.83 seconds; go for the aerodynamic bubble-top body in 1962, and it could hit an indicated 150mph (241km/h). By any standards, a 409-powered Chevrolet was fast.

If anyone remained unconvinced about the Impala's sporting aspirations, an SS package could be added by a local dealer. This could include power steering and brakes, heavy-duty springs and shocks, sintered metal brake linings, 8.00 x 14 whitewalls, 7,000-rpm tachometer and various 'SS' badges. But maybe Impala buyers were not hot-car types, as only 456 of them ordered the SS package in 1961, and of those, a mere 142 paid extra for the 409. But that hardly matters, as in every other way the Impala 409 (especially with the flashy SS parts) qualifies as a pre-muscle muscle car. By 1962, the SS package had degenerated

ABOVE
Chevrolet Impala SS421.

RIGHT
1965 Chevrolet Corvette Sting Ray.

into a badges-only option, so one could look the part even with a basic six-cylinder Impala. But if one could afford it, the 409 was still there to give tyre-smoking performance in the more conservative 1962 Impala.

If the downsized Impala represented an embryo muscle car, then the compact Chevrolet II Nova took this idea to its logical conclusion. The Nova was Chevrolet's answer to home-built compacts like the Ford Falcon and Chrysler Valiant/Lancer, not to mention imported Volvos and Rovers. After the avant-garde Corvair, Chevrolet seemed determined to make its new compact as unthreatening as possible; and so it was, with a 90-hp (67-kW) four-cylinder base

engine or 120-hp (89.5-kW) six. However, if one examined the options list hard enough, one would find that it was possible to have a choice of Corvette V8s installed by one's local dealer! The Nova had been designed to take both 283-cu in (4.6-litre) and 327-cu in (5.3-litre) V8s already, so no major surgery was involved. All the Nova V8s were the bigger motor, rated at 250, 300, 340 or 360hp (186.5, 224, 253.5 or 26.5kW).

That ultimate fuel-injected motor transformed the quiet, sensible Nova into a true muscle car, which could top 130mph (209km/h) and reach 60mph (96.5km/h) in a little over 7 seconds. To try to tame this performance, stiffer front springs were fitted to support the much heavier engine, with a front anti-roll bar, rear traction arms and metallic brake linings. Almost everything else was standard, so a hard-driven Nova V8 would have been quite a handful, though a lot of fun.

It was not cheap though. The basic car cost just $2,200, and a dealer-fitted V8 could inflate that price by 50 per cent, even before labour costs. But for lovers of subtlety, this was the one. There was nothing to indicate that the work had been done – no badges, special wheels or wide tyres. Only those who really knew their Novas would notice the dual exhaust tailpipes and 200-mph (322-km/h) speedometer. In fact, the whole option was distinctly low-key: a sporty SS package was offered in 1963, including bucket seats and extra chrome, but with no real performance aids. In the advertisement for

ABOVE LEFT
An early 1960s customized Corvette.

LEFT
A downsized Nova SS.

THIS PAGE
It may look innocuous, but this 1966 Chevy II has the L79SS race package. All the serious changes are under the skin.

OPPOSITE
A Chevrolet Bel Air, with the near-legendary 409-ci (6.7-litre) V8. So legendary, in fact, that the Beach Boys wrote a song about it.

the Chevrolet II Super Sports, Chevrolet didn't even mention the V8. Like the Nova itself, it seems they wanted to keep things quiet.

The same could not be said for the Corvette. America's only true two-seater sports car of the time, the Corvette is not always regarded as a muscle car: the classic muscle cars of the 1960s are all saloons or coupés. A Mustang might look like a sports car, but really it was a 2+2 coupé. Whether one includes the Corvette as part of the classic muscle car era or not, there is no denying that it was one of the fastest road cars one could buy in the early 1960s. In 1962, with Rochester fuel injection on the 327-cu in (5.3-litre) small-block V8, it had a better power to weight ratio than anything else, and could sprint to 60mph (96.5km/h) in less than 6 seconds. It also boasted 360hp (268.5kW), which was sky-high at the time.

Many Corvettes were raced, and the options list reflected that, with exotic items like an aluminium-cased transmission and large 24-gal (109-litre) fuel tank alongside the usual four-speed manual gearbox and sintered brake linings. There was all-new bodywork in 1963, for the Sting Ray Corvette, but the racing options were still there. Opt for the Z06 package, and one received the fuel-injected 327, a massive 36.5-gal (166-litre) tank, heavy-duty brakes and suspension, plus knock-off wheels. That big tank enabled the Corvette to compete in endurance races, though only 60 cars were actually fitted with it. The stylish-looking cast aluminium wheels were a mixed blessing: they were porous, and allowed air to leak out between rim and tyre. Those heavy-duty brakes were interesting too. Chevrolet had still not fitted new-fangled discs, making the drums as effective as possible instead: sintered metallic linings, power assistance, dual circuits and Ram Air

cooling. It sounded impressive, but the drum brake's sports car days were nearly over.

For 1964, there was cleaned up styling and more power, though all Corvettes had the small-block 327: the big-block 396 did not appear until the following year. In base form, the 327 gave 250hp (186.5kW) at 4,400rpm. Next up was the 300-hp (224-kW) L75 version, with Carter aluminium four-barrel carburettor. The 365-hp (272-kW) L76 added mechanical lifters, hotter camshaft and Holley carburettor, plus an 11.0:1 compression. However, the ultimate

Corvette still had fuel injection. Coded as L84 in Chevrolet-speak, the Ram-Jet injection motor produced 375hp (279.5kW) at 6,200rpm and 350lb ft (474.6Nm) at 4,400rpm, enough for 0–100mph (161km/h) in 14.7 seconds and a top speed of 138mph (222km/h). A Corvette may not have been considered a 'pure' muscle car, but it was certainly fast enough to qualify.

Meanwhile, another General Motors division was producing its own pre-muscle muscle cars. The Super Duty Pontiacs were, if truth be told, racing cars. Sure, they had

seats, and lights and a windshield wiper, and at a pinch they could be used on the road. But only if one were rich enough to buy one for personal use, and did not mind the stripped-out, lightweight interior. They remain a crucial part of muscle car history, however, paving the way for the GTO, the

ABOVE
Chevy Nova SS coupé.

OPPOSITE
Pre-Sting Ray Corvette.

car that arguably started it all. The Super Dutys took Pontiac's staid image by the scruff of the neck, picked it up and turned it around. By the time the GTO came along in 1964, the thought of a hot Pontiac was not only credible but desirable. Jim Wangers was a Pontiac promotions man who drag raced in his spare time. He and a group of keen young divisional engineers were instrumental in pushing the Super Duty options: after GM's racing ban in 1963, these same men turned to the next best thing, a hot Pontiac for the street. That was the GTO.

By their nature, the Super Duty Pontiacs were limited-production specials. Of all Pontiac models, Catalinas were the favourites, being the smallest and lightest of the full-sized Pontiacs. In 1962–63 these reached a nadir of development, before the GM racing ban called a halt. For 1961 they used the 389-cu in (6.3-litre) Super Duty, but the threat of Chevrolet's 409 led to the 421-cu in (6.9-litre) V8 in 1962. This became the ultimate Super Duty engine, strengthened with forged pistons and four-bolt main-bearing caps. It needed to be strong, as the unofficial power output was over 500hp (373kW), with twin Carter four-barrel carburettors. In the following year, a McKellar solid-lifter camshaft was added, with dual-valve springs, a transistorized ignition and 12.5:1 or 13.0:1 compression: in top tune, that equated to 540–550hp (402.5–410kW).

To maximize the effect, Super Duty Pontiacs came radically lightened, with lightweight front ends and aluminium bumper brackets, boot lids and radiator supports. As an option, one could junk the standard windows in favour of dealer-fitted Plexiglas. Most radical of all were the 'Swiss Cheese' Catalinas, with large holes drilled in their chassis. Weight was cut to

just 3,325lb (1508kg), but they were considered too radical for Super Stock drag racing, and were moved up to the new Factory Experimental class. Arnie Beswick drag raced one of these in 1963, managing a best quarter-mile of 11.91 seconds. Today, a Swiss Cheese with documented racing history would fetch over $100,000.

Of course, not all performance Catalinas were so exotic. By 1964, the 2+2 was being marketed as a sort of giant five-seat sports car '…as fine as you want – or as fierce'. Top engine was a 370-hp (276-kW) version of the 421HO V8, which came with Tri-Power (three two-barrel carburettors) and 460lb ft (623.8Nm) at 3,800rpm. It also weighed 4,000lb (1814kg), so the latest Catalina was no Super Duty, but with a quarter-mile time of 16.2 seconds it did qualify as a sort of muscle car, even if it was the boulevard type.

CHRYSLER

Chrysler's part in the muscle car story centres around the Hemi, that efficient, deep-breathing V8 that came to dominate the drag strip and NASCAR in the 1960s. But its origins lay much further back, in the 1951 Firepower V8. This motor's hemispherical combustion chambers allowed not only good breathing, but also a high compression plus plenty of space for big ports and valves. All well and good, except that the first 331-cu in (5.4-litre) Hemis were at a disadvantage, housed in heavy Saratoga saloons, and their performancefailed to set new records.

This all changed in 1955, when Chrysler unveiled the C300. With power increased dramatically to 300hp (224kW), hence the name, this first of the famous 'letter cars' set a new standard in performance. In fact, some people consider

that this, not the Pontiac GTO, was the first true muscle car. Not that it was a stripped-down special. The letter cars were never boy racer specials, but luxurious two-door saloons – spacious, elegant and well-appointed – but with blistering performance. Aimed at the top end of the market, Chrysler letter cars were expensive and exclusive, a fact reflected in a trickle of sales: in its best year, just over 3,600 were sold.

Some of the gloss was lost in 1959 when the Hemi was dropped in favour of Chrysler's new wedge-head V8, but the loss was more than regained the following year, when the 413-cu in (6.7-litre) V8 was given Ram-Air induction for the 300-F. A hotter camshaft, low back-pressure exhaust, twin four-barrel carburettors, freer-flowing air cleaner and special distributor and plugs helped push the power up to 375hp

BELOW
1955 Chrysler 300 grille.

OPPOSITE
ABOVE: Two-door 1955 Chrysler 300.

BELOW LEFT: Fin detail on Chrysler's muscle sedan.

ABOVE RIGHT: 1957 twin-headlamped 300.

(279.5kW). That was with the standard 30-in (76.2-cm) long stacks, which gave tremendous mid-range torque: it peaked at 2,800rpm, at which the torque was 495lb ft (671.2Nm). But performance suffered at higher revs, so just 15 cars were built with 15-in (38.1-cm) rams, an $800 option that also brought a four-speed manual gearbox, and 400hp (298kW). In truth, the 400-hp option was really intended for Daytona, but it paid off, with Greg Zigler setting up a Flying Mile record in a 300-F at 144.9mph (233.2km/h).

The same luxury-performance package continued as the 300-G in 1961, still with 375-hp long-ram and 400-hp short-ram options. Standard transmission was the Torquflite automatic, which in reality gave away nothing in acceleration to the three-speed manual (the four-speed had been dropped). Just to illustrate how luxurious the 300-G was, the options included air conditioning, remote control mirrors, a six-

way power seat and power door locks. An electric clock and front and rear centre armrests were standard.

For 1962, there were four bucket seats in tan leather, with alternative colours on special order. By this time, the 300 (300-H now) had been downsized slightly, sharing parts with the cheaper Newport. The upside was 300lb (136kg) trimmed off the weight and acceleration as quick as the original Hemi 300s. If that was not enough, a special engine option was announced in June. Overboring the 413 brought 226 cu in (6.9 litres) and a claimed 421hp at 5,400rpm on short-ram intakes.

Chrysler's downsizing did not last long, and for 1963 the 300-J was back up to full size, now with a 122-in (3.1-m) wheelbase and weighing over 4,400lb (1996kg). To compensate, the standard 413 V8 was squeezed up to 390hp (291kW) at 4,800rpm, enough for a top speed of 142mph (228.5km/h). The return of a convertible option, and lower prices (though it was still not cheap at over $4,500 for the open-top) made the following year's 300-K sell just over 3,000 hardtops and 625 convertibles. It was hardly Mustang numbers, but this was the best-selling letter car of all. In its final year, the 300-L of 1965 had grown more flab, now up to 4,660lb (2114kg), and the 0–60 mph (0–96.5km/h) time was now 8.8 seconds, a full second slower than the Hemi 300s. Still, it was mighty quick for such a big, heavy automobile, especially in 1965.

Remember that short-lived 426-cu in (6.98-litre) option for the 300? It lived on as the Max Wedge 426 in 1963, and thrived, as it fitted neatly into the new 427-cu in (7.0-litre) capacity limit for both NHRA Super Stock drag racing and NASCAR. In 1963, in 'Stage II' form, it was very different from that offered as an option in the Chrysler 300-H. It was a pure racing engine, with three power options: the single four-barrel carburettor version produced 400hp (298kW) and was intended for stock car racing, which specified a single carburettor; twin four-barrels and an 11.0:1 compression allowed 415hp (309.5kW) at 5,600rpm; finally, a 13.5:1 compression and twin carburettors brought 425hp (317kW). On paper, at least, this final development of the Max Wedge put out as much power as the second-generation Hemi which succeeded it.

FORD

Ford came late to the performance boom of the late 1950s: Chevrolet had its 409 and Chrysler its Hemi, but Ford's hottest was the 352-cu in (5.77-litre) 300-hp (224-kW) V8. That would have been impressive in 1955, but it was no longer so four years later. It is surprising, given Ford's commitment to 'Total Performance' in the 1960s, and the string of successes in all

forms of motor sport which followed. It really stemmed from the leadership of Robert McNamara, the Ford chief of the late 1950s, who saw cars as transportation rather than a source of excitement. That, and the company's strict adherence to the ban of the Automobile Manufacturers Association (AMA) on factory-sponsored racing. Chrysler and GM paid lip-service to the ban, but carried on helping private teams via the back door. But Ford followed it to the letter, and this was reflected in the cars it built for the road. Compare Ford and GM's range of performance V8s in the late 1950s: there is no clearer illustration of the way in which racing stimulated the production of hot cars for the road.

But from 1959, Ford's strict adherence to the rules began to relax. These things often come in cycles (remember that Ford had been first with a mass-production V8 in the 1930s) and in 1959 there were signs of a thaw, and of the realization that winning races really could help showroom sales.

The first sign came late in 1959, when a new 360-hp (268-kW) version of the 352-cu in (5.77-litre) motor was announced. Named 'Thunderbird Super', 'Interceptor' or 'Super Interceptor', it was fitted with single Holley four-barrel, solid-valve lifters, 10.6:1 compression and aluminium intake manifold. To cope with the extra power, the crank was of nodular cast iron. However, it was clearly not intended as an out-and-out

announced it was also getting back into NHRA drag racing. There was no doubt about it, Ford was back in the performance business.

But what did all this mean for ordinary drivers? The answer is simple: bigger engines, more power, and more speed. For 1961, a new 390-cu in (6.39-litre) version of the V8 was unveiled, with 4.05-in (102.9-mm) bore and 3.78-in (96-mm) stroke. Offered in the Galaxie Starliner, it came in three guises: 300-hp (224-kW) standard, 330-hp (246-kW) police variant and 375-hp (280-kW) Thunderbird Super/Special, the last with a single four-barrel carburettor. Ford was now feverishly working to keep up with the multi-horse race, and in the middle of the year announced the Thunderbird Special 6V: 6V stood for six venturi, thanks to three two-barrel carburettors, which helped produce 401hp (299kW). At first, the performance Fords came with a three-speed manual gearbox only, but now a four-speeder was optional. Better still, the Starliner was

LEFT
1958 Ford Thunderbird coupé.

BELOW LEFT
1969 Marauder: matt black strips were in.

BELOW
A 1978 sanitized Thunderbird.

OPPOSITE
ABOVE: 1955 Thunderbird.

BELOW: A stock Fairlane: hotter versions came later.

muscle power unit: first Ford chose to fit it to the imposing heavyweight two-door, the Galaxie. The Galaxie was full-size in every sense of the word: for 1959 it measured almost 214-in (5.44-m) long and over 81-in (2.06-m) wide. Big, brash and beefy, the Galaxie looked every inch the massive American cruiser that it was, though a new line in performance V8s was to give a further tweak to its image.

By 1961, however, the power race was

getting into its stride, and failure to produce extra horsepower, even for a single season, would result in its being left behind. Ford had already served notice of its corporate change of heart during the previous year, informing the AMA that it was suspending its support of the ban on stock car racing. To underline the fact, it took a Starliner Galaxie to Daytona and made 40 laps at an average 142mph (228.5km/h). Ford took 15 wins in Grand National races that year, and

OPPOSITE
Ford's Galaxie was hampered by its weight in drag racing.

BELOW
The lighter Thunderbolt (1964 model shown here) did rather better.

downsized slightly in the same year, so there was a little less weight to haul around. With a 6V under the bonnet, it could reach 60mph (96.5km/h) from rest in seven seconds, and run the quarter-mile in just over 15. At $425 extra for the 6V, most Starliner buyers, of whom there were almost 30,000 in 1961, opted for one of the smaller V8s or a straight six. There was no

doubt about it: Ford had finally built a pre-muscle muscle car.

But the company showed little sign of resting on any laurels, though the 390 had proved very competitive in drag racing. For 1962, its biggest V8 expanded again, this time to 406cu in (6.65 litres). It shared some parts with the 401-hp 6V, and those extra cubes, plus the 6V's three

carburettors, hot cam and solid valve gear which amounted to 405hp (302kW) at 5,800rpm. On paper this seemed something of an anti-climax, a lot of ballyhoo for a paltry 4-hp (3-kW) increase. But that would not be doing the 406 justice: it was actually a quite different engine from the 390. The block was all-new, with thicker cylinder walls. There were stronger pistons and connecting rods, while the transmission was substantially beefed up too: a 9-in (22.86-cm) ring gear was used in the four-pinion differential, and there were 3-in (7.72-cm) drive shafts. The Borg-Warner four-speed transmission was a performance item, and both springs and shocks were stiffened up to cope with the extra speed at which Galaxie drivers were now likely to approach corners. Harder brake linings helped too, and they were needed in a two-ton car that could top nearly 140mph (225km/h).

The 406 was not Ford's flagship for long, however, for it was announced late in 1962 and just six months later was topped by the 427. The 406 had not been in vain, however, for it was a stronger engine than the 390 and made a good basis for the still more powerful engines that Ford would be producing in the 1960s. However, it did give away a good 21 cu in (0.34 litres) to the NHRA/NASCAR 427.17-cu in (7-litre) capacity limit, which made the 406 look relatively puny against the 421 Pontiac and 426 Dodge.

So 427 it had to be. There were two versions for the road: a single four-barrel carburettor motor with 410hp (306kW), and a conservatively rated 425-hp (317-kW) version with twin four barrels. Both were options on the big Galaxie and 500XL (the latter with sporting trim) for 1963, in two-door hardtop form. They cost $461.60 extra, but that did not stop nearly 5,000 big

Ford buyers from signing the fatter cheque. So they impressed on the street, but on the drag strip even radically lightened Galaxies, festooned with aluminium and fibreglass parts, were still too heavy for all-out drag-strip success.

That is why Ford turned to the lighter mid-sized Fairlane to spearhead its drag racing campaign, complete with the 427 V8. The Galaxie concentrated on NASCAR, where its newly aerodynamic fastback proved a real boon, and weight was not such a handicap.

The 427 never found its way into a road-going Fairlane: that was restricted to the drag race special Thunderbolt, of which Ford built about 100 for 1964. But road drivers could drive a hot Fairlane too. It was not quite as muscular as the GTO, which was announced in that year, but still respectably fast. Its basis was Ford's 289-cu in (4.74-litre) V8, which was available in three rates of tune. In the mild 'C' code form, with a 9.0:1 compression ratio and lonely two-barrel carburettor, it produced 195hp (145kW); the 'A' code 289 (9.8:1 compression, four-barrel carburettor) bumped that up to 225hp (168kW), which was warm, but hardly hot; but the 'K', or 'Hi-Po' 289, with 10.5:1 compression, solid-lifter high-lift cam and Holley four-barrel, made that 271hp (202kW). This was the same engine that powered the top-model Mustang in its first three years, but worked equally well in the Fairlane.

As for Ford's luxury division, Lincoln Mercury, there were no real 'pre-muscle' muscle cars, though for 1964 the division did announce the Comet Cyclone. This was a higher performance version of the standard compact Comet, with Ford's 289 under the hood in 210-hp (157-kW) 9.0:1 compression guise. It was clearly not intended to out-gun the 271-hp Fairlane, and like most Mercuries

offered more luxurious trim than the Ford counterpart. It was not until 1966 that the Cyclone got serious. Now bigger, and sharing its bodyshell with the Fairlane, engine options included the 335-hp (250-kW) 390 in the new Cyclone GT. All the right parts were there, with a handling package, front disc brakes and four-speed manual gearbox all on the options list. The GT was truly Mercury's muscle car. But despite being handed the PR coup of running as pace car in the Indianapolis 500, sales were still disappointing, with less than 16,000 GTs sold that year: maybe Mercury drivers were not that bothered about performance.

STUDEBAKER

Studebaker? Pontiac built muscle cars, of course, as did Ford, Dodge and Chevrolet – but Studebaker? Sometimes ignored for not being part of the 'Big Three', little Studebaker did produce a couple of cars in the early 1960s that were indeed muscular, but being Studebaker it did it in a different way from everyone else, namely with supercharging.

The Avanti was a good basis for this, its exotic name reflecting long-hood coupé styling that was decidedly Italian in flavour. In some ways, it was quite advanced, the first full-sized American car with front disc brakes, which in this case were made by Bendix under licence from Dunlop. Shorter than the average American sedan at 192in (4.88m), the Avanti was also much lighter at 3,400lb (1542kg). That was just as well, as Studebaker had access only to its own 289-cu in (4.74-litre) V8, while rival muscle cars were breaking the 400-cu in (6.55-litre)

*RIGHT and OPPOSITE
The Euro-influenced Studebaker Avanti.*

barrier. In its standard form the Studebaker unit produced 240hp (179kW), enough to make the Avanti R1 competitive with the milder V8 Mustangs, but not enough to make it a muscle car.

But the R2 added a Paxton SN-60

ABOVE and OPPOSITE
Studebaker's coupé, the Hawk.

supercharger, boosting power to 289hp (215.5kW) at 5,200rpm (thus achieving the magic 1hp per cu in) and 330lb ft (447.5Nm) at 3,600rpm. As the R3, with a slightly enlarged 305-cu in (5.0-litre) unit, it made 335hp (250kW), though these were more expensive and few were made. The R3 was actually hand-built at Paxton, but only for serious and prosperous drivers.

Either way, both the R2 and R3 were

fast. A four-speed R2 recorded 158.15mph (254.51km/h) over the measured mile in 1963, and apart from its exhaust, that car was almost stock. An R3 broke records with just over 168mph (270km/h) over the mile. *Road & Track* reckoned a time of 7.3 seconds for 0–60 mph (96.5km/h) for the four-speed manual R2, and 8 seconds for the 'power-shift' automatic.

Just as importantly, the Avanti handled

well, unlike certain American-made muscle cars, and its standard disc brakes also functioned satisfactorily. Here was an American car, wrote John Gunnell in *American Muscle Cars*, that 'needed no apologies or alibis for either its acceleration or handling'. Unfortunately, the American public failed to be impressed, and less than 4,000 Avantis of all types were built in 1963.

If the Avanti was Studebaker's last brave attempt to turn its ailing fortunes around at the eleventh hour with a radical new design, the Super Hawk was more conservative. It stemmed from the elegant Hawk coupé of 1951, designed by that stylists' stylist, Raymond Lowey, the man who transformed everything from tractors to toasters. Updated by Brooks Stevens in 1962, the Hawk was clearly inspired by contemporary Mercedes, and Studebaker certainly marketed the car as a grand tourer: in one publicity shot, a smartly dressed woman perches on a set of cases next to her Hawk, surrounded by travel posters, and no doubt pondering on where her GT might take her.

It may not have looked like any sort of muscle car (it was just too refined for that), but the Hawk could be made to perform like one when it was equipped with the Avanti R2's supercharged V8. Andy Granatelli (boss of Paxton Products, which supplied the R2's supercharger) drove a Hawk GT to just over 140mph (225km/h) over the mile at Bonneville early in 1963: buyers who wanted a car to the same specification merely had to tick the 'Super Hawk' option box. That brought the R2 supercharged engine, power-assisted brakes, heavy-duty suspension with rear anti-roll bar and traction bars, a twin-traction rear axle, 6.70-15 four-ply tyres and a tachometer.

According to *Motor Trend*, this added up to a quarter-mile time of 16.8 seconds and 0–60 mph in 8.5 seconds. They

were supercharged, however. The R4 was yet another variation on the versatile little 289, ditching the Paxton blower in favour of twin four-barrel carburettors. It was not quite as powerful as the R2, with 280hp (209kW), but should have appealed to those who liked their muscle motors conventional. Studebaker chose the R4 for its Daytona, which was an updated restyled Lark, introduced in 1964. It seemed unassuming enough, but when R4-powered was capable of over 132mph (212.5km/h) and 0–60 mph in 7.8 seconds.

To put this into perspective, the Pontiac GTO, launched in the same year and hailed ever since as the first of the true muscle cars, was no faster to 60mph and 15mph (24km/h) slower on top speed. But then, as a hot car it looked the part, which the Daytona did not. Instead, Studebaker hoped to appeal to the man who favoured subtlety. As well as the R4 (or any of the high-performance R V8s), it could be ordered with an Avanti suspension package: stiffer springs and shocks, anti-roll bars and front disc brakes. So it handled and stopped as well. The Daytona may not have looked like a muscle car, but it performed like one just the same, and far better than some.

actually estimated the power at 300hp (224kW), though Studebaker itself never quoted figures for its top-range V8, and claimed the supercharger delivered up to 4lb (0.276 bar) of boost between 4,000 and 5,500rpm. One interesting alternative to the standard four-speed manual transmission was the 'Power-Shift' automatic, a Borg-Warner unit that was modified to suit the car. In position '1' and '2' it would not actually change up unless the driver did it manually, but in 'D' it operated like a conventional automatic. And kickdown (an automatic down change at full throttle) was available below 65mph (105km/h), with a manual down change possible up to 80mph (129km/h). The Avanti auto option was the same, reflecting the sporting bias of these cars.

Not all fast Studebakers of 1963–64

THIS PAGE and OPPOSITE
The pre-muscle Studebaker Starlight coupé.

29

Chapter Two
THE ORIGINAL:
The GTO Story

The Pontiac GTO was the world's first true muscle car, which is the consensus opinion of just about everyone who has written on the subject. Of course, there were rumbling, grumbling, growling V8 sedans well before the GTO came along, but most were big, heavy, full-sized cars. The difference was that the GTO married one of those full-sized V8s with a lighter, intermediate bodyshell. The result was stunning performance in an affordable package, and the muscle car was born. Pontiac could actually have sold more than it built in 1964, and it was soon apparent that it was a new class of car. The odd thing was that it nearly didn't happen at all.

There was no long-term plan behind the GTO, no systematic market research or seven-year research and development programme. The GTO came about because a few hot car fanatics were in the right

RIGHT and OPPOSITE
The car that started it all, the Pontiac GTO.

Catalina to trim further 'fat' from the vehicle. These were specialized racing machines that took time to assemble, so they were not cheap. There was one other thing: a prospective buyer could not just stroll into his local Pontiac dealer and order one for the grocery run. In the words of author Thomas DeMauro, one had to have the right credentials: 'Most required a National Hot Rod Association (NHRA) licence, a letter of recommendation from God and compromising photos of the auto maker's general manager driving a Volkswagen to get one.'

This was where the GTO broke new ground. It used a standard, smooth, reliable and docile 389-cu in (6.375-litre) V8 straight out of Pontiac's parts inventory. But it was fast (and this was the master stroke) because it was shoehorned into an intermediate saloon, the Tempest, that weighed a whole 400lb (181kg) less than a full-sized car. So it could do without rattly fibreglass panels, did not need the care and attention of a dedicated mechanic, and could afford to include all the hot car accessories like bucket seats and wide tyres without upsetting the weight balance. Best of all, being a mix-and-match of existing parts that slotted neatly together on the production line, it was cheap. The GTO

place at the right time, when it could so easily have been the wrong time. In 1963, General Motors decreed that none of its divisions would go racing any more, or even produce overtly sporting cars. Pontiac was also restricted to a 300-cu in (4.92-litre) capacity ceiling on standard engines in intermediate cars. It was a bitter blow, as of all the General Motors marques Pontiac, like Chevrolet, prided itself on building performance cars. But in the GM pecking order, it did not have the resources of Chevrolet to develop an all-new car to get around this decision.

It was even worse news for key Pontiac men like chief engineer John DeLorean, general manager Elliot 'Pete' Estes and his predecessor Semon 'Bunkie' Knudsen, engineers Russ Gee and Bill Collins, and advertising man Jim Wangers. All were hot car enthusiasts, convinced that the way to sell cars was by making image-building hot-rods. Fortunately for their fellow enthusiasts, all were in a position to do something about it.

Of course, Pontiac already made fast full-sized saloons, and Knudsen, Estes and DeLorean in particular had transformed the

division's image from staid to sporty in a few years. Super Duty engine tuning parts were aimed at NASCAR racing and the drag strip, but super-stockers also rolled off the production line, road-legal and ready to go.

They were certainly fast, but also loud, bad-tempered and decidedly spartan in comfort, while high-lift, long-duration solid-lifter cams and multiple carburettors made them temperamental. In an effort to reduce weight, aluminium or fibreglass body panels were often fitted: Pontiac even drilled out the chassis of the Super Duty

started at $2,700, which made for truly affordable performance.

This was the muscle car concept (a big V8 in a smaller saloon) and the GTO really did start it all. As it happened, the concept was easier for Pontiac to put into practice than anyone else, though was more by accident than design. Fitting a big-block V8 into a smaller car was not as easy as it sounds, as the big-blocks from Ford and Chrysler, not to mention Pontiac's in-house rivals, were physically bigger than the small-blocks, so one could not merely take one out and slot the other in. All Pontiac V8s, on the other hand, from the 326 up to the big 421 were physically the same size, so it was relatively simple to swap them around. That made a car like the GTO a relatively quick and easy variation to develop.

Better still, all those Pontiac V8s lost some weight in 1963. Without careful development, slotting a weighty big-block V8 into an intermediate car could result in a nose-heavy monster that would understeer at the slightest provocation. Pontiac's 389 was now light enough to minimize this problem. There was something else too. The unit-construction Pontiac Tempest of 1963 was not up to handling the power and torque of the 389. But for 1964, it was redesigned with a conventional perimeter frame, four-link rear suspension and solid rear axle, which could easily take a beefier output. Same-size engines, less weight, tougher chassis: it was almost as though the GTO was really meant to be.

Threading the Loops
But there was still one small problem: officially, no middleweight Pontiac could be offered with an engine larger than 300 cu in unless, of course, it was an option. So when it was announced in October 1963, the GTO was not a model in its own right, but a $295

option package which could be ordered with the LeMans Tempest in coupé, hardtop or convertible forms. The clever thing was that the GTO option was not just a big engine, but a whole range of detail parts that made the GTO a model in its own right. It was sneaky, but it worked, getting around the 300-cu in ceiling and kicking off a legend all at one and the same time.

The name, incidentally, stood for Gran Turismo Omologato, which was another piece of marketing sleight of hand. It implied that Pontiac had applied to the FIA (Fédération Internationale de l'Automobile, the world governing body for motor sports) to have the car homologated for racing. That is why the legendary Ferrari GTO was so named. Some people were horrified that this parts-bin special should take on such a hallowed badge without earning the right.

*ABOVE and OPPOSITE
1960s GTOs.*

ABOVE and OPPOSITE
A front body-coloured bumper featured for
1969/70.

Others could not have cared less. Either way, the controversy simply created more publicity for Pontiac in general and the GTO in particular: like a celebrity publishing his warts and all autobiography, Pontiac could not lose.

So what did one get for the $295? The basic engine was Pontiac's existing 389-cu in (6.375-litre) V8, which in standard tune produced 325hp (242kW) at 4,800rpm. The engine was not totally 'off the shelf', however: the standard heads were replaced with 421 HO items, with big valves, and allowing a 10.75:1 compression with the

flat-top pistons, and other changes included heavy-duty valve springs and a Carter four-barrel carburettor, plus different lifters and camshaft. If 325hp was not enough, one could change the option and specify Tri-Power, three Rochester two-barrel carburettors in place of the single four-barrel, which produced 348hp (259.5kW) at 4,900rpm. The triple carburettor set-up was a hangover from Pontiac's Super Duty days. Either way, one achieved eye-popping performance.

In January 1964 *Motor Trend* tested a GTO, a four-speed convertible which rocketed to 60mph in 7.7 seconds and covered the standing quarter-mile in 15.8 seconds. Meanwhile, *Car and Driver* published a now famous test between the GTO and a genuine Ferrari GTO. It was a nice idea, except that in its eagerness to out-GTO the Ferrari, Pontiac supplied two test cars, both fitted with tuned 421-cu in (6.9-litre) engines that managed 0–100 mph (161km/h) in 11 seconds (which *C&D*

headlined on its front cover) and turned in a standing quarter of 13.1 seconds. It really made a nonsense of the whole point of road-testing cars: no one could walk into his Pontiac dealer and order a GTO like that. On the other hand, it worked for Pontiac. *Car and Driver* declared that in many ways the U.S.-built GTO was better than the Italian vehicle. This delighted and infuriated so many enthusiasts that the magazine was still getting mail on the subject two years later.

But in the real world, it was not just a case of choosing between two states of tune: the GTO buyer could specify any of a bewildering array of other options, covering interior, exterior and mechanics. It was fun, it helped to 'personalize' the car, gave dealers and manufacturer extra profit mark-ups, and was always part of the muscle car buying experience. The basic transmission was a three-speed manual, with floor-mounted Muncie shift. Or one could have a wide-ratio or close-ratio four-speed, with at

least half a dozen different rear axle ratios. There was an automatic too, a two-speed Super Turbine, which was upgraded for the GTO with a high-output governor to allow higher speed and rpm up-changes, as well as higher clutch capacity, among other things. These detail changes to existing parts indicated that the GTO was not a hurried-through option, but well thought out and developed, notwithstanding what was said at the beginning of this chapter.

Suspension changes were limited to high-rate springs, specially valved shock absorbers and longer rear stabilizers than standard, backed up by wider 6-in (15.2-cm) rim steel wheels and low-profile red-stripe tyres. Not everything changed, though, and the 325-hp GTO carried the same 9.5-in (24.1-cm) drum brakes as the six-cylinder Tempest; this would be a GTO weak spot for quite a while. The only concession to the GTO's 115-mph (185-km/h) top speed was the option of semi-metallic linings, said to reduce fade.

The GTO was really a Tempest with some hot options included. This is a 1966 Tempest.

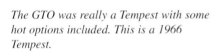

The Judge was really a GTO with bright paint and eye-catching graphics. Mechanically, it used the 400HO with Ram Air, plus heavy-duty suspension and wide, low-profile tyres.

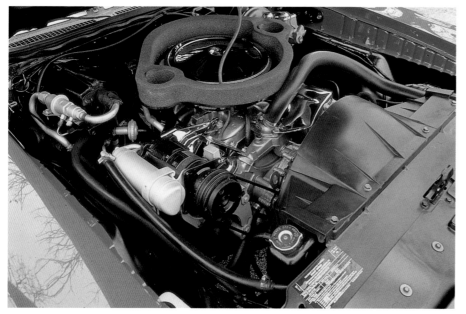

There was no chance of anyone mistaking the GTO for a pedestrian Tempest or LeMans, or for that matter an Oldsmobile Cutlass or F85, Buick Skylark or Chevrolet Chevelle/Malibu, all of which used the same A-body platform. As well as those wider red-stripe tyres, there were two fake hood scoops with chrome-ribbed trim and GTO badges on the grille, rear end and flanks. Inside, bucket seats were standard, with an engine-turned trim on the dashboard. What one did not get was full instrumentation, and the standard set simply comprised a speedometer and fuel gauge, backed by various idiot lights. Keen drivers could specify extras, such as a semi-circular tachometer which indicated an optimistic maximum 7,000rpm. It also proved to be wildly inaccurate, and was prone to emit a steady hum, later fixed: it is now a collector's item.

Most Judges were coupés, like this. The V8 under the hood was identical to that of the GTO, as was the hood-mounted tachometer.

OPPOSITE and ABOVE
Early Judges had a big rear spoiler.

PAGE 44
A GTO Judge, drag-racing.

PAGE 45
A Pontiac Royal Bobcat on the strip.

So what did the buyers think of Pontiac's latest option pack, the GTO? They loved it. Despite being on sale for only part of the 1964 season, over 7,000 coupés, 6,600 convertibles and over 18,000 hardtops were sold as GTOs, which was not bad for what was really just another option.

If there had been any annoyance among General Motors top brass at Pontiac's barefaced cheek with the GTO, it did not show. Anything the senior management may have felt was mollified by the 75,000-plus GTOs that were sold in 1965. In any case, the gates were open now, and in its second year the GTO faced in-house GM competition from the Oldsmobile 4-4-2, Buick Gran Sport and Chevrolet Malibu SS.

But one has a headstart, being first, and the GTO's first-year impact paid off in its second year. Pontiac made the most of that more aggressive front-end styling, with vertical twin headlamps and one large hood scoop in place of the two smaller ones. Bolder front grilles and concealed taillights completed the exterior changes, while inside there was a new Rally gauge option which brought a proper full-sized tachometer as well as water temperature and oil pressure gauges. The brakes remained unchanged except for optional aluminium finned drums, more efficient at dissipating heat and so reducing fade. The optional wire wheel covers now had slots to allow cooling air in, but the real solution was to ditch the drums altogether in favour of power-assisted discs.

The big news was more power, a clear indication that the Pontiac performance restriction had been swept away by the GTO's success. Both four-barrel and Tri-Power V8s received better breathing from altered cylinder heads and inlet manifolds. That boosted the base engine to 335hp (250kW), enough for a 16.1-second quarter-mile, and 0–60mph in 7.2 seconds. The triple-carburettor Tri-Power was fitted with a new camshaft as well, with 288/302 degrees duration, to produce 360hp (268kW) at 5,200rpm. To promote its new star, Pontiac emphasized the big cat theme. 'Have new tigers,' went one, 'need tamer. Apply at any Pontiac dealer'. There was also the 'GeeTO Tiger' record, revealing the sounds of a GTO being driven hard at the GM Proving Ground in Milford, Michigan. That was 50 cents, but if pocket money did not stretch quite that far, 25 cents bought a set of giant colour photographs of GeeTO Tiger in action.

The year 1968 was a high point for the GTO, the year when it finally became a model in its own right, not simply an option package. Better still, sales were up 28 per cent on the previous year, with nearly 100,000 cars sold. As ever, the hardtop was by far the most popular, making up 75 per cent of those 100,000 vehicles. A substantial minority (just over 10,000) plumped for the coupé and nearly 13,000 GTO buyers opted for convertibles. But they were not all performance freaks: less than one in five paid extra for the 360-hp Tri-Power set-up.

Whatever the model mix, the GTO was undisputed king of the muscle cars in 1966, selling more than anyone else, if one ignores the pony cars. It was quite an achievement, as the marketplace was now crowded with a host of rivals trying to muscle in on the quick-car scene. Ford fitted a 390-cu in (6.394-litre) V8 to the Fairlane GT and GTA, while Mercury did the same, turning the Comet into the Cyclone. More seriously, both could be had with a 427-cu in (7.0-litre) option, and Chrysler's 426-cu in (6.98-litre) Hemi was just coming on stream. GM cars were at a decided disadvantage, as the parent decreed that no GM intermediate car could be sold with an engine bigger than 400 cu in (6.55 litres), though Buick got a 401-cu in (6.57-litre) dispensation. This time they would make it stick: there would be no sneaky big-engine options to get around it.

But this did not appear to harm GTO sales, which were aided no doubt by the new Coke-bottle styling of that year. This little kick-up over the rear wheels, so ubiquitous in the late 1960s and early 1970s in cars built all over the world, rather than just in the U.S.A., had originated in Pontiac's full-sized cars of 1963. The hardtop got a semi-fastback, which combined rakish rear pillars with a more upright rear window. It looked good, but created a serious blind spot. Other changes were minor, though did include a Ram Air

option for the Tri-Power engine. As well as the foam-sealed air pan, it included a longer duration camshaft (301/313 degrees) and heavy-duty valve springs. Strangely, it was quoted at the same 360hp as the standard Tri-Power. Either way, this was the final year for the complex three-carburettor set-up.

But did the GTO deserve its best-seller status? Was the original muscle car still the best? In April, Car and Driver pitted the Pontiac against its five main rivals, and was ambivalent about the result. 'Certainly the sportiest looking and feeling car of the six,' went the write-up, 'Its shape, its paint, its flavor, say GO!… but it was its suspension that let it down.' It suffered severe axle tramp, 'bordering on the uncontrollable', and only the Comet was worse. The test driver for track sessions at Bridgehampton (racing driver Masten Gregory) was unimpressed by the GTO's cornering power as well: 'The suspension is certainly too soft … it tends to float and bounce in the corners.'

It might still have won out as a comfortable boulevard cruiser with a strong image, except that the test car came with the Royal Bobcat tuning package. An option offered by a Michigan Pontiac dealer, this consisted of richer jets, thinner head gaskets, positive locking nuts, and retuned distributor. These were not huge changes, but they made the GTO the most powerful car of the six, despite having the smallest engine. The trouble was, it turned the quiet, docile 389 into a recalcitrant beast. Hard to start and reluctant to keep going when cold, it idled noisily at 1,000rpm and guzzled gas at 11mpg (5.5km/litre) even at steady speeds. To add insult to injury, the fuel pump drive sheered off during the test, the 389 shed its fan belt on the drag strip and the left upper control

arm of the rear suspension broke. Twice the GTO had to be sent back for repairs before the test could continue. 'When [the GTO] was first produced,' concluded Car and Driver, 'we tended to forgive some of its handling foibles because of its newness and exciting originality, but now, in the face of sophisticated packages like the 4-4-2, it needs improvement.'

A Change of Climate

One generally associates the early 1970s with a downturn for muscle cars, when emission and safety standards were beginning to bite. But the climate had been changing from a time years earlier. California-bound GTOs had been fitted with closed crankcase ventilation from a time early in 1964, and with air injection from 1966. For 1967 the 'GeeTO Tiger' was dropped, and even John DeLorean emphasized safety in his public statements.

As for the GTO, it acquired a whole range of new safety features: dual-circuit brakes with those long-overdue and badly-needed discs (still only an option though), soft window handles and coat hooks, a breakaway mirror and a collapsible steering column. Just a few years' worth of muscular tyre-smoking antics, with the emphasis firmly on performance, had been enough to have safety campaigners up in arms. If one considered the number of people killed on U.S. roads each year, the critics had a point, especially while manufacturers paid so little attention to safety. So maybe it is possible to liken the 1960s muscle car era to a teenage party: it was not yet over, but responsible parents were standing around outside the house, tut-tutting the noise and bad behaviour, and it would not be long before one of them marched in and pulled the plug out of the stereo.

So Pontiac soft-pedalled its advertising for 1967, which merely disguised the fact that alongside the new safety features was a bigger engine. With a new block, the 389 was bored out to a full 400 cu in (6.55 litres) to take advantage of the GM capacity limit for intermediates. There was actually an economy version of this engine, with low 8.6:1 compression and two-barrel carburettor, rated at 255hp (190kW), and this came with an auto transmission only; less than 4 per cent of GTO buyers actually chose it. One suspects it was a sop to the safety campaigners. Most buyers went for the standard four-barrel 400, for which Pontiac claimed the same 335hp as the old 389. In place of the Tri-Power, there was a 400HO (High Output) version with 288/302 cam, free-flowing exhaust manifolds and a claimed 360hp, again exactly the same as its predecessor. The ultimate GTO power unit for 1967 was the Ram Air, which used a working air scoop to funnel cold, dense air straight into the intake at speed. As part of the package, it came with a peakier camshaft (301/313 timing) and low rear axle ratio of 4.33:1. That made it a mite buzzy on the highway, and the tuned Ram Air could get hot and bothered in warm weather.

Despite all the extra equipment, this engine put out the same 360hp as the HO, if one believed Pontiac. But really this was a sign of the times: manufacturers were understating power outputs to avoid drawing flak from the safety campaigners. Maybe they went too far, for only a small minority of GTO buyers paid extra for Ram Air in 1967. The actual figure was less than one in a hundred.

In the new climate, Pontiac would in any case have preferred to concentrate on the new disc brake option, which brought vented power-assisted front discs with four-

piston callipers. There were separate circuits for the front and rear, so there were still brakes if one of the circuits failed. A three-speed automatic, the TH-400, was another new option, finally replacing the ageing two-speed. More noticeable was the extra-cost hood-mounted tachometer. It was a neat and novel idea, though in practice tended to mist up in damp weather and was difficult to read at night, while its delicate components did not cope well with full-blooded hood slams.

As with most muscle cars, options were part of the fun. The GTO buyer faced lists and lists of options: quite apart from the three body styles, 12 different engine/transmission combinations and ten rear axle ratios, there were the endless detail touches available either on the production line, or dealer-fitted. The dealer could, for example, fit an engine block heater, ski rack or litter basket (the last in red, blue, black or beige). Factory options were extremely involved, with everything from the Ram Air engine to heavy-duty electrics or a reading lamp. If there seemed to be too much choice (there were nearly 100 individual factory-fitted options alone), there were various option groups. To give some idea of just how extensive this choice was, have a look at the tables. For the production planners, parts men and dealers, it must have been a nightmare.

TABLES

TABLE 1
Engine/Transmission Options – 1967

Engine	hp/kW	transmission
400 2-barrel	255/190	automatic
400 2-barrel with CCS	255/190	automatic
400 standard	335/250	manual
400 AIR standard	335/250	manual
400 standard	335/250	automatic
400 HO	360/286.5	manual
400 AIR HO	360/268.5	manual
400 HO	360/268.5	automatic
400 Ram Air	360/268.5	manual
400 Ram Air, with AIR	360/268.5	manual
400 Ram Air	360/268.5	automatic
400 Ram Air, with AIR	360/268.5	automatic

TABLE 2
Dealer-Fitted Options – 1967

Roof/boot ski/luggage carrier
Kar Pak roof luggage carrier
Ventilated driving cushion
Anti-theft barrier (convertibles only)
Vacuum gauge
Highway emergency kit (flag, fire extinguisher, tyre pump,
  warning flares, spare fuses)
Seatbelt retractors (for rear belts)
Chrome hood/bonnet retainers
Rally stripe package (red, black, white or blue)
Bonnet tachometer
Litter basket (red, blue, black or beige)
Tonneau cover (convertibles)
Chrome tissue dispenser
Engine block heater
Spare tyre lock
Car compass
Fire extinguisher

TABLE 3
Factory-Fitted Options – 1967

Power antenna
Push-button radio (manual antenna)
Push-button radio (power antenna)
Push-button AM/FM radio (manual antenna)
Push-button AM/FM radio (power antenna)
Manual radio (manual antenna)
Manual radio(power antenna)
Separa-Phonic rear speaker (not convertible)
Verba-Phonic rear speaker (not convertible)
Stereo type player
Heavy duty dual-stage air cleaner
Vinyl mat, luggage compartment
Spare tyre cover
Rear window demister (not convertible)
Door-edge guards
Passenger's side visor vanity mirror
Remote-control driver's side mirror
Luggage lamp
Glovebox lamp
Reading lamp (not convertible)
Courtesy lamp
Ashtray and lighter lamp
Under-bonnet lamp
Ignition-switch lamp
Custom retractable seatbelts
Rear centre seatbelt
Cruise control
Safeguard speedometer
Rally gauge cluster and tachometer
Wire wheel discs
Rally I wheels
Rally II wheels
Custom wheel discs
Deluxe wheel discs
Custom sports steering wheel
Console
Electric clock
Dual exhaust extensions
Stripes delete
Remote-control trunk/boot lid release
Power steering
Power brakes
Front disc brakes (includes power brakes)
Tilt steering wheel
Seven-blade clutch fan
Plastic inner wing liners
Custom four-speed gear knob
Soft Ray glass, all windows
Soft Ray glass, windscreen only
Power windows
Power bench seat
Power bucket seat
Bucket seat headrests
Reclining passenger's bucket seat
Air conditioning
Heater delete
Ride and handling kit
Front floor mats
Rear floor mats
Front & rear floor mats
Superlift rear shocks
Quick steering
CD ignition
F70 x 14-in whitewall tyres
Safe-T-Track differential
Economy axle
Performance axle
Automatic transmission
Four-speed manual transmission
Three-speed heavy duty manual with floor change
400 2-barrel V8 engine
400 HO V8 engine
Standard two-tone paint
Special single-colour paint
Special two-tone paint
Cordova top

SPECIAL EQUIPMENT

Notchback bench seat
Heavy load springs and shocks
Heavy duty frame (not convertible)
Full transistor regulator (not with air con)
Heavy duty 55-amp alternator and 61-amp battery
Heavy duty radiator
Whitewall four-ply tyres (7.75 x 14-in)
Whitewall eight-ply tyres (7.75 x 14-in)
Four-speed close-ratio manual transmission
  (3.90:1 and 4.33:1 axle only)
400ci Ram Air V8 (manual transmission)
400ci Ram Air California emissions V8 (manual
  transmission)
400ci Ram Air V8 (automatic transmission)

OPTION GROUPS

Basic Group

Pushbutton radio (manual antenna), dual-stage air cleaner & electric clock

Protection Group

Spare tyre cover, rear window demister, door-edge guards, custom retractable seat belts, front & rear floor mats

Mirror Group

Passenger's side visor vanity mirror and remote-control outside driver's mirror

Lamp Group

Luggage lamp, glovebox lamp, reading lamp, courtesy lamp, ashtray/lighter lamp, under-hood lamp & ignition/starter switch lamp

GTO sales fell in 1967, from that all-time high, to 81,722 vehicles. What with the new pro-safety climate and a horde of bigger, more powerful competitors, one might have forgiven Pontiac for expecting worse in 1968. But the GTO bounced back. With new more rounded styling and more power, sales crept back up to over 87,000, and the GTO was even voted Car of the Year by *Motor Trend*. (The new shape had much to do with this fresh lease of life.) Now in hardtop and convertible forms only, the GTO was more sporting than before, the classic long-hood/short trunk shape on a shorter 112-in (2.84-m) wheelbase. This was shared with the Tempest, but the GTO added trimmings like out-of-sight wipers and dual exhaust tailpipes. More obvious was the chrome-free Endura rubber bumper. Made from high-density urethane-elastomer, it would resist denting and even bounce back into shape after minor knocks. However, the standard chrome version was also available. The concealed headlamps were a new option, echoing the 1967 Camaro, and revealed by slide-away vacuum-operated doors in the grille. That was fine, until a leak developed in the actuator, and 'winking' GTOs (one headlamp door closed and the other open) were often seen as the cars aged.

There was an all-new interior as well, with lots of wood grain trim and a new three-pod instrument panel, though on this supposedly sporting car one still had to pay extra for a tachometer. Despite new moves to clean up emissions (redesigned combustion chambers and changed ignition timing) the 400-cu in (6.55-litre) V8 offered more power, with 350hp (261kW) in standard four-barrel form or 265hp (197.5kW) in two-barrel form. Meanwhile, a new Ram Air II system featured cylinder heads with bigger intake ports and freer-flowing exhaust ports, a cam with hotter timing and higher lift, plus bigger valves. Power was up, but only slightly, to 366hp (273kW), while the non-Ram Air 400HO remained at 360hp. There was just one drawback to Ram Air: it could not be used in the rain, as the open hood scoops let water in. So it came as a package in the trunk of the car; at the first sign of rain, the driver had to stop and swap back to blanked-off scoops. It is hardly surprising that Pontiac did not sell many.

TABLE 4

Sales by model – 1968

Hardtop 335-hp 4bbl manual	39,215
Hardtop 335-hp 4bbl auto	25,371
Hardtop 360-hp HO manual	6,197
Convertible 335-hp 4bbl auto	5,091
Hardtop 360-hp HO auto	3,140
Convertible 335-hp 4bbl manual	3,116
Hardtop 255-hp 2bbl auto	2,841
Convertible 360-hp HO manual	766
Hardtop 360-hp Ram Air manual	757
Convertible 360-hp HO auto	461
Convertible 255-hp 2bbl auto	432
Hardtop 360-hp Ram Air auto	183
Convertible 360-hp Ram Air manual	92
Convertible 360-hp Ram Air auto	22

The big news for 1969 was The Judge. Pontiac had long been pondering the fact that the GTO range fell short of both a budget muscle car and a premium model, during a period in which the competition offered both. There was a whole range of budget performers, such as Pontiac's own 350 HO-powered Tempest, which were cheaper than any GTO and cost less to insure, an important factor for younger drivers. But it was never promoted by Pontiac as a muscle car, and sales reflected the fact. So company engineers put a proposal together for a hopped-up Tempest to fill the gap and sent it up to John DeLorean. He rejected it, and ordered that the car be upgraded as a new range-topper for the GTO instead. This was The Judge.

It was, if truth be told, little more than an existing GTO with Ram Air and loud colours. Pop art was influencing car design in the U.S.A., and bright colours with suitable decals were becoming part of the muscle car look. Sure enough, the first 2,000 Judges were finished in Carousel Red, with extrovert 60-in (1.52-m) rear spoiler, bubble-letter 'The Judge' logos, and stripes. Mechanically, the Judge used the 1968 400HO power unit, but with Ram Air III, heavy duty suspension, Rally II wheels and G70 x 14 tyres. For an extra $332 over the price of the standard GTO, it offered a real eyeful, and came in both hardtop and convertible forms, though only 108 of the latter were built, compared with nearly 7,000 hardtops.

There were few other major changes for the GTO that year, though the latest Ram Air IV system now claimed 370hp

(276kW) at 5,500rpm as a result of improved intake ports and limited-travel hydraulic lifters, plus a slightly higher lift on the cam. Both this and Ram Air III, incidentally, were now driver-controlled. If it rained, the driver not longer had to stop, get out, find those closed-off hood scoops

and fit them. Now, the driver simply pulled a knob and the scoops closed themselves.

Seventies Slide
It was just as well that Pontiac had the Judge for 1969, and sold nearly 7,000 of them, for GTO sales slid to a little over

72,000 that year. That was a drop of almost 20 per cent, and heralded the rapid slump in GTO sales during the early 1970s. In 1970 they fell by nearly half, to 40,000, and to just over 10,000 in 1971, when the GTO was outsold ten to one by its bread-and-butter stable mate, the Tempest. Its fall

BELOW and OPPOSITE
For 1968, the GTO/Tempest acquired vertically-stacked headlamps. All GTOs were V8-powered.

from grace was sudden and dramatic, and its end was near. In a way, the GTO's tough performance image was biting back: along with other muscle cars in the early 1970s, it was suffering from spiralling insurance costs, especially for young drivers, as experience revealed that cheap tyre-smoking muscle cars and the under-25s were not always a good mix.

However, if the 1970 GTOs were anything to go by, it was simply business as usual. There had been complaints that the 1968 bodyshell left the GTO looking a little too refined and effete. So the 1970 version was given butch wheel-arch mouldings and a new aggressive front end with quad headlamps. There was a similar theme under the hood. GM had belatedly lifted its 400-cu in capacity limit, and Pontiac responded with a 455-cu in (7.46-litre) V8. However, this was not the high-horsepower option. Instead, the 455 was a relaxed, torquey engine in a mild state of tune, aiming to provide a suitable boulevard power unit for luxury GTOs: that was underlined by 360hp (268.5kW) but over 500lb ft (678Nm) of torque. Otherwise, the familiar 400s continued, offering from 350hp in the standard four-barrel to 370hp with Ram Air IV.

Incredibly, for 1970, 9.5-in (24.1-cm) drum brakes all round, with no power assistance, were still the standard brake set-up, though handling was at last improved with a rear anti-roll bar and a larger front bar. Spring rates were unchanged, but the suspension mountings were beefed up and a new variable-ratio power steering system was offered. The result was a great improvement, and the GTO finally had handling to match its straight-line performance. The Judge was still part of the line-up ('After a few moments of respectful silence,' went the 1970 advertisement, 'you may turn the page') and there was a new GTO-related budget muscle car, the GT37, based on a Tempest two-door. And there was an unusual new option that year. The Vacuum Operated Exhaust allowed the driver to move the exhaust baffles via an dashboard switch, giving more noise and horsepower at the pull of a dashboard knob. It was not quite as anti-social as it sounds, with the choice between a fully-legal standard GTO exhaust and the quiet LeMans equivalent. Only 223 GTO buyers specified the VOE.

By 1971, Pontiac seemed to have given up on the GTO. It was changed very little, apart from a bigger grille and hood scoops, and there was no advertising in the mainstream magazines at all. Compression ratios were dropped to allow all GTOs to run on regular fuel, and a new round-port version of the 455 HO was listed at just

ABOVE: The 2004 GTO was based on a Holden Monaro. It didn't enthral the US market who felt that the car did not reflect the GTO muscle car heritage.

RIGHT: The 2005 model really spelt the end for the GTO.

335hp (250kW). It was clear that Pontiac had better things on its mind than promoting the ageing GTO: the Trans Am was now its performance flagship, while the Firebird had been redesigned for 1971. Ram Air III and IV were dropped. Power started at 300hp for the standard 400 (now with an 8.2:1 compression), with the 335-hp 455 the hottest GTO one could buy, though the car looked as macho as ever.

Only 10,532 GTOs found buyers in 1971, and for 1972 Pontiac did the obvious thing, and relegated it to option status: the

GTO was now an option pack on the LeMans, though that did make it cheaper. Of course, this was exactly how the GTO had started, as a low-key option on a bread-and-butter model in 1964, which now seemed a lifetime away. Unless one was a GTO enthusiast, there seemed little point in buying one, as a LeMans could be specified at the same level of performance with a different range of options. Not surprisingly, GTO sales slumped again, to just 5,807 in that year. Of course, all muscle cars were suffering in the early 1970s, but the GTO

lost out more than most. There were very few changes to the car, though what looked like a drastic power cut was due to a change to net rather than gross power measurement. The base 400 now started at 250hp (186kW), with 300hp (224kW) from the 455 HO.

The year 1973, according to author Thomas DeMauro, was a lost opportunity for the GTO. Those 20-something baby boomers who had bought the original were now approaching comfortable middle-age: they wanted more comfort and prestige, maybe even four doors, and DeMauro reckons Pontiac had just the GTO for them. Instead, it was unveiled in 1973 as the Grand Am, which sold well. According to DeMauro, Pontiac wanted the GTO to return to its roots as a proper high-performance muscle car.

So the 1973 model was based on the latest LeMans coupé with the controversial Colonnade styling. Not everyone liked it: the single front headlamps and heavy chrome bumper seemed like retrograde steps, and it was certainly lacking the sheer threatening presence of the 1971 and 1972 GTOs. Early literature indicated that the car would be available with a 310-hp (231-kW) Super Duty 455, but when production started that was reserved for the Formula and Trans Am. Once again, the GTO option was not advertised, and even Pontiac's 1973 new model announcement contained just one, very small, reference to it. Only 4,806 people chose to add the GTO option to their LeMans in 1973, the worst sales figure ever.

By rights, the GTO should have died then and there. But at the eleventh hour Pontiac decided to give it another chance. This time they really did go back to the GTO's roots, reverting to the compact Ventura. Now this was promising. The

Ventura may have been an economy car, almost identical to other X-body GM siblings like the Chevrolet Nova, but it was up to 800lb (363kg) lighter than the LeMans. Even with a smaller engine, it should in theory have provided reasonable performance with better fuel efficiency. The 1974 GTO, available as an option on both the Ventura and Ventura Custom in two-door or hatchback forms, was more than just a badge and paint job. It was fitted with its own 350-cu in (5.735-litre) V8, which had actually been around since 1968, but there were some detail changes to suit this latest application. With Quadrajet carburettor and mild cam timing, it produced 200hp (149kW) at 4,400rpm. This was not in the 400-cu in class, but it did have that vibrating air scoop bulging out of the hood. The rest of the car betrayed its economy origins, with the bland bar speedometer only slightly offset by a little engine-turned appliqué, a reference to the 1964 original. Performance-wise, the Ventura GTO did not live up to its promise of a good performance/economy balance: road tests indicated a standing quarter mile

in around 16 seconds, but only 12mpg (5.5 litre/km). Still, some people liked it, and just over 7,000 GTOs were sold in 1974, a great improvement on the LeMans-based car of the previous year. It was not enough for Pontiac though, and the Ventura GTO experiment was not repeated in 1975.

But they say breeding will out. It did not take long for hot-car fanatics to realize that a 400 or 455 V8 could be slotted straight into the Ventura/GTO, to the point where original 350s are now hard to find. This equals a smallish car plus biggish engine, and that is where we came in.

The Pontiac GTO was relaunched in the United States in 2004, based on the Holden Monaro's V platform.

GM had high expectations to sell 18,000 units, but the Monaro-based GTO received a lukewarm reception in the U.S. The styling was frequently derided by critics as being too 'conservative' and 'anonymous' to befit either the GTO heritage or the current car's performance. In addition, the GTO faithful felt further insulted by GM's failure to present a U.S. built car that incorporated any design lineage from the muscular icons of the 1960s and 1970s. Given the newly revived muscle car climate, it was also overshadowed by the Chrysler 300, the Dodge Charger, Dodge Magnum and the new Ford Mustang, which all featured more traditional 'muscle' aesthetics. Sales were also limited because of dealer tactics, such as initially charging large markups and denying requests for test drives of the vehicle. By the end of the year, the 2004 vehicles were selling with significant discounts. Sales were 13,569 of 15,728 cars for 2004.

There were more modifications in 2005 but the car ceased production in 2006 marking the end of GTO's history.

Chapter Three
HEY, GOOD-LOOKIN':
The Mustang Story

It is likely that General Motors, Chrysler and AMC executives assured each other that it would never work when Ford launched its Mustang during April 1964. After all, the Mustang was neither one thing nor the other. It was American-made, but without the comfort or space of a full-sized Detroit sedan. It was styled like a sports car, but had none of the nimble responsiveness of an MG or Porsche. In any case, who in their right minds would pay extra for what was basically a run-of- the-mill Ford Falcon, but with less room for people and shopping? They were convinced that the traditional American car buyer would not like it (it's too small and looks too radical), neither would the sports car fanatics (it's too big for those guys), or so hoped the rival manufacturers.

How wrong they were. Twelve months later, the news arrived that Ford had sold an incredible 419,000 Mustangs in its first

RIGHT and OPPOSITE
Ford Shelby Mustang GT350.

54

year, a new first-year sales record for Detroit. Less than two years after the launch, the millionth Mustang was completed, and if anyone still harboured doubts about the car by that time, they were either out of touch or out of their minds. Not that any of Ford's domestic rivals could be accused of that: the moment the Mustang's massive success became clear, all of them began work on pony cars of their own, and the Chevrolet Camaro, Pontiac Firebird, AMC Javelin and reborn Plymouth Barracuda were all directly inspired. All sought to tap into that youth-oriented market, whose existence Ford had so amply proved. But all were at least two years behind Ford, which left the Mustang with the entire happy hunting ground to itself, at least for a while.

The secret of the Mustang's success was simple. It was a reflection of the fact that mainstream American car buyers might actually want a little sports car glamour. For decades, U.S. car makers had given buyers what they thought they wanted: two- and four-door saloons of ever-increasing weight, power and gaudiness. Though still heavyweights by European standards, more compact saloons had been built more recently, such as Ford's own Falcon in 1960, and the Chevrolet Corvair. But these were merely smaller versions of the same thing. The Mustang, with its long hood and short trunk, offered the sports car image at something close to saloon-car price. It was able to do this by taking most of its

RIGHT and OPPOSITE
The Mustang was based on this, the Ford
Falcon. This is a Falcon Sprint.

components from the Falcon, thus keeping costs down. Also, it was reassuring for buyers to know that under that Italianate styling lay reassuringly familiar components: straight six and V8 engines

OPPOSITE
1966 Ford Shelby Mustang GT350.

ABOVE
The engine bay of a race-prepared Mustang: note the strengthening brace.

which everyone (including their parents) had been driving for years.

Another Mustang strength was its breadth of appeal. It may have been a youth-oriented car, but times were changing, and such products were not always confined to the young. 'Within four months,' wrote *Car and Driver* of the Mustang's early prophets of doom, 'those oracles were watching 65-year-old retired druggists, school teachers and just about the whole population of every semi-fashionable suburb in the country, standing in line to buy a Mustang.' It was sporty and radical, but not over the top, and thus appealed to a wide spectrum of buyers. This was backed by a large range of engine and transmission options: by 1967 Ford was listing 13 different combinations. So the retired druggist could have a cheap, skinny-tyred, three-speed manual straight-six, which was nice and docile for shopping, but was still different enough to cause a stir as he rolled up for the bridge game; but his 20-something grandson also bought a Mustang, if he could afford it, in the form of the latest 390 big-block GT, with four-speed, full instrumentation, fat tyres and fancy wheels. In short, the Mustang had created something completely new: the pony car.

A Sense of Vision
It was all Lee Iacocca's idea. Countless others were involved, of course, and not everyone agrees as to just whose idea the Mustang originally was. Product planner Donald Frey and production expert Hal Sperlich, marketing man Donald Petersen and stylists Joe Oros and Dave Ash were all part of the Mustang project from an early stage. 'That car was developed seven months before [Iacocca] saw it,' said styling chief Gene Bordinat years later. 'That car

would have made it to the marketplace without Lee.' But even if the idea for a smaller, sportier Ford had been around before Iacocca became involved, there can be no doubt that he was the power behind its transformation into something with massively wide appeal.

Looking back, it is easy to see big corporations like Ford as giant monoliths, led from the top (in this case by Henry Ford II). In reality, there was intense competition between senior executives to move higher up the greasy pole, with more intrigue and political manoeuvring than in any medieval royal court. So grey suits on the way up (of which Iacocca was undoubtedly one) surrounded themselves with loyal acolytes: Iacocca's group called itself the 'Fairlane Committee', and met early on Saturday mornings to discuss a new type of car they called 'small-sporty'. At this point, Henry Ford II was not included in the deliberations.

The first clay model was for a sporty little two-seater, mid-engined and open-topped, with a gaping air scoop. It was shown to a group of sports car enthusiasts, who thought it was great. Iacocca later recalled: 'I looked at the guys saying it – the offbeat crowd, the real buffs – and said, "That's for sure not the car we want to build, because it can't be a volume car."' His gut feeling was backed by Ford's finance department, which thought the two-seater would sell a paltry 35,000 cars a year which, for a mass-producer like Ford, was not worth pressing the 'go' button for on the production line.

Then Iacocca dealt his master stroke, ordering that two bucket seats be added in the back, transforming the pure sports car into sporty family transport. 'Up until that point,' Donald Frey later recalled, 'we had been thinking two-seaters. But [Iacocca]

THIS PAGE and OPPOSITE
A different sort of muscle car. The AC Cobra used a Ford V8 squeezed into a tiny lightweight shell.

was right; there was a much bigger market for a four-seater.' Even the conservative money men agreed that four seats would widen the Mustang's appeal, perhaps to 100,000 a year, they said, though Iacocca thought it would be about twice that figure. Better still, basing what was now a 2+2 coupé on the existing Falcon platform and

engines meant it would cost relatively little to get the new Mustang into production: a $75 million investment for 100,000 sales a year was more like it. In the summer of 1962, the stylists got to work, and Dave Ash came up with the long hood/short trunk shape that would became familiar to several generations of American drivers. Clay mock-ups were complete by August, and the water was tested with the Mustang II show car in October 1963. The models looked good, but there were still doubters.

Not least among them was Henry Ford himself, who had never warmed to this idea of a small, sporty Ford. Eventually, Iacocca persuaded him to come back to the design studio for one last look. This was make or break time: Iacocca had been preparing the ground for months, dropping hints throughout the company, even to the motoring press, about the little car's huge

potential. 'I'm tired of hearing about this goddam car,' Ford is reputed to have said at that meeting. 'Can you sell the goddam thing?' Iacocca assured him that he could. 'Well you'd better.' It may not have been enthusiastic, but it amounted to a 'yes'. The Mustang was on.

'The best thing to have come out of Dearborn since the 1932 V8 Model B roadster,' declared *Car and Driver* when the Mustang was finally unveiled to the public and press on 17 April 1964. Gene Booth of *Road & Track* hit the nail on the head when he described the Mustang as 'a car for the enthusiast who may be a family man, but likes his transportation to be more sporting'. There were in fact two Mustangs at the very beginning, the notchback coupé and an open-top convertible, both with that big range of engines, transmissions and other options.

The basic powerplant was mild indeed, by later Mustang standards, in the form of a 170-cu in (2.785-litre) straight-six producing 101hp (75kW), though a few months later it was replaced by a sturdier seven-bearing version, of 200 cu in (3.28 litres) and 120hp (89.5kW). The V8 route started out with a 260-cu in (4.26-litre) 164-hp (122-kW) unit straight out of the Falcon. That too, was soon superseded by a gruntier version, in this case a 200-hp (149-kW) unit of 289 cu in (4.74 litres). At the same time, a higher-compression 289-cu in unit with a four-barrel carburettor was added, offering 210hp (156.5kW). But even that was not the most potent Mustang available during the first year. Three months after the initial launch, buyers could order the Hi-Po (High Performance) 289 Mustang, now with special cylinder heads, 10.5:1 compression, high-lift cam with solid lifters, 600-cfm (16.99-m./minute) Autolite four-barrel carburettor and freer-flowing exhaust manifold. To cope with the extra power, the main bearing caps were beefed up, and the quoted figure was 271hp (202kW). With the optional low-ratio 4.1:1 rear axle, that was enough for a 14-second quarter-mile, according to *Car and Driver*, with a terminal speed of 100mph (161km/h). Predictably, Hi-Po was the favourite of the motoring press, in that it backed up the Mustang's sporty looks with

So important was the Cobra concept, that for years after AC ceased production, others continued to offer their own interpretations, including Ford.

serious performance: '... the HP Mustang backs up its looks in spades,' said *Car Life*, while *Road & Track* summed it up as a 'four-passenger Cobra'.

But it was not just engines that forced new Mustang buyers to make choices. In place of the standard three-speed manual gearbox, they could have a four-speed manual or Cruise-O-Matic automatic three-speeder. And that was just the start. Assuming that one could afford them, power steering or brakes could be specified, as well as air conditioning and heavy-duty suspension. There were 14-in (35.6-cm) five-spoke steel wheels, a vinyl roof or wire wheel-style hub caps. One of the most popular was the 'Rally Pac', which was a steering column-mounted tachometer and clock, and proved popular because all first-year Mustangs came with the Falcon's standard instrument panel, which was anything but sporty.

In fact, there were so many options, both dealer and factory-fitted, that it seemed as if virtually every Mustang was different. It was the first 'personal car', which buyers could 'tailor' to their own requirements or ego. The reality was that with over 400,000 Mustangs sold in the first year, many would be identical, but the customers thought differently. One other point was crucial to the Mustang's feel-good factor: all of the cars, even the cheapest six, had bucket seats, a floor shifter and sporty three-spoke steering wheel, three items guaranteed to make an immediate (and favourable) impact in the showroom. To American car buyers in the early 1960s, these were icons of sporty, upmarket cars. They might have added a little to the cost of each and every Mustang, but first impressions count, and they were well worth having.

The Mustang made so huge an impression in its first few months that one

could have forgiven Ford for leaving the design as it was, and concentrating on churning out units as fast as possible for, after all, it could sell every single one. But Ford had rested on its laurels once too often, and did not relish a repeat. So three months into production came that Hi-Po V8; three months after that a third body shape, the

'2+2' fastback, appeared, complete with fold-down rear seat: it complemented the long hood/short trunk look perfectly, and over 77,000 were sold in 1965. That figure made it a specialist model compared to the coupé and open-top Mustangs, over 600,000 of which were sold in that year.

The 'Rally Pac' was all very well, but

ABOVE
1968 Mustang GT.

OPPOSITE
Details counted on the Mustang GT: note the grille on the fastback.

it soon became clear that Mustang buyers wanted something extra to differentiate the cockpit of their 'small-sporty' from that of a next-door neighbour's Falcon. In April 1965 they got it. The 'interior décor group' soon became known as the 'pony interior', thanks to the galloping horses embossed on all four seats. It may seem rather quaint now, but then it was cool, and that was not all that the buyer got. As part of the package, there was simulated walnut for the steering-wheel rim and various other bits and pieces, door-mounted courtesy lights, various bright mouldings and 'pistol grip' door handles. Best of all, that boring Falcon instrument strip was replaced by a proper sports car set-up with five round dials.

That took care of the inside. At the

same time, Ford introduced the GT option, which brought power-assisted front disc brakes, a quicker steering ratio (22:1 rather than 27:1) and stiffer springs, bigger shocks and front stabilizer bar. And in case bystanders were in any doubt, the GT package also included look-at-me parts:

body stripes, twin tailpipes and fog lamps. Only the powered-up 225-hp and 271-hp V8s could be had with the GT pack, so there was no disguising your bargain basement six. If one were really strapped for cash, the Sprint 200 of 1966 offered a flashier version of the basic 200-hp Mustang, with pinstripes, wire wheel covers, centre console and chrome air cleaner. It was all very well, but in the meantime there were new kids on the block. With the new Camaro and Firebird imminent, the Mustang would not be having its own way for much longer.

Meeting the Challenge

In 1967, the Mustang changed, as part of its first major facelift becoming longer, wider and slightly taller. It put on 130lb (59kg) in weight and the new styling reflected this, making it slightly more beefy and bulbous, as if the lithe young contender of 1964 was starting to acquire middle-aged spread. Not everyone appreciated the change, especially Iacocca, who saw the upsized Mustang as a dilution

OPPOSITE
Mustang with GT equipment.

THIS PAGE
GT badges, wood-rimmed wheel and five-dial instruments were part of the GT package.

Mustangs excelled at circuit racing, and were successful in the Trans Am series, with drivers like Parnelli Jones, who won the SCCA Trans Am championship for Ford in 1970. The Boss 302 was specifically intended for this sort of racing. For the NASCAR ovals, however, the superior aerodynamics of bigger cars (below) proved more suitable.

of his original concept. It was, he later wrote in his autobiography, 'no longer a sleek horse, it was more like a fat pig'.

But there was a need for change. For its first two and a half years, the Mustang had the pony car market to itself: it had, after all, created the niche in the first place. But in late 1966 serious competition appeared in the forms of the Chevrolet Camaro and Pontiac Firebird. GM's own pony cars were aimed right at the Mustang's jugular: the styling may have been a little conservative by comparison, but there was a crucial difference. From the start, the Camaro came with a big-block 396 V8 and the Firebird a 400, and either of these could blow even the hottest Mustang GT into the proverbial weeds.

For a car with sporting pretensions, this was embarrassing, so the priority was to give the Mk II Mustang some extra horsepower. That was partly why it had to grow, as Ford's big-block V8 would not otherwise fit under the hood. The engine they chose was the FE-series, in 390-cu in (6.39-litre) form, which put out 320hp (238.5kW). The former range-topping Hi-Po 289 was still available, though it would soon disappear, and both engines came with or without the GT option package.

It looked good on paper, but was not quite enough to keep up with the opposition. Early in 1968, *Car and Driver* tested a Mustang 390 GT against five rivals: every major U.S. manufacturer was now in on the pony car act, so Ford had an even tougher job on its hands. Running a 14.8-second quarter made the Mustang slightly quicker than the Camaro 396SS, but C&D reckoned it to be 'a lame gazelle in the street racers' sweep stakes'. The test car was not helped by a substandard engine that was recalcitrant from cold and needed a tune-up before it was finally up to speed.

Even with a 100 per cent healthy power unit, the Mustang would not have fared well. Testers criticized its tendency to understeer and very heavy steering. Nor did they like the 2+2 fastback shape, which was exceeding awkward for rear seat passengers and difficult to see out of, with poor luggage room. On a points basis, the Mustang 390 scored lower than any other car. In short, it had gone from toast of the town to turkey in just three years.

In its conclusion, however, Car and Driver admitted that although the Mustang scored lowest, none of the testers considered it the worst car, so it must have had some redeeming features. The American public seemed to agree, and continue to buy the Mustang in large numbers: the Camaro did not finally overtake it until the early 1970s. As ever, there was huge scope for personalizing the Mustang: 13 engine/transmission permutations alone, thanks to the new big-block V8, plus new options like a sun roof, cruise control and integrated air conditioning. However, these luxury touches suggested that the Mustang was going a bit soft, forcing the true performance enthusiasts to look elsewhere. Late in 1967, one Ford dealer revealed that 390 sales, healthy at first, had dwindled '... to practically nothing. We found the car so non-competitive,' he went on, 'we began to feel we were cheating the customer.'

Looking to the future, it was crucial for Ford to win the performance crown back from GM, though the lead was actually taken by Ford dealer and tuner Bob Tasca, who blamed the 390's lack of 'pizzazz' for falling sales among the performance buffs. To regain this factor, Tasca used no expensive, hand-crafted tuning parts, just regular off-the-shelf Ford components that happened to perform better than the

standard 390. Tasca removed the engine from one 390, replacing it with a 428 Police Interceptor unit with big-valve heads and a 735-cfm (20.81-m_/minute) four-barrel Holley carburettor. The result transformed the Mustang into a real hot-rod, able to run the standing quarter in 13.39 seconds. They nicknamed it KR for 'King of the Road', and it was.

Ford very quickly realized the potential and introduced its own production version, the 428 Cobra Jet Mustang, during April 1968. This was not a mere existing engine shoehorned under the bonnet. Instead, Ford mixed and matched parts to create a 335-hp (250-kW) V8 that brought it back to the top of the performance pile. The Cobra Jet unit

ABOVE
The Boss Mustang, with all-black interior.

OPPOSITE
Boss 351 Mustangs, in SportsRoof form.

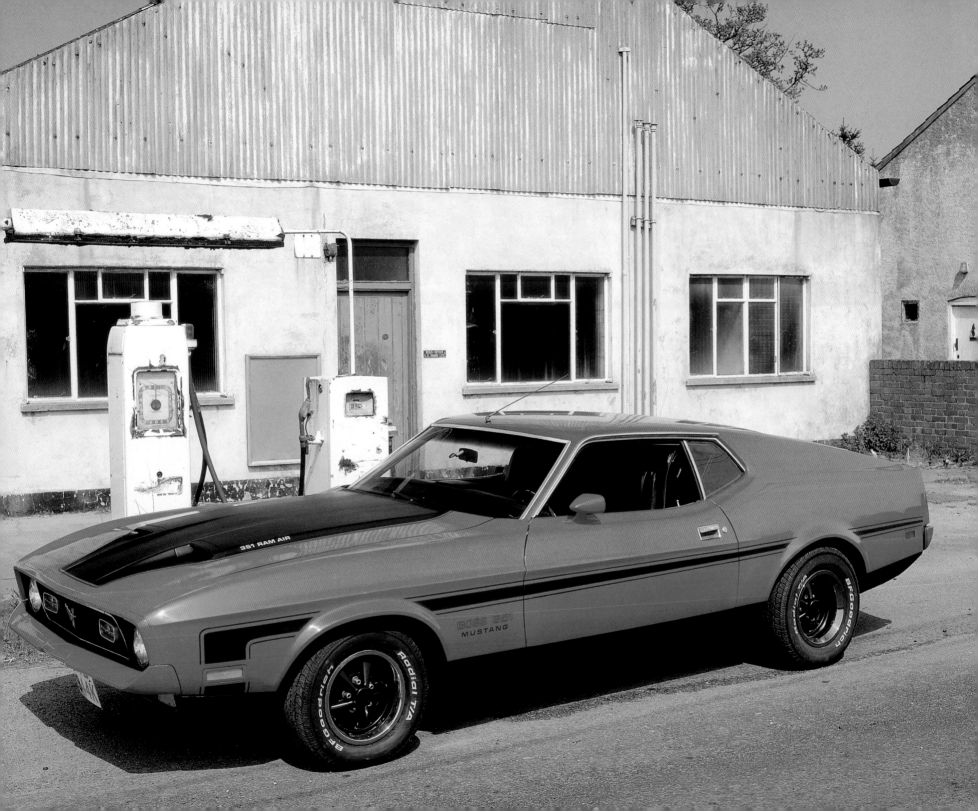

was based on the existing 428-cu in (7.0-litre) V8, but with high-compression 10.6:1 pistons, a 390 GT cam, Holley four-barrel carburettor, a free-flowing exhaust and Ram Air. To cope with a claimed 335hp, the CJ Mustang came with power-assisted front discs, braced shock towers, staggered rear shocks and limited-slip differential. *Hot Rod* magazine was delighted, summing it up as 'probably the fastest regular production saloon ever built'.

In fact, the late 1960s would be a real performance-fest as far as the Mustang was concerned. Much of this was down to Semon E. 'Bunkie' Knudsen, who joined Ford from General Motors in February 1968. He loved performance cars, and made no bones about his ambitions for Ford: to become top dog in that particular market. Knudsen was also president of Ford, so the next 18 months saw three high-horsepower Mustangs that were faster than anything seen before.

In a way, these three were the Mustangs closest to the muscle car tradition, but each one was carefully targeted at a different market: the Mach 1 was a relatively civilized road car; the Boss 302 was aimed at handling prowess, and the Boss 429 was a hairy, straight-line machine pure and simple. Now with new smoother styling for 1969, the Mach 1 SportsRoof (the latest name for the fastback) was powered by a small-block 351-cu in (5.75-litre) V8 in a fairly mild state of tune. But to do justice to its name, hood scoop and go-faster stripes, buyers could specify a hotter four-barrel 351, the 320-hp (238.5-kW) 390 GT or of course the 335-hp 428 Cobra Jet. But even with the standard 351, Mach 1 buyers could enjoy wide E70 tyres, 'Special Handling' suspension and interior upgrades like high-backed bucket seats and a centre console. The Mach 1 was a

Mustang Boss 351.

success, with well over 70,000 sold in its first year.

The Boss Mustangs were very different, being sold in far fewer numbers, and were really aimed at the race track and drag strip, though of course they were also road-legal. Knudsen had ordered a new Mustang that would be 'absolutely the best-handling street car available on the American market'. So the Boss 302 sat on lowered suspension and wide F60 tyres on 7-in (17.8-cm) rim wheels, with power from a high-revving small-block V8, the

by 1 inch (2.54cm) to make room. With 375hp (279.5kW), the Boss 429 was without doubt the most powerful factory Cobra yet, though its 13.5-second quarter-mile was no faster than that of the original Tasca 428. The truth was that the biggest Mustang was no more than a convenient means of homologating the 429 'semi-hemi' (its hemispherical combustion chambers owed much to the Chrysler Hemi) for NASCAR racing. Regulations did not specify the car in which the engine was used, only that at least 500 be sold, and in this case it happened to be the Mustang. In any case, the ploy worked, as 859 Boss 429s found buyers in 1969: peanuts really, but worth it for the media exposure.

The big-selling Mustangs were cheaper, more practical cars like the Mach 1 and the new Grande hardtop offered in the same year. This was a luxury Mustang, with softer suspension, deluxe interior, wire wheel covers, more sound insulation and a vinyl roof. Over 20,000 were sold in 1969, and nearly 13,600 in the following year. Still, those figures underlined the fact that in overall terms sales of the Mustang were down. Although still the best-seller in its class, the Mustang now shared its cake with five hungry rivals. Who would win?

Serious Downsizing

The early part of the 1970s was not a good time to be making muscle cars. For a decade, manufacturers had been happily pursuing a horsepower war, each year bringing ever more tyre-melting, fuel-guzzling monsters onto the roads. But now the new challenges were not in the manufacture of the most powerful car on the market, but keeping up with ever tighter

302-cu in (4.95-litre) with Ford's free-breathing Cleveland heads. Surprise, surprise, it also got the Mustang conveniently inside the 305-cu in (5-litre) capacity limit for Trans Am racing. Less than 2,000 people ordered Boss 302s in 1969, but the stripes, spoilers and bold colours ensured that all of it would be noticed.

The Boss 429 was different again, relying on the brute force of a big, heavy engine rather than a smaller higher-revving one. So big was the engine, indeed, that the front shock towers had to be moved apart

Mustang Boss 351.

safety and emissions legislation, while insurance premiums hit the roof. Bunkie Knudsen did not foresee all of this (though as president of Ford maybe he should have done so), so the new Mustang that was authorized by him was the fattest, heaviest yet. Officially, Knudsen had been 'let go' from Ford, and after a mere 18 months at the top. The real reason was that there was insufficient room for both Knudsen and Iacocca at the top of the same company, and while Iacocca was a Ford man through and through, Knudsen was an outsider. Henry Ford had once said that history is bunk. 'Bunkie is now history,' was the gleeful adaptation throughout Ford after this ex-GM man packed his bags in September 1969.

But before he left, Knudsen had given the nod to a new Mustang. Just like the 1967 version, the Mustang for 1971 was longer and wider than before. It also weighed an extra 250lb (113kg), while the basic price for a V8 coupé jumped to over $3,000. If the 1967 Mk II Mustang had shown early signs of middle-age spread, then this one was heading for outright obesity. Predictably, Lee Iacocca was no more impressed by this latest Mustang than he had been by the 1967 'fat pig'.

It was the power race that was behind it all: to keep up with the competition, the Mustang had to keep growing. Sure enough, 1971 saw the 429 Cobra Jet replace the old 428, using Ford's all-new 429-cu in V8, which replaced the FE unit. Claiming 370hp (276kW), it gave the new Mustang a 13.97-second quarter-mile time, according to *Super Stock* magazine. Complementing this was the latest SportsRoof, now with a radical 14-degree fastback: *Car Life* magazine thought 'flatback' would be a better term, pointing out that the extreme angle reduced rear-

view vision to almost nothing. Not that there was anything new in that, as Mustang fastbacks had always sacrificed practicality to looks.

But whatever bodywork they wore, the days of the old-style heavyweight muscle cars were numbered, and less than 2,000 Cobra Jets were sold in 1971. There was also a spiritual successor to the Boss 302, the Boss 351 from November 1970. It carried on the line of high-revving, small-block V8s, in this case the 351-cu in (5.75-litre) 351 HO with ultra-high 11.7:1 compression, 715-cfm (20.25-m_/minute) four-barrel carburettor and 330hp (246kW). To back that up as part of the Boss package, there was a Hurst four-speed shifter, competition suspension and F60x15 tyres, with full instrumentation inside. The press liked it: *Motor Trend* reckoned it was as quick as the big 429 Cobra Jet, and in truth the Boss 351 was one of the fastest production Fords of all.

However, times were changing, and the market was adopting new priorities so different from the free-living, high-horsepower, high-octane 1960s. That was reflected in falling Mustang sales, by 22 per cent in 1971 alone, and it was clear that Knudsen's timing could not have been worse as the biggest Mustang was already starting to look like a dinosaur. Reflecting that feeling, the basic power unit for the Mach 1 was downgraded from the 351 to a 302-cu in (4.95-litre) small-block. A sign of the times, sales fell again in 1972, and though they recovered slightly in the following year, the changing market was underlined by that luxurious Grande. As the fat-tyred sporty Mustangs sat in showrooms, Grande sales climbed 28 per cent in 1971, and by 1973 made up one in five Mustang sales.

Iacocca got his revenge on Knudsen. In

late 1970 he was appointed president of Ford. Now it was payback time for the Mustang humiliations of 1967 and 1971, which in Iacocca's view were mere travesties of the original concept. Sales between 1971 and 1973 seemed to bear him out. Iacocca wanted to return the Mustang to its roots as a sporty-looking, easy-to-drive car, cheap to buy and economical to run, and above all, small. Iacocca was not talking European small here, but when it was unveiled in 1974, the Mustang II looked like a true pony car next to its predecessor. It was 4in (10.2cm) narrower, over 1ft (30.5cm) shorter in the wheelbase and with 300lb (136kg) trimmed off the kerb weight. Previous Mustangs had kept a family resemblance to the 1964 original, but this machine, styled by Ghia of Italy, was all-new. However, like its grandfather, the Mustang II was based on a small bread-and-butter Ford, the Pinto.

By no stretch of the imagination could it be described as a muscle car. Purists must have gazed, horrified, at the press reports. The base engine unit was a mere 140-cu in (2.3-litre) four, with a 171-cu in (2.8-litre) V6 optional and, worse still, there was no V8 option at all! However, it did fit the mood of the times, and as the Ford ads said: 'The right car at the right time'. Well, maybe it was in the short-term. In its first year, the Mustang II recreated that original 1964 stampede, with almost 386,000 sold. Would a rip-snorting V8 have sold that many in the dark days of fuel crisis?

The honeymoon was short-lived, however, and as gas prices began to ease down again, so did sales of the economical Mustang II. They slumped by half in 1975, then more gradually in 1976 and 1977, though actually bounced back again in the car's final year, up by 25 per cent. Reflecting the times, Ford introduced a V8

option in 1975, albeit a mild-mannered 302, and butched-up the Mustang II with the striped and spoilered Cobra II in 1976 and low-production King Cobra two years later. Power front discs, power steering and heavy-duty suspension were part of the King Cobra package, as was a four-speed manual gearbox. But its 302 V8 was a pale shadow of its fire-breathing predecessors, with just 139hp (103.5kW) at 3,600rpm. Scorned by a generation of enthusiasts since, the Mustang II deserved better: it sold in greater numbers than its immediate predecessors, and kept the name alive until performance was back in fashion.

A New Generation
At first, the third-generation Mustang of 1979 seemed like more of the same. The project had begun back in 1973, with Ford already looking forward to what would replace Mustang II: the company wanted a light, fuel-efficient coupé, and that is what (by American standards) it got.

Like the Mustang II and the original 1964 model, the newest Mustang was based on an ordinary platform, in this case the Fairmont saloon, which had been launched in August 1977. It was wider, longer and taller than the car it replaced, had 20 per cent more room inside, but was 200lb (91kg) lighter. The top and bottom engine options were unchanged, in the forms of a 139-hp 302 V8 and 140.4-cu in (2.3-litre) four respectively, but the big news was a turbocharged version of the four delivering around 130hp (97kW), indicating that Ford was serious about offering performance again, but in a more efficient package. Suspension was by MacPherson strut at the front, with four-link suspension at the back, in either standard or sports TRX form (with attractive alloy wheels as part of the package). At first, it came as a two-door

notchback or hatchback only, though a convertible followed in 1983.

History repeated itself when the new Mustang went on sale in 1979, with almost 370,000 cars finding homes. Just like the first Mustang in 1964, and the second ten years later, the first year was the most successful. The new Mustang was given another boost when it was chosen as official pace car for the Indianapolis 500, just as the original had done 15 years earlier. Ford made the most of that by selling 11,000 Indy pace replicas, with either V8 or turbo four power. Neither of these power units did much to excite true muscle car freaks but, over the next few years, the Mustang would gradually creep back into the performance market, recovering the crown from the Camaro.

The first sign that the Mustang would not remain meek and mild forever came

ABOVE and LEFT
The Mach 1 SportsRoof, shown here with optional wide tyres. The 351-ci (5.75-litre) V8 was standard (in two- or four-barrel forms) but a 390 or full 428 were options.

OPPOSITE
A Mach 1 from 1969 or '70. The lack of big side stripes marks it out as a non-Boss Mustang.

THIS PAGE
The Boss 302 placed handling above outright power, being more at home on twisty circuits than the drag strip.

OPPOSITE
A 1962 Mustang Roadster concept car, before Lee Iacocca turned it into a four-seater and broadened its appeal.

performance-orientated, with all-round disc brakes, a Traction-Lok rear axle and aluminium wheels with 7-in (17.8-cm) rims. Ford claimed a top speed of 134mph (215.5km/h) and a 0–60mph time of 7.5 seconds. If press reports were anything to go by, that was no overblown claim either. 'The SVO outruns the Datsun 280ZX,' said *Road & Track*, 'outhandles the Ferrari 308 and Porsche 944, and it's affordable.' It got a power boost in 1985, to 205hp (153kW), and nearly 10,000 SVO turbos were built in three years.

So did that mean the end of the V8 as the muscle Mustang's power unit of choice? The simple answer is, not a bit of it. The 302-cu in (4.95-litre) motor had been downgraded to a 255-cu in (4.18-litre) in 1980, but from 1882 onward power crept up and up. 'The Boss is Back,' announced the ads, when the full 4.95-litre returned in 1982, in 157-hp (227kW) two-barrel form and with the High Output (HO) tag. The

less than two years after its launch. The McLaren Mustang was a low-production product of Ford's new Special Vehicle Operations (SVO) department. Its real purpose was to act as a showcase for what SVO could do, and stimulate existing Mustang owners' interest in aftermarket tuning parts. So only 250 were built (some say fewer than even that) and the price was a sky-high $25,000. For the money, one had

a 175-hp (130.5-kW) version of the turbocharged four, with turbo boost turned up to 11lb/sq in (0.76 bar) from the figure of 5lb/sq in (0.345 bar) in the standard car. To avoid confusion with the standard production line Mustang, the McLaren carried a full body kit of flared fenders and big spoiler, with BBS wheels and 225/55 Firestone tyres. There was even a roll cage!

It would be another four years before a

production version of the McLaren appeared. Named after that specialist department, the Mustang SVO also squeezed 175hp out of the turbo four with the aid of fuel injection and an air-to-air intercooler. A large hood scoop delivered cold, dense air to the turbo, helping boost torque to 210lb ft (284.8Nm) at 3,000rpm, and a five-speed manual transmission was standard. The whole package was

Scoops aplenty on this 428 Cobra Jet – no one ever said muscle cars must be subtle. The 428 also brought the Mustang back into contention as a performance car.

year after, a four-barrel Holley carburettor boosted that to 175hp. All Mustangs, incidentally, came in LX or GT trim.

The V8s were proving popular. This was not only because they remained first choice for U.S. gas heads, but also because they were substantially cheaper than the SVO turbo: in Mustang GT hatchback form, the latter was priced at $14,521, the V8 less than $10,000. With economics like that, and the oil crises of the 1970s fast becoming folk memories, the new breed of Mustang V8s could hardly fail. So for 1985 Ford introduced the latest 4.95-litre HO Mustang, now with 210hp (156.5kW) at 4,400rpm and 270lb ft (366.1Nm) at 3,200rpm. The extra power came from a high-lift cam, roller tappets and two-speed accessory drive. It was hardly surprising, therefore, that over 36,000 V8s were sold in 1984, and over 45,000 the year after.

Less than 2,000 SVO turbos found buyers in 1985, making it clear that it was back to the good old days for American car buyers: one could still have a Mustang in basic 88-hp (65.5-kW) four-cylinder or V6 form, but the V8 was king.

So successful was the third-generation Mustang that Ford abandoned plans to replace it with a front-wheel-drive Mazda-based car (this became the Probe) and allowed the Mustang to carry on. There were fewer changes in the late 1980s, though the 4.95-litre HO V8 was now up to 225hp (168kW) at 4,200rpm and 300lb ft (406.8Nm) at 3,200rpm, thanks in part to sequential fuel injection. Fundamental to its appeal, as had been the case with the original Mustang, was performance per dollar. In 1989, V8 prices started at just $11,410 for the LX coupé, and a GT hatchback was $13,272, though

convertibles were $17,000 or more. That led *Motor Trend*'s Automotive Yearbook to sum it up succinctly: 'It's a very hot package with a 1960s ring and a torque curve that'll tighten your skin, all for the price of a Honda Accord.'

So the 1980s Mustang had reinvented the good-value V8 muscle car, not long after many drivers thought those days had gone forever. It also enjoyed a very long production run, and was not replaced until 1994; but for its last year, Ford unveiled something special. The Mustang Cobra for 1993 was a product of Ford's Special Vehicle Team (SVT), the 1990s equivalent of the SVO. But it was not only an end-of-line boost: Ford needed to hot-up its now ageing Mustang in the face of the new 275-hp (205-kW) Chevrolet Camaro and Pontiac Firebird. Ford had actually considered building a 351-cu in (5.75-litre)

Mustang in the previous year but rejected the concept as too costly. Instead, the familiar 302 was given cast-iron big-valve GT40 cylinder heads, a two-piece intake plenum and manifold, a peakier camshaft, higher-flow fuel injectors and freer-flowing exhaust system, among other things. To cope with the extra power, the Borg-Warner gearbox was strengthened, there were all-round disc brakes and 7.5-in (19.05-cm) wide wheels. The suspension was actually softened a little: the art of suspension tuning had come on since the 1960s. The final 1993 Mustang was certainly quick, but not as fast as a Z28 Camaro, though that reflected its claimed 235hp (175kW) against the Chevrolet vehicle's 275hp (205kW); the 0–60mph and quarter-mile figures were 6.2 and 14.4 seconds respectively, while those of the Camaro were 5.6 and 14.0, according to a *Road &*

Track head-to-head test. It was fast enough, however, and for lovers of traditional V8 rear-drive muscle cars, a good note on which to end.

The 1990s Generation

The Fox platform had served the Mustang well, reviving the concept of a V8 muscle car and selling in reasonable numbers for a dozen years. But by the early 1990s it was looking decidedly old. It says much for the Mustang's viability that Ford rejected the idea of basing the fourth generation on a front-wheel-drive Mazda, and decided to spend money on an all-new home-grown car.

Away went the boxy 1980s look, and in came sleeker, more streamlined styling, though still based on a rear-drive chassis. The suspension layout (front MacPherson struts and live rear axle) was actually

carried over from the old Mustang, but the new unitary bodyshell was claimed to be 56 per cent stiffer in bending and 44 per cent in torsion. The old bodyshell was known to flex in extreme circumstances, so this was a welcome improvement. From the start, a convertible was planned alongside the coupé: the previous Mustang convertible

Bright colour, matt black stripes, spoilers and louvres, all-black interior: this was the late-1960s/early-'70s muscle car personified.

was a limited edition from SVT. The engine had an interesting lineage, with a block from a marine application, coupled with special cams, GT40 heads, aluminium alloy pistons and various other parts. Now with 300hp at 4,800rpm and 365lb ft (494.9Nm) at 3,750rpm, this Mustang was evidently aimed at the track. This was underlined by the stripped-out interior, with no radio, air conditioning or rear seat. Part of the package was a large racing fuel cell holding 20 U.S. gal (75.7 litres), 9-in (22.9-cm) wide rims and a price tag of $35,449 (plus a $2,100 gas-guzzler tax). In theory, the latest Cobra R, with its white paintwork and beige cloth interior, was as road-legal as any other, and it complied with road emissions standards. In practice, it was a racer, pure and simple. Only 250 were built, and just about all of these were snatched up by race teams.

In the following year, the 1990s Mustang finally got the engine it needed to meet the competition. The new 281-cu in (4.6-litre) overhead-cam V8 used aluminium-alloy heads and was rated at 215hp (160kW). That alone would not have been enough, but there was also a special all-alloy version, with DOHC four-valves per cylinder and a grand total of 305hp

had been something of an afterthought, and as a result was far heavier and more expensive than its coupé counterpart. There were also disc brakes front and rear, with a new 232-cu in (3.8-litre) V6 for those who wanted a pony car minus the muscle.

So far so good, except that the genuine Mustang still used that old pushrod 4.95-litre V8. This had done sterling service through the 1980s, but was no match for the latest Camaro Z28, which boasted 275hp against the Mustang's 215hp (160.5kW). The Chevrolet machine also had a six-speed gearbox where the Ford had a five-speed unit. Not surprisingly, it was decisively quicker both to 60mph and over the standing quarter-mile. In the following year, Ford attempted to redress the balance with a new Mustang Cobra. It was business as usual, relying on GT40 heads, fuel injection and a different camshaft, much as in the 1993 model. With Bosch ABS, wide rubber and tweaked suspension it looked just the thing to make the Cobra king once again. But the goalposts had moved, and even 240hp (179kW) was not enough to keep up with the Z28, Firebird and Trans Am any more. A hotter Cobra R appeared in 1995, bolstered by Ford's 351-cu in (5.75-litre) Windsor V8 with 300hp (224kW), but this

ABOVE and OPPOSITE
Shelby's ultimate Mustang was the GT500.

(227.5kW) at 5,800rpm. This was no production-line item. Each one was hand-assembled by a two-man team in Ford's Romeo, Michigan engine plant. It took them an hour per engine, and at the end of each hour, they would autograph the cam cover! It was exclusive and therefore expensive, and worlds away from the original Mustang concept of cheap, straightforward performance.

As for the standard 215-hp unit, it was smoother and higher-revving than the old 302, but no more powerful. *Road & Track* found the 1996 Mustang marginally slower than its 1994 counterpart, both to 60mph and over the quarter-mile. It was still no Camaro beater; for that, one needed to take a much fatter chequebook along to the local Ford dealer and order an SVT Mustang Cobra with its all-alloy, autographed powerhouse. It was not cheap, but it did the job. *Road & Track* pitted one against a Z28

Compare and contrast the Shelby GT500 (opposite) with the final Fox-chassised Mustang of 1993 (above left) and the '94 Mustang GT (below left) which replaced it. Above right is the 1999 SVT Cobra Mustang.

Camaro (now with identical power) and found that there was nothing between them on acceleration. Ford had caught up at last, and 10,000 Cobras were sold in both 1996 and 1997.

The Mustang received a facelift in 1999, with slightly more angular styling. Underneath, there was a new independent rear suspension set-up, with a 1.4-in (3.56-cm) wider rear track for improved handling. There was a large power boost too, to 260hp (194kW) for the standard GT and 320hp (238.5kW) for the Cobra. The latter turned out to be a little optimistic, as owners found it to be anything but 320hp. The cars were recalled and retuned, and no Cobras were offered at all for 2000, while the work was done. It was back for 2001 though, with 320hp guaranteed. As for the Cobra R, this now utilized another mix-and-match V8 with some parts from Ford's own warehouse, some of its own. Based on a cast-iron truck block, it added special aluminium four-valve heads, which alone increased airflow by 25 per cent over the standard Cobra. There were forged aluminium pistons, billet steel connecting rods and a large racing oil pan. Together, they allowed this 330-cu in (5.4-litre) unit to push out 385hp (287kW) at 5,700rpm, and 385lb ft (522.1Nm) at 4,500rpm. A six-speed Tremec transmission completed the mechanical package, along with Bilstein shock absorbers. Unlike previous Cobra Rs, this retained its electric windows and central locking, so maybe that was partly why it weighed 160lb (73kg) more than a standard Cobra. Were racers getting soft? Or maybe Ford was subtly aiming this latest Cobra R at well-heeled road drivers, though at a list price of over $55,000, they would need a fat cheque book. Unlike previous Cobra Rs, one did not need an SCCA or NHRA competition

licence to buy one. Meanwhile, nothing could slow the R: *Motor Trend* blasted one through the quarter-mile in 13.09 seconds, and to 60mph in 4.82 seconds, electric windows and all.

But as ever, this was the rarefied end of the Mustang range. For the road driver who simply wanted a boost of image, there was still a basic 3.8-litre V6 Mustang coupé or convertible on offer in 2003. Muscle power was in evidence too: the GT Coupé came with the 260-hp version of the 4.6-litre V8, plus Traction-Lok and a Quadra Shock rear end. The Mach 1 had returned, with the four-valve version of that same motor, while the Cobra was supercharged. The muscle-bound Mustang had returned.

At the 2004 North American International Auto Show, Ford introduced a completely redesigned Mustang, codenamed 'S-197,' that was based on an all-new D2C platform for the 2005 model year. Developed under the direction of Chief Engineer Hau Thai-Tang and exterior styling designer Sid Ramnarace, the fifth-generation Mustang's styling echoes the fastback Mustangs of the late 1960s.

LEFT
2003 Mustang GT, with the famous badge.

OPPOSITE
The 2001 'Bullit' Mustang owed much to Steve McQueen.

PAGE 90
2003 Mach 1 Mustang.

PAGE 91
For 2004, Ford unveiled this GT concept car, which makes clear references to the original Mustang.

The fifth-generation Mustang is manufactured at the AutoAlliance International plant in Flat Rock, Michigan. The base model is powered by a 210 hp (157 kW) cast-iron block 4.0 L SOHC V6, which replaces the 3.8 L pushrod V6 used previously. The Mustang GT features an aluminum block 4.6 L SOHC 3-valve Modular V8 with variable camshaft timing (VCT) that produces 300 hp (224 kW). The 2005 Mustang GT has an approximate weight to power ratio of 11.5 lb (5.2 kg)/bhp. The base Mustang comes with a standard Tremec T-5 5-speed manual transmission while Ford's own 5R55S 5-speed automatic, a Mustang first, is optional. Though the Mustang GT features the same automatic transmission as the V6 model, the Tremec T-5 manual is substituted with the heavier duty Tremec TR-3650 5-speed manual transmission to better handle the GT's extra power.

A new option for the 2009 Mustang was the glass roof. This $1,995 option is in effect a full roof sunroof that splits the difference in price and purpose of the coupe and convertible models.

For 2010, Ford unveiled a redesigned Mustang prior to the Los Angeles International Auto Show. The 2010 Mustang remains on the D2C platform and mostly retains the previous-year's drivetrain options. The Mustang received a thoroughly revised exterior, with only the roof panel being retained, that is sculpted for a leaner, more muscular appearance and better aerodynamic performance (coefficient of drag has been reduced by 4% on V6 models and 7% on GT models).

The V6 for base Mustangs remains unchanged, while the Mustang GT's 4.6 L V8 has been revised to specifications similar to that of the 2008-2009 Mustang Bullitt's 4.6 L V8, resulting in 315 hp (235

kW) at 6000 rpm and 325 lb·ft (441 N·m) of torque at 4250 rpm. Other mechanical features for the 2010 Mustang include new spring rates and dampers to improve ride quality and control, standard traction control system and stability control system on all models, and new wheel sizes. For the Mustang GT, two performance packages were made available. Other new features and options for the 2010 Mustang include Ford SYNC, dual-zone automatic climate control, an updated navigation system with Sirius Travel Link, a capless fuel filler, and a reverse camera system to aid in backing up. Note that SYNC, navigation, and the reverse camera are not available on the basic V6 coupe

LEFT: The GT500 for 2010 has retro styling of earlier Shelby Mustangs.

OPPOSITE: The GT comes in an array of colours and custom paint jobs.

Chapter Four
MUSTANG-HUNTING:
The Camaro Story

General Motors had a problem, and it was called the Ford Mustang. Not that GM recognized the problem as such, at least at first. In fact, there seemed to be a consensus in Detroit that the Mustang would fail. Despite its massive advertising budget, the biggest ever in the industry, this was a mere Falcon with less practicality and radical styling. Who would buy it?

The answer, as it turned out, was just about everyone: in the first year, over 400,000 Mustangs found buyers, and suddenly General Motors realized the magnitude of the problem after all, with Chevrolet taking it personally. Although Chevrolet constituted the budget end of GM, producing simple, straightforward and fairly conservative cars, it was also the sporty marque, and Ford's new baby was aimed directly at this sector. When the sales figures were published, and it was clear that the Mustang was more Model T than Edsel in its massive appeal, GM and Chevrolet had a rude awakening: they had to come up with a Mustang rival, and quickly.

The trouble was that both companies had been caught on the hop, like everyone else in the industry, and it would be a couple

of years before Mustang rivals finally began to hit the showrooms. But this very embarrassment seemed to give Chevrolet fresh impetus, seeing an opportunity to better the Mustang. So the new car would have to be better-looking than Ford's pony car, both inside and out; it would be longer, wider and lower with better legroom; faster and better-engineered, nicer to drive with better responses; and of course it had to be cheaper as well.

There had been a couple of similar proposals at Chevrolet already, one of which could have been on sale before the Mustang. The chief designer at Chevrolet, Irv Rybicki, had the notion of a smaller sporty car to rival the European imports, which by then were selling so well in the U.S.A. He was supported by Bill Mitchell, GM's overall styling vice president. But Chevrolet's general manager, Bunkie

Knudsen, vetoed it: 'the one thing we don't need right now,' he said, 'is another car.' Knudsen did say yes to the Super Nova in 1964, however, a sporty show car designed to test public reaction; this time his boss Jack Gordon was the one to give the thumbs-down. Then those Mustang sales figures found their way on to top brass desks, and everything changed.

A design team under Hank Haga immediately set to work. The team knew what it wanted: not a small two-seater for sports car fanatics, or a hotted-up four-door sedan, but a two-door coupé, clean-looking, and with a clear Italian influence. They were also thinking of Chevrolet's own Corvair and a feature that had been there almost from the start: the hidden headlamps behind that egg-box front grille, a startling concept for 1966 and one that became the early Camaro's trademark. Standard on the

ABOVE and OPPOSITE
The Camaro. Was it the car to topple the Mustang?

RIGHT
Not a Camaro, but a Impala. Chevy's mid-size car later came with its own hot options.

RS and SS at launch, the headlights were revealed when that part of the grille pivoted sideways electrically, though there was a manual control should the electrics fail. Finally, like the Mustang, the new car would have that coke bottle kick-up over the rear wheels, suggestive of raw power.

But since the Camaro (though the name had not yet been chosen) was a feel-good car, the interior design was equally important. At the time, American-built cars were, from the driver's seat, uninspiring. Seated on the big bench seat, gazing at a bland strip speedometer, the driver could never feel special: he or she was really only one of the passengers. Chevrolet's designers realized that drivers in the Mustang class wanted something different. They needed to be flattered, made to feel important, as if they were in control of a precision, powerful machine: it was no coincidence that the Camaro ended up with several features influenced by fighter planes. Chief of interior design George Angersbach was so convinced of the wisdom of this that he had a four-speed manual gear shift built into his office chair, so that he could get into character! The result was an all-enveloping interior that wrapped around the driver: a triple pod of main instruments, with a central console stretching back between the front seats to carry more instruments, the radio, heater controls and gear shift. It also placed a solid barrier between driver and passenger, so tight-lipped parents would probably approve as well.

Meanwhile, the engineering work was proceeding apace. There would be nothing radically new about the Camaro's mechanics, with drum brakes all round and a choice of existing Chevrolet engines, straight-sixes or V8s. The new body was unitary-constructed, but like the Chevrolet

II Nova (Chevrolet's compact saloon that bridged the gap between Corvair and Impala) also had a front ladder frame to support the engine and front suspension. The latter had independent coil springs and wishbones, while at the back monoplate leaf springs supported a solid rear axle.

Four existing engines were selected from the Chevrolet parts shelf: a 230-cu in (3.77-litre) six of 140hp (104kW), a 250-cu in (4.1-litre) six of 155hp (115.5kW), and a 327-cu in (5.36-litre) V8 in 210-hp (156.5-kW) and 275-hp (205-kW) forms, the latter aided by a four-barrel carburettor. But the Camaro would not have been convincing without a true performance option, so Chevrolet engineers produced a new 350-cu in (5.74-litre) 4bbl V8, producing a claimed 295hp (220kW). Even if few buyers actually opted for the projected high-performance Camaro SS, it would have done its job of letting its power/speed glamour rub off on the cheaper models. After all, that was what most buyers in the Mustang-class were laying out their hard-earned dollars for – image.

This wide range of power options naturally meant a wide range of running gear to suit. Transmission options covered a two-speed automatic as well as three- and four-speed manuals; a five-speed manual would not reach the Camaro until the mid-1980s. Transmissions were no problem, but

wheels and tyres were. From the start, the Camaro had been designed to look beefy and muscular, sitting on wide wheels and tyres. That was fine for the powered-up V8 SS, with its D70 tyres on 6-in (15.2-cm) rims, but the standard set-up for all other Camaros was 7.35 rubber on 5-in (12.7-cm) items. It looked, said Haga, 'like a car on roller skates'. Unfortunately, the designers and engineers would just have to live with it, for at General Motors the accounts department invariably had the last word. Whatever else it was or pretended to be, the Camaro had to make a profit.

Work proceeded swiftly. By mid-1965, prototypes were running around, heavily disguised, but recognizable as a new car: it was an open secret that Chevrolet was working hard on a Mustang competitor. One of the few major problems to come up was that of severe scuttle shake on the

The 1968 Camaro.

convertible, though this was sorted out with counterweights. Road testing continued over the winter of 1965–66, and by the spring much of the work had been done and the Camaro was on target for its autumn launch. But it did not have a name, and 5,000 contenders were considered. 'Panther' and 'Wildcat' were among the front-runners, a wild animal name having obvious attractions

as a Mustang rival. But in the end, Chevrolet settled on Camaro because it sounded vaguely European and exotic: it also began with a C, which was a classic Chevrolet feature. But it was a fraught process, especially when a journalist discovered that a Spanish meaning of the word was a 'shrimp-like creature'. Then someone else found another meaning: 'loose bowels'. GM

was to get a repeat experience many years later, when it discovered that the name of its new hatchback, Nova, translated into Spanish as 'no go'.

Names are not the most important feature of selling cars, however, and the bottom line was that the Camaro fulfilled its aims of outgunning the Mustang in a number of key areas: it handled better; all the various

models were cheaper than their Mustang equivalents; and there was better trim and more options, like electric windows and folding seats. There were more safety features, too, such as twin-circuit brakes, collapsible steering column and hazard warning lights. It was time for Chevrolet's copywriters to do their stuff, and they did not disappoint. 'Meet the masked marvel,'

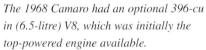

The 1968 Camaro had an optional 396-cu in (6.5-litre) V8, which was initially the top-powered engine available.

trumpeted one early advertisement. 'Meet Camaro. Masked because it carries Rally Sport equipment with hideaway headlights. A marvel because it's an SS350: telltale domed hood, rally stripe and Camaro's biggest V8. Over 3200 pounds of driving machine nestled between four fat red-stripe tires, an SS350 carries the 295-horsepower 350-cubic-inch V8…Try one on at your Chevrolet dealer's. It's a ball and a half.' Somehow, those unfortunate translations of its nametag were soon forgotten, and the Camaro was well-received when launched in late 1966. It was, wrote one road-tester, 'a tasteful American interpretation of the European Gran Turismo'. Haga and his boys were surely pleased with that one.

But it wasn't a clear-cut victory. In

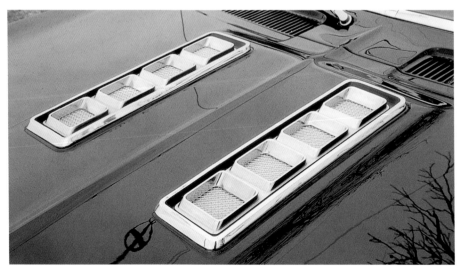

LEFT, OPPOSITE and OVERLEAF
The Z28, initially a race-car option,
became a legend in its own right.

May 1967 *Motor Trend* magazine reported how the Camaro, in all its options, compared with the Mustang and Plymouth Barracuda. The magazine liked the wide range of engines on offer in the Chevrolet, including a new 396-cu in (6.5-litre) V8 option producing 325hp (242kW), not to mention the 400-hp (298-kW) Z28, there were seven. If the standard 396 did not have enough power, it could be hopped-up to 375hp (279.5kW) with a dealer-fitted camshaft; the Camaro was also the only one of the three to offer a larger-capacity (the 250-cu in/4.1-litre) six. With the 396 under the hood, the Chevrolet was decisively

faster than the equivalent 320-hp (238.5-kW) Mustang as well: 0–60mph (95.5km/h) in 6.0 seconds, compared with the Mustang's figure of 7.4 seconds, and the standing quarter-mile (402m) in 14.5 seconds to reach 95mph (153km/h), as opposed to the Mustang's 15.6 seconds and 94mph (151km/h).

All three cars were available with stiffer suspension set-ups, but as standard there was not much to choose between them: the Camaro understeered a little less than both the Mustang and Barracuda, but was more prone to power oversteer than the Ford. But (and this was the one major criticism of early Camaros) it suffered severe rear axle hop under hard acceleration and braking. The optional suspension package (offered on the SS350 and 396) came with a traction bar that overcame this, and was thought to feel better than its rivals on tighter turns, the equal of the Mustang on higher-speed corners, despite the latter's heavy understeer. All three cars came with drum brakes as standard, and the Camaro's were judged the best, being without side pull.

The Camaro lost out to the Barracuda on interior space, however, and the Camaro convertible was judged to be more of a 2+2 than a full four-seater, just like the Mustang. The Barracuda won out on ride quality too, thanks to its longer wheelbase. Moreover, despite all the time George Angersbach and the interior designers had spent replicating a fighter plane's cockpit, the cheaper Camaros came with just a speedometer and fuel gauge. If one wanted extra instruments set into the central console, one had to pay extra, and one had also to choose between these and the stereo, as there was insufficient room for both. The bean counters had won out once again.

The Z28 is Born

But there was something else General Motors needed to out-Mustang the Mustang. It was not enough to be faster, better to handle and cheaper. Since the Mustang class was all about image, it had to win races as well. This presented a problem, as GM had set its face against helping private race teams, let alone running its own. This was in accordance with the 1957 SCCA ruling, which banned factory-sponsored teams outright. However, Ford was flouting the rules by supplying plenty of support to the privateers, and if the truth be told, so was Chevrolet. But GM knew that to succeed in the new Trans Am series, a few warmed-over parts bolted into a standard Camaro would not be enough: what was required was a substantially new Camaro, designed specifically for racing. In making that decision, the company was on the threshhold of launching a legend, the Z28.

One can always tell when a car name is worth its weight in gold in marketing terms and image: it keeps coming back, year after year. So just as Pontiac's Trans Am tag was still in use up to the end of the 20th century, so were Ford's Mustang and Cobra. Over at Chevrolet, it was Z28, which made a comeback in 1977 and again in 2000. Legends die hard.

The substance of this particular legend was a new V8. Actually, it was not that new, merely a clever mix-and-match of existing parts. Trans Am racing had a 305-cu in (5.0-litre) capacity limit, and at first Chevrolet thought its existing 283-cu in (4.64-litre) V8 would neatly fit the bill. But it soon became clear that it would stand no chance against special 302-cu in (4.95-litre) Mustangs. So instead, Chevrolet combined the existing 327-cu in (5.36-litre) cylinder block with the 283 crankshaft, then added a large Holley four-barrel carburettor, L79 cylinder heads

from the Corvette and an aluminium high-rise intake. Those heads had big 2.20-in (5.59-cm) intake valves and 1.6-in (4.06-cm) exhausts, with dual exhaust ports, and the ignition was boosted with high rpm distributor points. The result was a high-revving motor that produced 350hp (261kW) at 6,200rpm, and 320lb ft (433.9Nm) of torque. In the event, it was a more conservative 290hp (216kW) and 290lb ft (393.2Nm) , but the effect was the same and it was enough to win races.

In theory, a buyer could order the Z28 engine on his new Camaro for an extra $358. In practice, the high-powered V8 came with a set of compulsory options such as heavy-duty suspension, close-ratio four-speed manual transmission, 3.73:1 rear axle and power-assisted front disc brakes. Thus the complete car cost a hefty $4,100 at a time when the basic price of the hardtop Camaro was $2,608.

But that did not seem to matter. Trans Am racing stipulated that a minimum number of cars be built, so that in theory Joe Public could go to his local dealer on Monday morning and order the same model that had won the weekend race. In practice, most of these cars (and certainly all of the early ones) went to established racers. They had to, to make it in time for the first race of the season. The first production Z28 rolled off the line on 29 December 1966.

Roger Penske, the high-profile Chevrolet dealer and racer, took delivery of his on 10 January 1967 and immediately began to prepare it for the Daytona round of the Trans Am, then only ten days away. It was not quite a fairy-tale debut: Penske led for a while before retiring with engine problems, but Canadian Craig Fisher finished second in his Z28, ahead of two Mercury Cougars and a Mustang. Weeks later, it was announced that an SS Camaro convertible would be pace car for that year's Indianapolis 500, the dream exposure ticket for any muscle car market. By the end of its first year, just over 200,000 Camaros had been sold: not quite Mustang figures, but good enough. Really, the Camaro could hardly have got off to a better start.

For 1968 the Z28 got a new induction system with twin four-barrel carburettors, the intake carefully designed to send peak waves of fuel/air mixture into the cylinder

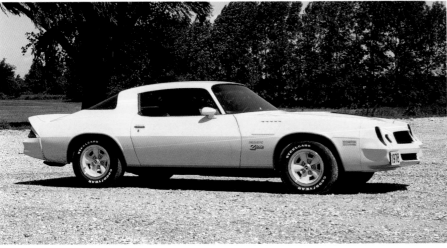

at precisely the right time. Available as an add-on part for existing Camaros, it was in theory road-legal, but in practice its sole raison d'être was success in Trans Am racing. Chevrolet rated the new package, again conservatively, at 280bhp (209kW), though *Road & Track* considered that 350bhp (261kW) at 6,200rpm was a more realistic figure.

The magazine was probably right, as the Z28 proved marginally quicker than the equivalent Mustang, which was lighter in weight. The 0–60-mph time came up in 5.3 seconds when compared with the Mustang's figure of 5.4 seconds, and the standing quarter-mile in 13.77 seconds to the Mustang's 13.96: it also outpaced the Ford by just 1mph (1.6km/h) on top speed, at 132mph (212.5km/h). With this much performance, the old criticism of axle hop was back, and the ride was described as stiff (not unexpected, in a race-bound car) and not everyone liked the gear-change. Still, everyone was impressed with the brakes (the Z28 needed 39 ft/12m less than the Mustang to panic stop from 80mph/129km/h) and power steering. The bottom line was that a Z28 won the championship that year.

While race-prepared Camaros tore up the tracks and drag strips, the design team began to plan variations for the road. An attractive Kammback, a sort of high-performance estate, got to the mock-up stage but was rejected as being too expensive to produce. Similarly, a fastback Camaro was rejected by the top brass, but this time because they had been tempted into building fastbacks before, but had failed to secure the anticipated sales. For the time being, the Camaro would have to soldier on as a hardtop or convertible only.

None of this was hurting its popularity. In 1969, the Camaro was voted top sporty

car by readers of *Car and Driver* magazine. An advertisement of the time celebrated the fact with a to-the-point headline: 'A word or two to the competition: You lose.' Chevrolet could be forgiven for crowing over the Camaro's success. That year sales boomed to 235,147. Of those, over three-quarters were V8-powered, underlining the fact that straight-six 'muscle cars', if they can be described as such, were often seen as price leaders. Their main job was to

attract buyers into the showroom, whereupon the salesmen would do their job of talking customers into buying an optioned-up V8, which meant fatter profit margins all round. The same thing was true of the Z28, which made up only 3 per cent of total sales: it too had to tempt potential Camaro buyers into their Chevrolet dealer, thanks to its exploits on the racetrack.

One thing that probably added to the Camaro's wide appeal was its styling,

ABOVE, OPPOSITE and OVERLEAF
An early-1970s Camaro coupé. The wide wheels and tyres are later additions.

which was not overly aggressive, and the fact that women were often shown at the wheel in promotional advertisements; consequently, women were one in four Camaro customers. Actually, there were signs that Chevrolet thought it had gone a little too far in that direction, and the 1969 Camaro was given a little more aggression, with wider tyres, bigger arches and horizontal lights. Meanwhile, a three-speed Turbo-Hydramatic transmission replaced the old two-speed, and the manual option was four-speed. There was also the exciting ZL1 V8 engine, a 427-cu in (7.0-litre) all-aluminium unit that promised more power than ever before. But it was no Z28 replacement, being intended purely to challenge the Boss 429 Mustang in drag racing. Just 70 were made.

A new era for the Camaro began in February 1970, when Chevrolet general manager Pete Estes, who had overseen the

Camaro launch, was replaced by the dynamic John DeLorean. DeLorean, of course, would much later become associated with a much less successful car, but in 1970 he was on the way up GM's corporate ladder. And he was adamant about one thing: under his leadership, the Camaro would have to knock the Mustang from its pedestal, and become the U.S.A.'s best-selling sports car. He also had in mind the fact that the Camaro was a popular first-time car; among the under-25s no less than 40 per cent of Camaro buyers were purchasing their first car. Brand loyalty being what it was, many of those people would go on to buy another Chevrolet, and another, so it made sense to give a big push to the first-car favourite.

Announced in February 1970, the Mk 2 Camaro was designed to look lower, wider and more expensive than the car it replaced. Where the old Camaro was almost subtle in

its performance pretensions, the latest one was clearly aspiring to an Italian look, certainly upmarket. It worked as well. There were other touches like hidden windscreen wipers, bucket seats and a redesigned instrument panel. The lowest-powered six was dropped, and the three standard engines were now a 155-hp (115.5-kW) 250-cu in (4.1-litre) six, and 307-cu in (5.0-litre) and 350-cu in (5.74-litre) V8s of 200 and 250hp (149 and 156.5kW) respectively. In SS form, a 300-hp (224-kW) version of the 350-cu in was

standard, with a 350-hp (261-kW) 396 optional. For the Z28 there was a new 350-cu in (5.74-litre) unit rated at 406hp (303kW).

The press liked it. 'The first of a new generation of American GT cars,' hailed *Car and Driver*. *Motor Trend* recorded a 7-second 0–60-mph time for the new Z28, with a quarter-mile time of 14.9 seconds. Oddly, *Sports Car Graphic* could manage only 8.7 and 15.3 seconds with the same model. Whatever the truth, it was clear that the Camaro was swiftly becoming a four-

seat family alternative to the Corvette, with much the same performance. At first, sales went well, so well in fact that three-shift working was introduced to keep up with demand: in April 1970 the Camaro actually outsold all its rivals. But overall, sales were down, and the new car only sold 148,301 in its first year, whereas the Mustang managed 170,000.

In fact, the whole future of the performance car appeared to be in doubt during the early 1970s. The U.S.A. was leading the world in an ever stricter regime

of safety and anti-pollution legislation. GM began a policy of reducing compression ratios to accept low-octane fuel, and with power now quoted net instead of gross, it made the 1971 Camaros seem weedy indeed. The engines were the 250-cu in (4.1-litre) six at 110hp (82kW), 307-cu in (5.0-litre) V8 at 140hp (104kW), 2bbl 350-cu in (5.7-litre) V8 at 165hp (123kW), 4bbl 350-cu in (5.7-litre) V8 at 210hp (156.5kW), SS 396-cu in (6.5-litre) V8 at 260hp (194kW) and 350-cu in Z28 at 275hp (205kW). There was a proposal for a new 400-cu in (6.55-litre) V8 to power the Z28 but this was turned down. The reality of the time was that car sales were falling and money was tight; in 1972 fewer than 117,000 Camaros found buyers.

In an attempt to drum up some interest, the marketing department put together three new packages, selling the Camaro as a four-seat sports car that could do everything a Corvette could, but for less money. Cheapest of the new set-ups was the Budget GT, which bought the 165-hp (123-kW) V8, four-speed transmission, F41 sports suspension, power steering and a few other extras for $3,850. Then there was the Luxury GT, with all the interior touches like air conditioning, tinted glass and a tilting steering wheel, for $4,365. Finally, the Performance GT was basically a Z28 with automatic transmission and Rally Sport interior, for $4,558.

It was not enough. The last straw was

LEFT
A T-roof later replaced the full convertible.

new standards for fenders, which looked like costing a great deal of money to apply to the Camaro. The car was selling reasonably well by pony car standards, but not in terms of other GM models. In mid-1972, Ed Cole made the announcement: the Camaro would have to die. But at the eleventh hour Chevrolet engineers found a way of meeting the fender standards at lower cost, by using extra struts and guards. After much argument, the Camaro was given a reprieve, and the threat of cancellation was lifted. It was just as well, since only 70,809 Camaros were sold in that year, though this was due in part to a long strike. Some half-completed cars were actually scrapped, as they had not sold and would not meet the 1973 safety and emissions standard.

The year 1973 was a slightly better one for the Camaro, with just over 90,000 sold, of which one in ten was a Z28, despite a power drop to 245hp (183kW), while the entry-level 250-cu in six was down to 100hp (74.5kW). But there was more equipment all round, with sports steering wheel, new seat harness, and floor shifter across the range. A new luxury Camaro, loaded with equipment, sought to tempt older, more affluent buyers: the Luxury Touring featured the 350-cu in V8, power steering, remote-control mirrors, special paint, trim and instrumentation, plus 14 x 7 Rally wheels. It was little more than tinkering, but it seemed to work.

Nineteen-seventy-four arrived, when the Camaro seemed to be recovering from its sales low-point. First, DeLorean left Chevrolet, promoted even further up the GM greasy pole after his four-year stint, during which the marque had broken all sales records, overtaking Ford in the process. Then there was a whole new raft of safety and emissions standards: an ignition

cut-out until seatbelts were fastened, for example, and in the following year the catalytic converter was introduced. In the Camaro, catalysts did come along with some other improvements, as well as a cleaner exhaust: electronic ignition was part of the package, which gave better economy and longer service intervals. The car was improved too, with power steering on all the V8s, a bigger fuel tank, and new air conditioning in 1974. The year 1975 saw a big wraparound rear window and many minor changes, while the RS was reintroduced: it had been dropped the year before, which had turned out to be a mistake.

But what of the 1974 oil crisis? Surely rocketing fuel prices and a 55-mph (88.5-km/h) speed limit really did spell the end of cars like the Camaro? Oddly enough, the opposite happened. By European standards, the Camaro is a big gas guzzler, but Americans saw it as a relative compact, which actually used less fuel than the average big sedan. As a result, sales soared to over 135,000 in 1974, and there was a repeat performance the following year. So high was demand that another GM factory, at Van Nuys in California, was turned over to Camaro production.

Times were changing fast, and Chevrolet advertising reflected the fact. 'Camaro lets you limit your speed without cramping your style,' went one advertisement. 'Look good and feel good at 55…', which of course referred to the 'double-nickel' speed limit, not the average age of Camaro buyers. 'As long as you've got to go slower, you may as well do it in style.' The whole language of car advertising had changed. The handling was no longer 'race-bred' but 'smooth and stable', and the Z28 was not 'eye-popping' but 'heavy-duty'. It seemed like a complete

culture shift for Detroit: rubber-burning, gas-guzzling monsters were out, cool, safety-conscious cruisers were in. As if to underline the fact, the Z28 was dropped altogether in 1975.

It was a short-lived change of heart, however. In 1976 Chevrolet began to make advertising capital out of the International Race of Champions (IROC), in which well-known drivers from all types of motor sport raced against each other in identical Camaros, with the result that IROC became irrevocably linked with the car. Sales climbed to over 160,000 in that year (still not the happy hunting ground of the late 1960s, but a whole lot better than the low point), not far behind those of the Mustang. In the following year, there were actually power increases (5hp/3.7kW) across the range, but the big news was that the Z28 was back. 'The Camaro Z28 is intended for the macho enthusiast …a special breed of aspiration car…aggressive, quick, agile and dependable.' It was clearly back to business as usual!

The new Z28 was not as quick as the old one (Car and Driver recorded 8.6 seconds to 60mph and 15.35 seconds for the quarter-mile) but the motoring press was delighted to welcome back an old friend. Under the bonnet was the latest 350-cu in (5.74-litre) V8, bolted to a Borg-Warner four-speed manual transmission, with new suspension system incorporating stabilizer bars, different spring rates and rear shackles. Chevrolet sold over 14,000 examples of the new Z28 in that year, which helped boost sales again almost 200,000. Meanwhile, Ford sold 161,000 Mustangs, so the Camaro had finally fulfilled its original brief to outsell its arch-rival.

It was time for another facelift, and 1978 saw a freshened-up Camaro, with soft

front end in body colour, incorporating the bumper, and the same treatment at the back with wide tail lamps. Reflecting the times, the 'Budget' had disappeared from the line-up, which now comprised the Sport Coupé, LT, RS, Rally Sport LT and Z28. The last had a T-hatch roof, aluminium wheels and a power boost to 185hp (138kW). Car and Driver now put it at 7 seconds dead for 0–60mph, but slightly slower over the standing quarter-mile at 16 seconds. The two millionth Camaro was made that year, and tuner Bill Mitchell was offering a turbocharged version. And it was the best sales year yet, with 247,437 cars finding homes, the Mustang trailing with 180,000. The good news for Camaro lovers continued in the following year, with a new luxury Berlinetta replacing the LT, while the EGR system was changed to improve economy and driveability. Sales were down slightly, to just over 230,000, but the Chevrolet M-car seemed to have put the 1974 oil crisis way behind it.

Then in 1980 came another oil crisis. There were few changes to the cars in that year, unless one counted new striping on the Z28, and sales slumped to barely 131,000, with another bad year in 1981. But the old Camaro was only treading water, because a new one was on the way.

A Camaro for the 1980s
When the new Camaro was being planned in the troubled 1970s, one thing was crystal clear: to survive, it would have to be smaller, lighter and more fuel-efficient than the old one. But it also had to retain a family resemblance, as Camaros were now part of the fabric of American motoring society, driven by an entire generation; one does not reject that sort of heritage lightly.

When it was finally unveiled in 1982, the new car did represent a radical change, but not as radical as it might have been. All sorts of things had been considered in the quest for lightweight efficiency: front-wheel drive, sliding doors with fixed glass, short, squat front ends. As it turned out, the new Camaro had none of those things, but the new wedge shape clearly contained Camaro genes. It looked thoroughly modern, but also slightly retro, the big glass hatchback styled like a traditional notchback coupé. The big rear glass, with its double bend, was a challenge in itself, and the windshield was raked back at 63 degrees, in keeping with the car's overall wedge shape.

Under the bonnet, the base engine was a 2.5-litre four-cylinder unit – a mere four cylinders in a Camaro! It was enough to make the 1960s gas heads spinning in their graves. Of course, it was not any old four, having the benefit of throttle body fuel injection, and if that were not enough, next

up came a 434-cu in (2.8-litre) carburettor-fed V6, and if one really insisted, there was a 775-cu in (5.0-litre) 4bbl V8 in normally-aspirated and fuel-injected versions. All came in that cheese-wedge body, with body-coloured soft-nosde fenders of a urethane-covered honeycomb. Despite being smaller, the new car was roomier than the one it replaced, though there was less luggage room, and had better visibility. Had the Camaro gone all sensible?

There were just three models now, namely the Sport Coupé, Berlinetta and Z28, all of which gained a five-speed manual gearbox and four-speed auto in 1983, an option on the SC, standard on the other two, while the ultimate 5.0-litre V8 on the Z28 now had Cross-Fire fuel injection. That year, *Motor Trend* voted it Car of the Year, and the Camaro continued to lead its class in sales. As for the Z28, purists may have looked down on it as a lesser

descendent of the original, but in reality it was just as fast: with the L69 High Output (HO) V8 it produced 190bhp (141.5kW) at 5,800rpm, which allowed the 0–60-mph dash in 7.2 seconds. It could accelerate from 0–100mph (161km/h) and brake back to a stop again in 23.8 seconds. The HO was the option to have for performance freaks, with high-lift camshaft and improved ignition, intake and exhaust systems.

A decade after that first oil crisis, performance was back with a vengeance, and for 1985 Chevrolet announced the IROC-Z28, based on the cars supplied for the IROC series, which apart from a break between 1981 and '83, was still ongoing and still using Camaros. Lowered all round, the IROC-Z28 used gas-filled Delco/Bilstein shock absorbers and ventilated disc brakes. The fuel-injected LB9 V8 was not more hugely powerful than the standard Z28, but with 215bhp (160kW)

and 275lb ft (372.9Nm), it was fast enough: *Motor Trend* reckoned on 6.87 seconds to 60mph and 15.32 for the standing quarter-mile. That performance was complemented by a high-ratio power steering set-up (2.5 turns lock to lock) and 245/50-16 tyres. Both Sport Coupé and Berlinetta continued with the V6, now with fuel injection.

Performance was back in fashion, and the IROC-Z28 proved most popular, doubling its sales in 1986. Meanwhile, the

ABOVE
A convertible Camaro returned in the late-1980s.

LEFT
1988 Coupé.

base Sport Coupé was powered-up with the 171-cu in (2.8-litre) V6 with multi-port injection, wide wheels and five-speed gearbox. It was also the last year for the luxury Berlinetta, suggesting that the Camaro might be returning to its performance roots: in fact it was, for nearly half of all Camaro sales now consisted of the Z28 and IROC-Z28.

Sensing that horsepower was back in fashion, Chevrolet uprated the IROC-Z28 in 1987, with the L98, a 348-cu in (5.7-litre) fuel-injected V8 straight out of the Corvette.

Now with 220hp (164kW) or, according to some, 225hp (168kW) at 4,200rpm and 320lb ft (433.9Nm), the fastest Camaro could reach 60 mph from rest in just 6.3 seconds, and took 14.5 seconds for the standing quarter-mile. Apart from a 3.27:1 Australian-built Borg-Warner rear axle, the running gear was the same as in the standard 5.0-litre version. But just as with the original Z28, one could not buy the engine option alone. It came with a whole list of mandatory 'options': upgraded four-speed auto transmission, limited-slip differential,

four-wheel disc brakes and engine oil cooler. Together, these almost doubled the price of the engine, but *Hot Rod* magazine thought the result was worth it: 'It could be,' a journalist wrote, 'the closest facsimile to a full-bore road-racing car you'll ever drive.'

By the early 1990s the wedge-shaped Camaro, which had seemed so radical back in 1982, was looking old. In the meantime, it had had to face a new generation of Japanese sports cars, two- and four-seaters that made up in technical sophistication what they lacked in sheer cubic capacity. So the fourth-generation Camaro looked very different from the old one, with soft, rounded lines that could only be a product of the 1990s. But under the skin, was there front-wheel-drive and a high-revving, small-capacity V6 perhaps, or maybe an ultra-economical turbo-diesel? No, the Camaro was still rear-wheel-drive, as it always had been, with the performance options provided by big, beefy V8s.

At first, it came only as a hatchback coupé, with a convertible following in 1994, whose sleek new body consisted of composite panels based on a steel structure. The front suspension was new (short- and long-arm with coil springs) as was the rack-and-pinion steering set-up. The baseline engine was a 160-hp (119-kW) 208-cu in (3.4-litre) V6, but this was not really a muscle car. For that, the familiar Z28 package provided the answer (the IROC-Z28 had gone) with 275hp (205kW) provided by the LT1 348-cu in (5.7-litre) V8 with aluminium cylinder heads. Also standard (and accounting for a premium of more than $3,000 over the baseline model) was a Borg-Warner six-speed manual gearbox, ABS brakes and 8-in (20.3-cm) aluminium wheels with Goodyear 235/55R16 tyres. For the first time, a Camaro was artificially speed-limited, to a maximum of 108mph

had ABS brakes, twin air bags and daytime running lights, with engine options including the 285-hp (212.5-kW) Z28 and 305-hp (227.5-kW) LT1 V8 from the Corvette. The aluminium LS1 V8 became the base engine for 1998, when the car got a mild restyle, now with 305hp, while the WU8 SS 320-hp (238.5kW) was an option. The days of a complete range of Camaros, with seven engine options alone, were long gone. Pitted against a Firebird Trans Am and Ford SVT Cobra Mustang in the following year, the Camaro was judged to be not quite as quick as its rivals, but with excellent handling; it was the best choice if one needed to drive it every day.

The original Camaro designers would have been pleased with that judgement. After all, their baby had never been intended as an out and out sports car, but as a four-seater with sporting pretensions and, if one picked the right options, performance. For 2000, a smaller 232-cu in (3.8-litre) V6 became the new baseline engine, though even that now claimed 200bhp (149kW). If that was not enough, one could still have the venerable 348-cu in (5.7-litre) V8 in 305-bhp (227.5-kW) or 320-bhp (238.5-kW) form. And in the early 21st century, 35 years on from birth, the Camaro (in base Z28 or SS, with the same V6 or V8 options) was still in business. As the Chevrolet slogan of the time went: 'We'll be there'.

(174km/h) that was achievable in fourth, fifth and sixth gears. However, pay $144 extra for Z-rated tyres, and the top speed exceeded 150mph (241km/h). The 0–60-mph time was 5.3 seconds, according to *Car and Driver*, with the quarter-mile covered in 14 seconds for a maximum speed of 100mph (161km/h). In other words, the latest Z28 was the fastest road-going factory-built Camaro yet. The magazine also declared the 1994 version to be the best car in its class.

There were few changes over the next

couple of years, but in 1996 tuner Ed Hamburger developed a hotted-up Camaro that could be sold through Chevrolet dealers as a factory-approved option. The SS name was resurrected for this car, which boosted the LT1 to 305bhp (227.5kW) at 5,000rpm and 325lb ft (440.7Nm) at 2,400rpm. There were plenty of changes: sequential port injection, new intake and exhaust arrangements, and a 10.4:1 compression ratio. Part of the package consisted of 9-in (22.86-cm) wide Corvette ZR1-style wheels, a Torsen limited-slip

differential and Bilstein shock absorbers. According to the figures, the new SS accelerated only marginally more quickly than the Z28, but if one had to have the latest, hottest Camaro, here it was.

By this time, the Camaro had become an institution, and marked 30 years in production in 1997, with a 30th Anniversary Package for the Z28. This brought a colour scheme of white with orange stripes, similar to that of the 1969 Indy pace car, plus white aluminium wheels and special interior trim. All Camaros now

LEFT
The 1994 Camaro, still Mustang's rival.

OPPOSITE
2001 Camaro.

Chevrolet carried on producing the Camaro into the mid-2000's. and in 2006 production of the fifth-generation Camaro was approved on 10 August 2006.

In 2009 Oshawa Car Assembly produced the new Camaro which went on sale in spring of 2009 as a 2010 model year vehicle.

Production began on March 16, 2009. The 2010 Camaro is offered as a coupe only in LS, LT, and SS trim levels. LS and LT models are powered by a 3.6 L (220 cu in) V6 producing 304 hp (227 kW) mated to either a 6-speed manual or a 6-speed automatic with manual shift. The SS is powered by the 6.2 L (380 cu in) LS3 V8 producing 426 hp (318 kW) and is paired with a 6-speed manual. The automatic SS gets the L99 V8 with 400 hp (300 kW). The RS appearance package is available on both the LT and SS and features 20-inch rims with a darker gray tone, halo rings around xenon headlamps, and red RS or SS badges.

LEFT & OPPOSITE: Still going strong, the 2010 Camaro.

Chapter Five

BREATHE DEEP:
The Hemi Story

When one thinks of American muscle cars of the late 1960s and early 1970s, or indeed of any time, the one engine that stands head and shoulders above the rest is the Chrysler Hemi. It was quite simply the most powerful production engine of its time, so powerful, in fact, that Chrysler understated its real power by a substantial amount. In print, the Hemi produced a claimed 425hp (317kW) at 5,000rpm. In practice, it was more like 500hp (373kW) at 6,000rpm.

But despite offering more power than anyone else, even at that 'official' figure, during an age in which horsepower was king, the Hemi sold only in tiny numbers. It was an option on several Chrysler muscle cars, but there were few takers. In the five years that it was available as a road-going option, only 11,000 Hemis were sold, a miniscule number by U.S. mass-production standards. Maybe history is playing tricks

RIGHT and OPPOSITE
Dodge's Charger had the Hemi treatment.

on us, and the legend that has grown up around the Hemi in the 30-odd years since, its domination of drag racing and NASCAR, has given it more prominence than it deserves. Maybe at the time a stock 383-cu in (6.28-litre) engine was quick enough, and a 426-cu in (7-litre) Hemi simply did not seem worth its higher insurance rating. What was uppermost in the minds of most buyers was probably the option price, anything between $500 and $1,100 or more, which was quite a chunk on a $2,700 car. Whatever the reasons for its limited sales, it has left us with quite a legacy.

Chrysler, in particular, had much to thank the Hemi for, because its effect on the public's perception of Chrysler muscle cars was out of all proportion to the numbers actually made. A clue to its secret lay in that name: Hemi was short for Hemispherical, indicating the use of a half-sphere-shaped combustion chamber. It is now recognized that this shape allows more room for larger ports and valves, and a higher compression ratio in relation to the size of the combustion chamber. With higher volumetric efficiency than a comparable engine, a hemi breathes deep, and deep breathing is one of the holy grails in the search for high horsepower.

But the 426 Hemi of the 1960s was not Chrysler's first such engine. A smaller 331-cu in (5.42-litre) engine was launched in 1951. The Firepower V8, as it was called, produced 180hp (134kW), though maybe it was wasted in the heavyweight Saratoga sedan: at 4,000lb (1814kg) that tended to blunt the Firepower's performance somewhat. A smaller 241-cu in (3.95-litre)

THIS PAGE and OPPOSITE
Dramatic grille, Hemi V8 and fastback.

version followed in 1953, fitted to Dodges, and in 1955 the new Chrysler C300 made a huge impact with its 300-hp (224-kW) 331-cu in (5.42-litre) Hemi. At the time, this was a stratospheric figure for a production car, and Dodge backed it up with a 270-cu in (4.42-litre) unit rated at 193hp (144kW) in Super Red Ram form. There was also an even higher-performance D-500 from Dodge, with more cubes and horsepower.

Chrysler dropped its first-generation Hemi in 1959, replacing it with a 413-cu in (6.77-litre) V8 with wedge-shaped combustion chambers. Nicknamed Max Wedge, it proved a formidable performer, especially once the race-tuned version had appeared in the early 1960s, as the Dodge Ramcharger or Plymouth Super Stock. With 11.0:1 compression, twin four-barrel carburettors and an aluminium short-ram inlet manifold, the Max Wedge was soon making a big impression on the drag strip. Officially, it was designed for 'police pursuit work': in other words the drag strip! There was also a hotter 420-hp (313-kW) version with 13.5:1 compression. In 1963 the Max Wedge was taken out to 426 cu in (7.0 litres), which meant 425hp (317kW) in high-compression form.

THIS PAGE and OPPOSITE
Less dramatic, the Plymouth Belvedere.

The Hemi-equipped Plymouth Belvedere added up to a practical performance car, with a large trunk. Details show auto gearshift and 1967 brochure.

OPPOSITE.
1965 Plymouth Belvedere II Commando.

ABOVE
An impressive air cleaner atop the
Commando V8.

FAR RIGHT
Those extra dash-top dials would be a hot-
rodder's dream.

A Racing Start

The Max Wedge was merely a preamble to the main act, the Hemi. Unveiled in 1964, it owed much to both the original Hemi and the Max Wedge, combining the deep breathing of one with the sheer cubic capacity and wild tuning of the other, but was really an all-new engine. At first, this was a pure race unit, with a compression of 12.5:1 and double-roller timing chain. Carburation was a single four-barrel carburettor for stock-car racing, or two four-barrels on the drag strip, the latter version rated at that infamous 425hp, with a true figure of over 500hp. Installed in radically lightened B-body Chryslers, the Hemi soon made a name for itself,

ABOVE
1967 Dodge Coronet R/T.

LEFT
The R/T stood for 'Road and Track'.

OPPOSITE
The Hemi fits neatly into the Coronet engine bay.

especially in drag racing, where it rapidly achieved near-complete domination. The engine itself was lightened with aluminium heads in 1965.

So before it set foot anywhere near a road car, the Hemi was already well known by the driving public and, crucially, the sort of public that bought hot cars. It was only a matter of time before the two were put together, when for 1966 Chrysler announced the street Hemi as an option for certain models. It was obviously detuned from racing spec. The compression was lowered to a more moderate 10.25:1, there was a milder hydraulic lift cam and twin four-barrel Carter carburettors. Quoted power was still 425hp at 5,000rpm, with 490lb ft (664.4Nm) at 4,000rpm.

The Hemi road era had begun, but it was a low-key start. One could hardly miss the flashy Pontiac GTO or the imposing Ford Fairlane, for these were muscle cars with presence. But the Dodge Coronet and Plymouth Belvedere/Satellite were inoffensive-looking sedans. They were the sort of thing retired insurance salesmen would drive, or maybe a great aunt, as likely to rip away from the traffic lights in a plume of tyre smoke as they would fly to the moon. There was a '426 Hemi' badge, but blink and one missed it, it was so small. But despite their dowdy exteriors, these were the fastest, most powerful cars on the market in 1966. Moreover, looks certainly did not bother *Car and Driver*, which tested a Satellite Hemi in 1966. This just missed a test of six 'Super Cars' the previous month, but *C&D* made no bones about what the outcome would have been if the Hemi had made it in time. 'Without cheating, without expensive NASCAR mechanics, without towing or trailing the Plymouth to the test track, it went faster, rode better, stopped better and caused fewer problems than all six of the cars tested last month.' For the record, it dashed off 0–60mph (96.5km/h) in 7.4 seconds, with a time of 14.5 seconds for the standing quarter-mile. And there was another factor: despite its racing origins, the Hemi proved as reliable and docile a street engine as one could hope to find. Far from being trailered to the test (and for magazine tests of the time, some muscle cars were) the Satellite was driven from Detroit to New York, and was used every day of the week before the test. About the only complaint *C&D* could find to say about the fastest muscle car ever was its styling.

If, on the other hand, one really considered the Coronet and Belvedere too staid, one could always opt for the Charger,

OPPOSITE.
Stripes and badges indicate muscle car status.

LEFT
Neat door trims.

a fastbacked version of the Coronet which actually looked quite different, thanks to the fastback's almost wedge shape and full-width grille with concealed headlights. The little doors that hid the lights were powered by electric motors. Underlining the upmarket approach, there were four bucket seats and full instrumentation. The

Hemi was, of course, optional. As part of the Hemi package, the buyer received heavy-duty suspension, larger brakes and 7.75 x 14 Blue Streak tyres. Transmission was a four-speed manual or TorqueFlite automatic. However, of 37,000-plus Charger customers in 1966, only 468 (a little over 1 per cent) paid extra for the

Hemi package, split roughly 50/50 between TorqueFlite and four-speed. But over 1,500 Belvedere/Satellite buyers went for the Hemi, so maybe there were a few drivers out there who appreciated the combination of conservative looks with stunning performance.

As for engine longevity, Chrysler

ABOVE and RIGHT
There is no mistaking the performance potential of this 1968 Charger.

OPPOSITE
The Hemi: Chrysler owed a great deal to this engine.

ABOVE
There are clues as to the Charger's performance in the interior.

RIGHT
Charger was long a Dodge performance brand.

played safe with a reduced 12,000-mile (19310-km)/12-month warranty on the Hemi, and even this would be invalidated by what they euphemistically called 'extreme operation'. Still, it was a sensible move. With a car this fast, it seemed almost inevitable that keen owners would take it racing at weekends, before turning up at the dealer come Monday morning, with some broken parts and a warranty claim form in hand. They played even safer with the Hemi cars built for Super Stock: these had

does not apply to this vehicle.'

For 1967, Chrysler attempted to catch up with the flashier muscle car competition. The GTX was really a Belvedere with a massive hood scoop, stripes, rally wheels and bucket seats. Although basically a Belvedere, it looked the part of a muscle car, and in Super Commando form came with the biceps to back it up, the choice of 440-cu in (7.21-litre) Max Wedge or Street Hemi V8s. Although smaller than the Max Wedge, the Hemi offered an extra 50hp (37kW) for an extra $564, which included heavy-duty suspension. So it was good value, but again, few GTX customers opted for it: 720 out of around 12,500 (and at least one author puts the figure at just 125; but, either way, the Hemi was in a minority).

Alongside the GTX, Dodge launched the R/T (Road & Track), a rebadged version of the same car with slightly tweaked styling. But neither was the fully styled muscle car that the opposition was offering. From Chrysler, that was still to come.

Chrysler may have come late to the muscle car scene, but lost little time getting in the swing, though of course with engine options like the Hemi and Max Wedge, that was not too much of a problem. Muscle cars were getting increasingly expensive by the late 1960s, and out of the reach of

no warranty at all. A notice under the bonnet reminded owners of the fact: 'NOTICE: This car is equipped with a 426-cu in engine (and other special equipment). This car is intended for use in supervised acceleration trials and is not intended for trials or general passenger car use. Accordingly, THIS VEHICLE IS SOLD 'AS IS' and the 12-month or 12,000-mile vehicle warranty coverage and 5-year or 50,000-mile power train warranty coverage

younger buyers, so Mopar led the field with the first budget muscle cars, or what *Car and Driver* magazine called 'Econo-Racers.' It was a simple formula: take the lightest, cheapest two-door body available, strip off all the options, and stick in the most powerful off-the-shelf V8. For car fanatics who loved trawling through the options lists this was no big deal, but the new Plymouth Road Runner did all that for one, offering a ready-made Q-car at a bargain price.

The Road Runner (and its Dodge Super Bee equivalent) was an instant hit, selling well over 40,000 cars in its first year. That made up nearly one in five of all intermediate Plymouths, quite a sales feat. It certainly did not look like a muscle car, lacking chrome, bulges and hood scoops. Inside, rubber mats, rather than carpets, covered the floor and there was a plain bench seat: bucket seats were not obtainable, even as an option. Only the discreet Road Runner badges hinted that there was something special under the bonnet. That of course, was the Road Runner's raison d'être. The standard power unit was a special 335-hp (250-kW) version of Chrysler's 383, but more interesting by far was the $700 Hemi option. For this amount, Hemi buyers also had a larger radiator, power front disc brakes and 15-in (45.7-cm) wheels with F70 Polyglas tyres.

Dodge should not be forgotten, of

course; its equivalent to the Road Runner was the Super Bee, based on the Coronet and aimed at the same concept of muscle car performance in a more affordable package. That was made clear in this gem of the 1968 copywriter's art: 'Announcing: Coronet "Super Bee". Scat Pack performance at a new low price. Beware the hot-cammed, four-barrelled 383 mill in the light coupé body. Beware the muscled hood, the snick of the close-coupled four-speed, the surefootedness of the Red Lines, Rallye-rated springs and shocks, sway bar and competent eleven-inch drums. Beware the Super Bee. Proof that you can't tell a runner by the size of his bankroll.' As with the Road Runner, a 383 V8 was standard, but a Hemi topped the options list. Without the Hemi, the two-door sedan cost less than $3,500, but 166 customers chose to pay the extra $712. Actually, the acceleration figures were not much different: the standard Super Bee reached 60mph (96.5km/h) in 6.8 seconds, and the Hemi was just 0.2 seconds quicker, though it did lop a whole second off the quarter-mile time, at 14 seconds. For 1971, with the Coronet out of production, the value-for-money Super Bee option was available on the Dodge Charger only.

Meanwhile, Road Runner sales nearly doubled to 80,000 in 1969, and *Motor Trend* named it Car of the Year. Not many of those 80,000 were Hemi-powered, partly because a new triple two-barrel carburettor

LEFT and OPPOSITE
The 1969 Charger R/T. Concealed headlamps were in vogue at the time.

145

option was added to the 440-cu in (7.21-litre) V8, which offered Hemi style acceleration at half the price. But for the full experience one had to have a Hemi, a fact underlined by *Car and Driver* when it tested the Hemi Road Runner against five other econo-racers, the Chevrolet Chevelle SS396, Ford Cobra, Mercury Cyclone CJ, Dodge Super Bee and Pontiac The Judge. Put simply, it was in a different class. The Hemi option made this Road Runner several hundred dollars more expensive

ABOVE, LEFT and OPPOSITE
Brilliant white bucket seats, trim and vinyl roof took a lot of care to keep them in pristine condition.

than any of the others, but if the following statement is correct, it was worth it: 'Where the Chevelle, Cobra and Cyclone CJ give the impression of being hot sedans, the Road Runner comes in from another direction – a tamed race car… [At full throttle] the exhaust explodes like Krakatoa and the wailing howl of surprised air being sucked into intakes turns heads for blocks. Baby, you know you're in the presence.' In short, the Road Runner accelerated faster than any rival (5.1 seconds to 60mph and a 13.54-second quarter-mile), stopped more quickly and rated second out of the six on handling. They also warned about 'incredibly stiff' suspension. And yes, it was worth it.

In the same year that *Car and Driver* was eulogizing the Road Runner, Dodge announced something far more outrageous, the Charger Daytona. From its 1966 luxury fastback origins, the Charger had gradually become more and more of a muscle car. Sales slumped in 1967, so for 1968 it was completely restyled to distance it from the Coronet on which it was based. There was a coke-bottle kick-up to the side panel, flared wheel arches and more aggressive fastback shape. The Hemi option came only with the R/T version of the Charger, and in 1968 475 were sold, a figure that had dropped to just 42 by 1970.

The new Charger's high-speed performance was hampered by that deep-set grille and tunnelled rear window, so for 1969 the Charger 500 was launched with a smoother, more aerodynamic shape in loud colours, big stripes and a 440 base engine option. The '500' came about as a result of NASCAR rules, which stated that 500 production-line cars had to be built to qualify for racing. But meanwhile Dodge's main NASCAR rivals, Ford and Mercury, had equalled the 500's aerodynamic

improvements. So Chrysler spent an alleged $1 million on a car specifically developed for NASCAR. It was developed in a wind tunnel, the wedge-shaped nose adding a whole 18in (45.7cm) to the car's length. At the rear, there was a massive spoiler, 58-in (1.47-m) wide and nearly 2ft (61cm) clear of the boot lid. It looked like the ultimate street racer's weekend toy, but really did reduce lift at high speeds. As a result of all these changes, drag was cut by 15 per cent and in race trim the Charger Daytona could reach 200mph (322km/h). It won first time out, too, at Talladega. Bobby Isaac set a world closed-course speed record in one at 201.104mph (323.64km/h), and went on to set an unlimited class record at Bonneville Salt Flats, with 217mph (349km/h).

Outrageous though they were, the Daytonas really could be road cars. Five hundred of them had to be, to qualify for NASCAR racing, and the first was delivered to a Dodge dealer in Lafayette, Indiana in June 1969, the last reaching the saleroom in September. Most were powered by the base 440 engine, but 70 Daytonas came Hemi-powered. Interestingly, the rules were changed in 1970. Instead of 500 cars to qualify, manufacturers had to build one for each dealer. Plymouth produced its own version of the Daytona, the Superbird, in that year, and so nearly 2,000 were built, just 135 of which had the Hemi option. Although it looked very similar to the Daytona, with the same droop snoot and high rear spoiler, the Superbird was quite different, being based on the Road Runner. In the early 21st century Chrysler's 'Winged Warriors', as they were known, look faintly ludicrous. One can imagine them being shown on the Thunderbirds TV show, or driven by Batman on his day off. But that is unfair: as road cars they were outrageous, but behind that was a list of

race wins that justified the outlandish looks – they weren't for show.

The Pony Hemis
But times were changing in the muscle car world. The 'Winged Warriors' were a symbolic last flamboyant gesture in a world where sheer brute power was going out of fashion. Emissions and safety legislation was getting tighter by the year, insurance premiums were going through the roof, and there was a growing climate of public opinion opposed to what was seen as a profligate use of resources. In truth, it was the end of the pure, no-holds-barred muscle car era.

But there is another piece of the Hemi story still to be told. Cars like the Charger and GTX, even the Road Runner, were too big and heavy to compete with the pony cars, the immensely successful Mustang and Camaro. For that market, Plymouth had launched an all-new Barracuda in 1966, in fastback, coupé and convertible forms. But it was not until 1970 that a Hemi option was added: the mighty 426 was simply too big to squeeze in before that, even after the Barracuda's 1968 facelift.

In that year Chrysler contented itself with building some lightweight Dodge Darts and Plymouth Barracudas for drag racing. The front spring towers were prized apart to allow the big Hemi to be squeezed in. But a purely road-going Barracuda/Dart had to wait for the 1970 E-body, which was designed specifically to allow bigger engines such as the Hemi and 440. In the words of author Robert Genat, 'Chrysler was determined to build the most potent pony car ever.' To handle that power, the cowl, front subframe and rear axle were taken from the B-body cars (the Coronet/Charger) and a new muscular body was designed to suit, lower and wider than

the old Barracuda, and in the classic long hood/short trunk mould. There would be both a Plymouth Barracuda and an upmarket Dodge Challenger, both based on the same platform, but with subtly different bodywork. Flush door handles, hidden wipers and streamlined mirrors were all period touches. Fat 60-series Polyglas tyres emphasized the aggressive stance. What it did not have was a urethane front end like the Pontiac GTO. Chrysler did not have the budget, but offered the Elastomeric, a steel bumper covered in high-density foam, painted in body colour.

Once one had decided to buy a Barracuda or Challenger, this was just the beginning. There was a base Barracuda, a luxury Gran Coupé and sporty 'Cuda, the latter with a Hemi option. Challenger trim levels covered base, SE and R/T. The Barracuda engine range was huge, starting with two non-muscular slant sixes (125 and 145hp/93 and 108kW) plus a 318-cu in (5.21-litre) V8. Then one stepped up to a 275-hp (205-kW) four-barrel 340-cu in (5.57-litre) unit, and the 383-cu in (6.28-litre) engine in 275-hp (205-kW) two-barrel and 300-hp (224-kW) four-barrel forms. Topping out the non-Hemi range was the

OPPOSITE
1969 Dodge Super Bee.

'Six-Pack' 440-cu in (7.21-litre) unit that produced as much torque as a Hemi but a 'mere' 385hp (287kW). But for true performance freaks with deep pockets and thick wallets, there could only be one choice, the Hemi. Choose the latter for one's 'Cuda, and it came as standard with the famous Shaker scoop, that burst through the hood and lived up to its name, trembling and quaking in sympathy with the V8 to which it was bolted. The Hemi option was one of the most expensive, at $1,227, which added over 40 per cent to the price of the basic car. Despite this penalty, 666 customers ordered it, making the 'Cuda

the second most popular Hemi-powered Chrysler. They would not have been disappointed either, as *Motor Trend* tested one in September 1969, with TorqueFlite transmission, 4.1:1 rear axle and power steering. Despite considerable wheel spin, it tripped the quarter-mile clocks at 13.7 seconds and 101.2mph (162.9km/h).

The Hemi 'Cuda option may have been short-lived and rare, but it achieved fame a quarter of a century after it disappeared from the Dodge price lists. Don Johnson, who had played a Ferrari-driving cop in the TV show *Miami Vice*, wanted a Hemi 'Cuda convertible for his new cop show

series, and called in Hollywood car supplier Frank Bennetti. The trouble was, Hemi 'Cudas are rare, expensive collectors' items. Even if they could find a car in time, explained Bennetti, it would cost a fortune. So in true Hollywood style, they cheated. Four Barracuda convertibles were painted an identical yellow, trimmed with a correct 1971 Parchment white interior, and went filming. Under the bonnets were 360-cu in (5.9-litre) or 440-cu in (7.21-litre) V8s, far less valuable than the real thing. But as far as the viewing public was concerned, or those who knew their muscle cars, it was fame at last for the Hemi-powered 'Cuda.

ABOVE
Super Bee front and rear lights, with Super Bee logo.

OPPOSITE
The Six-Pack (three two-barrel carburettors) V8.

Page 152
The no-frills Super Bee was the budget muscle car.

PAGE 153
Removing the hood.

ABOVE
That boot stripe was common to the Dodge
'Scat Pack'.

OPPOSITE
Matt black, big scoop, QR fixings.

As for the Challenger, one could have the Hemi option only in sporting R/T trim, though in any of the body styles: hardtop, SE hardtop (a special for 1970) and convertible. As ever, it was the most expensive engine option. In place of the standard 383, one shelled out an extra $130 for a 375-hp (279.5-kW) 440-cu in (7.21-litre) Magnum V8, or $249 for the hotter 390-hp (291-kW) version. The Hemi was in a different league, adding nearly $780 to the basic price. The Challenger was a big

hit for Dodge, in 1970 alone selling 76,000, of which just under 20,000 were R/Ts. Of those 20,000-odd, there were only 356 Hemi-equipped cars. Not that Dodge would have been too bothered: the Challenger outsold its arch rival, the Mercury Cougar, that year, which was sweet for Chrysler.

Sweet perhaps it was, but it was only a brief moment of glory. In 1971 all muscle car sales slumped, because of the pressures mentioned above. Naturally, all-out performance options like the Hemi suffered

even more. In that year Chrysler sold just 115 Hemi-equipped 'Cudas and 71 Challengers. By now, the only B-models available as Hemis were the GTX and Road Runner: in 1971 Plymouth sold just 55 Hemi Road Runners and 35 GTXs. Nothing more clearly spot-lighted the fact that the age of the full-horsepower muscle car was drawing rapidly to a close. And let there be no doubt, a Plymouth or Dodge with a 500-hp (373-kW) race-bred V8 under the bonnet was certainly one of those.

SPECIFICATION
Street Hemi

Engine Type	Water-cooled, overhead valve 90-degree V8
Engine Codes and	H (1966), J (1967-69) R (1970-71)
Bore x Stroke	4.25 x 3.75in (108 x 95mm)
Capacity	425 cu in (6964cc)
Compression Ratio	10.25:1
Combustion Chamber Volume	168-174cc
Valve Size	Inlet 2.25in (57.15mm) and Exhaust 1.94in (49.3mm)
Carburettors	Dual Carter AFB
Camshaft	Mechanical (1966-69), and hydraulic (1970-71)
Cam Duration	276 degrees (1966-67), and 284 degrees (1968-71)
Ignition	Dual point distributor
Firing Order	1-8-4-3-6-5-7-2
Power (see text)	425hp (316.9kW) at 5,000rpm
Torque	490lb ft (664.4Nm) at 4,000rpm

For 1970, the Hemi finally appeared in the Chrysler pony cars, the smaller, lighter Dodge Challenger (shown here) or the Plymouth Barracuda.

157

Buy New

As late as 1999, one could still buy a new Hemi, but the cost was dear. Complete engines were listed by Mopar Performance Parts dealers as Hemi Crate Motors. There were two of them. The mild one (though that is a relative term) utilized the same 425 cu in (6.96-litre) capacity as the original, based on a cast-iron block containing forged 9:1 pistons. The stainless steel valves were the same size as the original Street Hemi, at 2.25in (57.15mm) inlet and 1.94in (49.3mm) exhaust, though the distributor was now electronic. There was a hydraulic-lifter cam of 278 degrees duration, and

with the 750-cfm (21.24-m³/minute) carburettor that Mopar recommended, claimed power was 465hp (346.7kW) and 520lb ft (705.1Nm) of torque. Even considering the Hemi's improvement over the years, it puts that official figure of 425hp (316.9kW) into perspective.

Or one could go for the comprehensive 528-cu in (8.65-litre) version, bored and stroked to 4.5in (114.3mm) by 4.15in (105.4mm). The block was unchanged, but topped with aluminium heads, and used high-compression 10.25:1 pistons; Mopar reckoned one would need an 850/900-cfm (24.07/25.49-m³/minute)

carburettor. The result was 610hp (454.8kW) and 650lb ft (881.4Nm). It was not cheap at nearly $17,000 for the complete engine, but for some people, worth every cent.

So why, nearly 30 years after the last Hemi road cars left production, could one still buy a new motor? Put simply, the answer lay in the fact that the Hemi was still a serious force in drag racing and still winning, and Mopar was not about to let all those drag racers down, not after 30 years.

A 1970 Lemon Twist Challenger convertible. Other colours offered by Chrysler were Vitamin C, Lime Light and Go-Mango. Sunglasses were optional.

ABOVE
The Hemi was expensive, and consequently found few buyers.

ABOVE RIGHT
An imposing view of 1970 Challenger R/T.

RIGHT
True-blue interior

OPPOSITE
1970 Dodge Challenger R/T.

OPPOSITE
1968 Plymouth GTX convertible.

THIS PAGE
The 440 Super Commando engine option was a little slower than a Hemi, but much cheaper.

PAGE 164
Front view of the GTX.

PAGE 165
A non-sporting interior on the GTX.

ABOVE
1969 Plymouth Road Runner.

RIGHT
The Road Runner lived up to its cartoon
inspiration.

OPPOSITE
The frill-free Road Runner, stripped of all
chrome.

PAGE 168
The rear of the Road Runner was plainer
still.

PAGE 169
Bench seat and strip speedometer revealed
the car's low-priced origins.

LEFT and OPPOSITE
The E-body Barracuda had a Hemi option.

BELOW LEFT
This one has the cheaper 440 V8.

BELOW
The E-body was designed to accept big engines from the start.

171

ABOVE
Two-spoke steering wheel, black interior.

ABOVE LEFT & LEFT
Simple front and rear treatments.

OPPOSITE
The big-cube 440 was a potent engine.

OPPOSITE
1970 Plymouth 'Cuda 440/6.

LEFT
The Shaker scoop was a popular option.

ABOVE
'Cuda interior, with high-mounted three-spoke wheel.

ABOVE
The Shaker scoop.

ABOVE LEFT and LEFT
The 'Cuda was the second most popular
Hemi-powered Chrysler.

OPPOSITE
Details of the 440 'Cuda, whose engine
was the biggest available.

177

OPPOSITE
1976 Plymouth 'Cuda Hemi.

ABOVE
The interior was similar to non-Hemi
'Cudas.

ABOVE RIGHT and RIGHT
The Hemi option was powerful but
expensive. The Shaker scoop was standard.

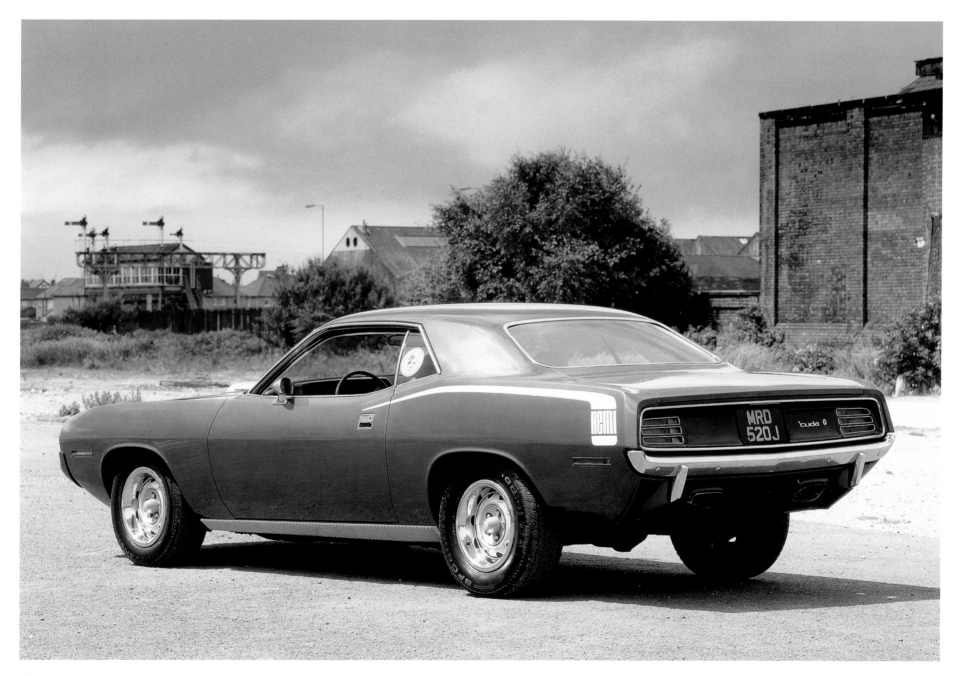

TOP
The Road Runner logo defined the car.

ABOVE and RIGHT
440/6 stood for 440 cubic inches, with three two-barrel carburettors.

OPPOSITE
1971 Plymouth Road Runner 440/6.

ABOVE and FAR LEFT
The Road Runner interior, still with the afterthought tachometer.

ABOVE LEFT
Road Runner was restyled for 1971.

OPPOSITE
1971 Road Runner 440/6: only 55 customers followed the Hemi route that year.

OPPOSITE
The Daimler-Chrysler Vehicle Collection.
Administrator Brandt Rosenbusch (left)
and restoration expert Dean Reitsnider
remove the hood of a 1964 Dodge Coronet
to expose the Hemi engine.

ABOVE
Dean Reitsnider positions a classic Hemi
engine in the exhibition.

ABOVE RIGHT
Frank Klegon, Vice President of truck
engineering for the Chrysler group, unveils
the new Hemi V-8 in 2001. This legendary
engine was re-intoduced in that year in the
Dodge Ram.

RIGHT
The Dodge Ram with Hemi V8 engine.

OPPOSITE
2001 Dodge Super 8 Hemi concept car. The car took centre stage when it made its debut at the North American International Auto Show. The styling is based on a Dodge truck and a sports utility vehicle. It features a prototype 353-cu in (5.8-litre pushrod V8 Hemi engine.

LEFT
The 2003 Dodge Durango HEMI (R) making its world debut at the Detroit Motor Show.

OPPOSITE and LEFT
Another vehicle using Hemi technology.
The 2000 Chrysler 300 HEMI (R) C
concept vehicle, powered by a V8 rear-
wheel-drive Hemi engine.

Hemi carried on developing engines into 2010.

ABOVE LEFT: Dodge Ram 3500.

ABOVE: The new Dodge Challanger.

LEFT: Dodge Magnum.

OPPOSITE: Dodge Charger.

Chapter Six
SURVIVOR:
The Firebird/Trans Am Story

In many ways, the Pontiac Firebird is the forgotten muscle car. Like every other non-Ford pony car, it was a reaction to the Mustang. General Motors' pony car was really a Chevrolet project, which Pontiac tagged on to late in the day; for the first few years of its life it played second fiddle to its GM sibling, the Chevrolet Camaro. The Firebird, moreover, did not sell as well as its Camaro cousin, let alone the Mustang itself.

And yet the Firebird turned out to be the great survivor among muscle cars, persevering with a big, hairy 455-cu in (7.47-litre) V8 in the uncertain 1970s, when every other muscle car was downsizing, downgrading or hiding its horsepower beneath a bushel. It was all due to the Trans Am, which started off as a Firebird derivative but ended up as a model in its own right. There was a paradox here too, for the Trans Am, one of America's legendary hot cars, was named after the famous race series but was never a successful racer itself. Yet up to 2002 one could still buy a brand-new Firebird or Trans Am.

In 1964 the Mustang had been let out of its stable and, contrary to the predictions of the industry, was selling in huge numbers.

Over at General Motors, Pontiac top management was peopled by individuals who loved and understood performance cars, most notably Bunkie Knudsen and John DeLorean. In a few short years they had helped to change Pontiac's image from fuddy-duddy to hot and desirable, with the Super Duty racing specials. On the back of that, they had recently launched the GTO, which was destined to become the first of a new generation of muscle cars. If any GM division was equipped to meet and beat the Mustang, it was the newly performance-aware Pontiac.

They got to work. Chevrolet had already proposed the XP-836, a sporting four-seater, but John DeLorean in particular wanted a proper two-seat sports car, a cheaper competitor for Chevrolet's own Corvette. This was the XP-833, with a streamlined, futuristic plastic body. But it was too avant-garde for GM's top management, who in any case did not want any in-house competition for the Corvette. Consequently, the XP-833 died a swift death.

Meanwhile Chevrolet has been working hard on the XP-836, the car that would become the Camaro. GM decreed that

instead of producing its own Mustang rival, it would work with Chevrolet on the XP-836, which subsequently became a joint project. This put Pontiac at a disadvantage, as Chevrolet was already some months down the design road, and coming to the project so late meant that Pontiac would have little influence on the car's fundamentals. 'Pontiac didn't like the decision,' wrote Bill Holder and Phillip Kunz in their book *Firebird & Trans Am*, 'but that was the way the game would be played.' The Camaro's styling had already been finalized, and to cut costs (and time) the new Pontiac would have to share its wings and doors: only the nose and tail could be altered to make the car different in character from the Camaro.

They managed to do this by giving it a GTO-style split-front grille with recessed twin headlights and narrow rear lights in two tiers, instead of the Camaro's conventional lights. It was not much, but at least the cars now looked like cousins rather than clones. The downside was that the extra design work pushed the Pontiac's launch date back to February 1967, five months after that of the Camaro. However,

the Firebird did have a suitably evocative name.

Late Starter
'After this', went the advertising copy, 'you'll never go back to driving whatever your driving.' That ran below an almost full-page colour picture of an open-top Firebird 400 roaring along an open mountain road, devoid of traffic (in car advertisements, roads never have any other traffic). The advertisement also referred to '400 cubes of chromed V8…heavy-duty 3-speed floor shift, extra-sticky suspension and a set of duals that announce your coming like the brass section of the New York Philharmonic.' If Pontiac was attempting to sell a politically incorrect fantasy, it was doing a pretty good job.

Hot pants, hot car?

That 400 was the top model of five: Firebird, Sprint, 326, 326HO and 400. The base model came in at only $2,600, powered by Pontiac's own overhead-cam 230-cu in (3.77-litre) straight six with 165hp (123kW). Despite all the components it shared with the Camaro, the Firebird used Pontiac's own power units. That also allowed Pontiac to offer the Sprint, which was surely unique among muscle cars in using a highly-tuned six-cylinder engine instead of a V8. For only $116 extra over the base Firebird, the straight-six was given a Rochester four-barrel carburettor, higher-lift cam, 10.5:1 compression ratio, split exhaust manifold and freer-flowing air cleaner, plus 215hp (160kW), 50hp (37kW) more than standard. As part of the package, the three-speed shifter was floor-mounted, and the suspension was firmed up. By American standards, this was a relatively small-engined high-revving performance car. Both the Sprint and base Firebird could be had in open-top forms, as a $237 option. Despite that seductive advertisement, convertibles were only ever a minority of Firebird sales: less than 16,000 were sold

in that first year, or about one in five of the total.

If the Sprint seemed too frenetic, and for many traditionalists it probably did, the more laid-back 326-cu in (5.34-litre) V8 was a better choice. Slightly more powerful than the Sprint at 250hp (186.5kW), but with far more torque as it provided 330lb ft (447.5Nm) at 2,800rpm, this was the most relaxed of the new Firebirds. Pontiac underlined the point by equipping it with a non-sporting three-speed column shifter, and billing the buyer for $21 less than the Sprint owner. A three-speed transmission was not synonymous with boulevard cruising: even the top-performance Firebird 400 stuck with a three-speed. For an extra

$47, Firebird 326 owners could make that a floor shift, while a centre console and bucket seats were also on the options list. As ever, the interior design of mass-market muscle cars was just as important as the way they looked on the outside. Owners were paying for something that made them feel special. Not for nothing had the Camaro's designers aimed for a fighter plane feel for the interior.

But it was the two top Firebirds, the 400 and the 326HO, that finally entered true muscle car territory. The HO took the standard 326-cu in engine and added a 10.5:1 compression, Carter four-barrel carburettor and dual exhaust, among other things. According to Pontiac, this boosted

power by a modest 14 per cent to 285hp (212.5kW). This figure is generally considered to have been underrated, with the true figure at 300hp (224kW) or more. The official torque figure seems more believable, at 359lb ft (486.8Nm). To proclaim to the world that one had bought an HO, the car sported long body stripes and 'HO' badges: in this instance, the HO stood for High Output.

At the end of that first 1967 model year, 82,560 Firebirds had found buyers, which was surely not as many as Pontiac would have liked, but the car was hamstrung by missing the first five months of the sales season. That was partly why Chevrolet managed to sell over 200,000 Camaros in the same year. Both were a long way off Mustang figures, but the figures were good enough. And in 1968, the Firebird's first full year on sale, 107,000 cars were sold. In fact, 1968 would head the Firebird's sales record for eight years. This, of course, was the height of the muscle car boom; only a few short years into the future and Pontiac salesmen would be looking back to these times with feelings of nostalgia.

There were few major changes in that year. The straight six got a capacity boost to 250 cu in (4.1 litres) which gave 175hp (130.5kW) and 240lb ft (325.4Nm), though it was still a mildly tuned unit, with a lowly 9.0:1 compression ratio. Oddly, although the Sprint enjoyed the same increase in cubes, it was still quoted at 215hp (160kW), though rated torque was up to 255lb ft (345.8Nm): maybe the original had proved just a little too 'European' for traditional U.S. buyers. Of more significance was the replacement of the 326-cu in unit with the Firebird 350. Like its predecessor, this 350-cu in (5.74-litre) V8 came in two forms: mild-mannered

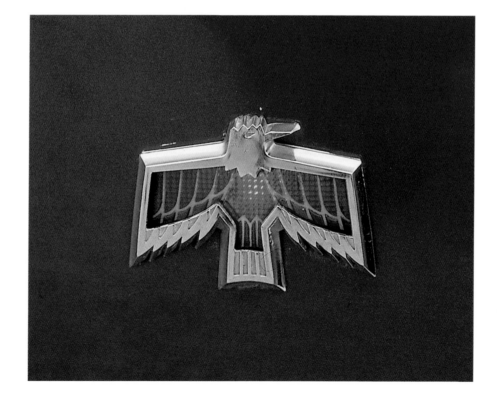

RIGHT
The distinctive Firebird badge

OPPOSITE
1969 Pontiac Firebird.

The Firebird (1969 model shown here) was Pontiac's version of the Camaro. But it came to the project late, and could only make limited changes to Chevrolet's design.

Two-piece rear lights distinguished the Firebird from the Camaro.

been banished by a six-car test in *Car and Driver* during May 1968. A Firebird 400HO was compared with a Camaro SS396, AMC Javelin SST, Mustang 2+2 GT, Mercury Cougar XR-7 and Plymouth Barracuda Formula S. The Pontiac product came out head and shoulders above them all.

Car and Driver loved its big engine, though admittedly it had been very well prepared, and scored it top of the six in every category. It was the fastest-accelerating of the six, and by some margin, attaining 60mph (96.5km/h) in 5.5 seconds when compared with the 6.6 and 6.3 seconds recorded by the Camaro and Mustang respectively, and the quarter-mile time of 14.2 seconds. Moreover, it revved so quickly and smoothly that it was easy to overshoot the 5,100rpm shift point. The variable-ratio power steering (the first on an American-made pony car) came in for particular praise, as did the handling. There was no mention of the axle hop which early Firebird tests criticized, so the changes for 1968 (multi-leaf springs and staggered shocks) seem to have worked. The ride was thought to be a little too firm, but the Firebird scored bottom only on front fender protection and the effectiveness of its wipers, hardly major points. When all the points were added up, the Firebird scored 118, ahead of the Barracuda (111), Javelin (91), Cougar (90), Camaro (79) and Mustang (73).

'For sheer enjoyment and confidence behind the wheel,' the *Car and Driver* testers concluded, 'the Firebird was almost

cruiser with a single two-barrel carburettor, three-speed column shifter and now 265hp (197.5kW) at 4,600rpm, and as the 350HO with four-barrel Rochester, 10.5:1 compression and 320hp (238.5kW). As with the original HO, there were plenty of cues on the outside as to what lay beneath the bonnet, such as dual exhaust and F70 x 14 tyres, plus all the usual stripes and badges. The 350HO's power output was not far behind that of the 400, now boosted slightly to 335hp (250kW) at 5,000rpm as

the 400HO and still offered with or without Ram Air. This was due to a higher 10.75:1 compression and power-flex fan. Any performance difference between the 350 and 400 engines may have been small, but for many buyers there was still one very good reason to pay the extra $435 for a 400: it still had more cubes than any other pony car – even the latest 1968 Camaro had only 396. Of course, that could be coaxed up to 375hp (279.5kW) with a dealer-fitted hot camshaft. The Z28 Camaro produced

400hp (298kW), but for many buyers, the Firebird 400 remained the cubic-capacity king. To maintain interest, Pontiac offered an updated Ram Air system, the Ram Air II, late in the model year, though the real significance lay not in the Ram Air itself, but in the fact that the new engine was significantly stronger than the old one, with forged pistons and four-bolt main bearings.

Any doubts Pontiac may have had about adopting and adapting what was basically a Chevrolet design would have

in a class of itself.' By contrast, the Camaro was 'built to be all things to all people, and as a result, it was a disappointment.' That surely was the sweetest victory for the Pontiac engineers. They had succeeded in taking a Chevrolet design and transforming it through careful use of their own components. As *Car and Driver* acknowledged, the division seemed to have a knack for taking unpromising material and producing something very different. If *Car and Driver*'s test was to be believed, it certainly succeeded with the Firebird.

The Arrival of the Trans Am
It had not escaped the Pontiac management that the Mustang had come last in that *Car and Driver* test. The reason was simple: the Mustang had barely changed in three years, while newer rivals were coming thick and fast. They were determined that no such

fate should befall the Firebird, so for 1969, after less than two years on the market, the Firebird received some major changes. As well as the subtle alterations to the sheet metal enjoyed by the Camaro that year, the Firebird's front end was restyled, with the quad headlights now carried in body-coloured mouldings, with the famous split grille squeezed inward to make room. Inside, there was an improved dashboard and new safety features.

The Sprint got a power boost to 230hp (171.5kW), but the best-seller of the entire range remained the softer Firebird 350, its power unchanged. The 350HO could boast an extra 5hp (3.75kW), which was not much but which counted on the all-important specification sheet, to 325hp (242kW), as a result of new cylinder heads, larger valves and a higher lift cam. The base 400 now offered only 5hp more than

the 350, but 13 per cent more torque at 430lb ft (583.1Nm). It was also given all the visual cues of the largest-engined Firebird on offer: hood scoops (which was available even without Ram Air), dual exhausts and floor shifter. An extra $435 brought Ram Air III, which gave those hood scoops something to do, and according to Pontiac delivered an extra 5hp and identical torque to the standard 400. If that was not enough, there was a new Ram Air IV for 1969. It was expensive at $832 extra (and not many were sold) but promised much, with a hotter cam, aluminium cylinder heads and different valve train. Another clue as to why not many Firebird customers chose to tick the Ram Air IV box lay in Pontiac's official power figures, which put Ram Air IV at 345hp (257kW) at 5,400rpm, with identical torque. Most considered that 10hp

(7.45kW) more for $800 was not an outstanding deal. However, the very same engine in Pontiac's GTO was quoted at 370hp (276kW). Either Pontiac had made a slip, which was unlikely, was being modest, which was very unlikely, or wanted to take the heat off its top-performance car in the face of the criticisms of safety campaigners.

Whatever the truth, it was overshadowed by a new option for the Firebird that, with hindsight, was more significant than any of those: the Trans Am. Mention that name today, and most people will not think of the race series for pony cars, but a hot Pontiac that made the name its own. Pontiac's plan went like this: it did not have a suitable competitive engine for the popular Trans Am series, so it started to develop a 303-cu in (4.965-litre) V8 based on the 400. In the meantime, Firebirds were raced using Z28 Camaro power units. After

racing a while, the special 303 would be fitted to a road-going Trans Am named after the series. But it took too long to develop, and by the time 303 was ready, the rules had changed, and it was not legal for Trans Am racing.

Faced with race-heritage rivals like the Z28 and Boss Mustangs, moreover, Pontiac did not want to delay its road-going spin-off, so the Firebird Trans Am was launched anyway, at the Chicago Auto Show in March 1969, though powered by the existing 400-cu in motor rather than the special 303. Consequently, when it was launched, the new Trans Am had never actually turned a wheel on a race track. Pontiac even had to pay the Sports Car Club of America a $5 royalty on every car. Still, it was a good investment, given that the car was still going strong 30 years later and was better known than the race series!

So what was the basis of the Trans Am? It seems almost sacrilegious to suggest it, but without that special 303-cu in race-bred engine, the early Trans Am was little more than a Firebird 400 with a spoiler and a different paint job. Engine-wise it was identical to the top 400s, with 335-hp (250-kW) Ram Air III or so-called 345-hp (257-kW) Ram Air IV. It looked very different, however, and this was part of its reason for being. John DeLorean was the power behind the Trans Am. As GM's Pontiac chief, he could not help but notice how well the Z28 Camaro had been selling. What the Firebird needed was its very own Z28, and the project that was initiated was codenamed 'Pontiac Firebird Sprint Turismo'.

When launched, the Trans Am looked as though it would be loud even before it was started up. All the early cars came in white, with blue racing stripes running the length of the hood, roof and trunk lid. Two gaping scoops gaped hungrily out of the hood, two more extractor scoops were fitted just behind each front wheel and there was a large rear spoiler, which the engineers calculated to produce 100lb (45kg) of down-force at 100mph (161km/h). So the Trans Am was flashy (tame by the standards of the 1970s, but a rabid extrovert for its time), but there were some suspension changes over the standard Firebird as well, namely heavy-duty springs, a 1-in (2.54-cm) stabilizer bar and 7-in (17.8-cm) wheels. It was not a mere paint and badges job, but it was close.

Nor was the first Trans Am a mass-market car. Pontiac made only 697 in its first year, most of which were fitted with Ram Air III, and most were automatics. But despite the extra glamour of the Trans Am,

This is the Bridgehampton round of the Trans Am, a race series that gave one hot Pontiac its name. There are no Trans Am cars here, but Pontiac made the name its own.

RIGHT
1973 Trans Am with SD-455 engine.

OPPOSITE
1973 Trans Am SD-455.

Ram Air IV and the restyling, Firebird sales as a whole were actually down in 1969, to 87,000, and that was over an extended 15-month model year, as a strike delayed the launch of the1970 cars.

For 1970, the Firebird, and of course the Trans Am, shared new single headlight styling with the Camaro: the Chevrolet and Pontiac vehicles would share bodies until 1981. Most people liked the cleaner look, with more subtle hood scoops and an inbuilt rear spoiler on the top Formula 400. But the times were reflected in other changes. To rationalize and save money, Pontiac's overhead-cam six was dropped in favour of the equivalent Chevrolet six, which brought the power down to 155hp (115.5kW). The peppy Sprint was replaced by the Esprit, which made luxury, rather than performance, its top selling point. It was powered by the 350 V8, now with lower 8.8:1 compression and single two-barrel carburettor, producing 255hp (190kW). Meanwhile, the three 400-powered Firebirds were replaced by the Formula 400, offered with either 330-hp (246-kW) base-model engine or the 335-hp (250-kW) Ram Air III. Ram Air IV was now only available to special order. The Formula's suspension was upgraded along Trans Am lines, with front and rear stabilizer bars and heavy-duty springs.

The 1970 Trans Am ('1970+' in official

ABOVE
Interior of the 1973 Trans Am SD-455.

OPPOSITE
Rear view of the 1973 Trans Am SD-455.

Pontiac jargon as it had been launched late, in March 1970) went along with the more subtle approach of the Firebirds. The rear spoiler was the muted, inbuilt unit seen on the Formula, and new front spoiler (giving up to 50lb/23kg of downforce according to Pontiac) was also smoothly styled in. The standard power unit was Ram Air III; here again Ram IV was available on special order, but was taken up by only 88 Trans

Am buyers. Nevertheless, they still got a Shaker hood (in place of the twin front-facing scoops), Rally II wheels, power brakes and steering, concealed wipers and dual horns., while the front stabilizer bar was a beefier 1.25in (3.175cm). The changes worked, and more than 3,000 Trans Ams were sold in that year. This was not enough to worry Ford or anyone else, but was a useful boost to the Firebird, whose

sales collapsed disastrously in 1970 to less than 46,000, or half the 1969 figure. The muscle car bubble had burst, but could the Pontiacs cope?

The 455
In many ways, Pontiac made the same efforts at retrenchment as every other muscle car manufacturer in the early 1970s. Compression ratios were scaled back to cope with lower octane fuel and stricter emission limits, and there was as much emphasis on luxury muscle (in the new Esprit Firebird, for example) as on sheer horsepower. The whole atmosphere had changed as horsepower figures tumbled. Much of the latter was the result of a change in measurement from gross to net horsepower, but it served only to reinforce the idea that the performance car was retreating.

In the midst of all this, Pontiac launched the biggest ever V8 fitted to a pony car, a 455-cu in (7.46-litre) unit. Fitted only to the Formula Firebird or the Trans Am, it came in two guises: 8.2:1 compression for 325hp (242kW) gross or 255hp (190kW) net, or 8.4:1 and a four-barrel carburettor HO with 335hp (265kW). Naturally, these massive motors pushed out a great deal of torque, and even the low-compression version managed 455lb ft (617Nm): in other words, one pound per foot per cubic inch, more likely to have been the result of careful development rather than sheer coincidence.

If the 455s seemed over the top, one could still buy a Formula 400 (now detuned to 300hp/224kW gross or 250hp/186.5kW net) with a lower-powered, budget-priced Formula 350 which cost only $29 more than the Esprit. The idea of the new, cheaper Formula was to provide all the performance add-ons (bucket seats,

LEFT
Rear view of the 1973 Trans Am SD-455.

OPPOSITE
1979 Firebird Trans Am, now with four rectangular headlamps.

suspension package, hood scoops) with lower purchase, insurance and running costs. With this car and the 455s, Pontiac was offering Firebirds in tune with the incoming tide of safety and emissions legislation, but at the same time struggling to come to terms with the inevitable.

The Esprit, meanwhile, came with 350 or 400 two-barrel V8s, both in modest states of tune, and buyers of the basic Firebird had a choice of the 250-cu in (4.18-litre) straight-six or the 350. Not surprisingly, the Trans Am came only with the new 455 motor, but delivered 335hp at 3,500rpm and 480lb ft (650.9Nm). In fact, despite the hard times for muscle cars, there were more Firebird models to choose from than ever before. Not that it helped sales much. They were up marginally, to 53,000 (excluding just over 2,100 Trans Ams) but, to put that in perspective, the Pontiac was outsold by Camaro and Mustang by three to one.

The year 1972 proved to be the Firebird/Trans Am's low point: this was in fact the year that GM considered dropping both the Chevrolet and Pontiac pony cars, though both just managed to survive. In keeping with the times, the best-selling model was the basic Firebird, which made up 40 per cent of the 1972 total. It still came with a choice of detuned 250-cu in six (now derated to 110hp/82kW net) or

Other muscle cars fell by the wayside, but the Trans Am struggled on.

problems) and sales of the whole range amounted to 28,700. It was little wonder that the GM top brass considered dropping the whole lot.

But having decided to hang on in, Pontiac took no half-measures. For 1973, while almost every other muscle car was in retreat, the Firebird and Trans Am were given extra power. It came in the form of the SD-455 V8, which was the existing 455 with many tweaks and changes to produce 310hp (231kW) net. That was equivalent to around 350hp (261kW) gross, so this 1973 V8 was offering the same sort of power as muscle cars of the late 1960s. To underline a return to what some would see as the good old days, Pontiac resurrected the 'SD' or 'Super Duty' tag, the name given to all those drag racing special parts of the early 1960s.

SD was no misnomer, as it was a very different motor from the standard 455, with a reinforced block, forged rods, aluminium pistons, Quadra Jet carburettor, dry sump lubrication, special cam, four-bolt main bearings and dual exhaust. In fact, so hot was the SD that it failed to meet emission limits, and Pontiac had to hurriedly derate it by 20hp (14.9kW). With a milder cam and cleaner exhaust it could manage 290hp (216kW), still more than any other muscle car. Moreover, the Firebird/Trans Am still

two-barrel 350-cu in (5.74-litre) V8 offering 160hp (119kW). It was closely followed by the Esprit (still majoring on chrome and interior fittings), now available with a 400 V8 as well as the 350. And the performance Formula? This had greater engine choice than ever before: 160- or 175-hp (119- or 130.5-kW) 400 or 300-hp (224-kW) 455. Despite

these options, only a little over 5,000 vehicles were sold, so despite the extra choice and the reflected glamour of the Trans Am, it seemed as though buyers really were abandoning muscle cars. The Trans Am itself came only with that top 455 motor, and about two-thirds of buyers opted for the M-40 automatic rather than the Hurst shifter four-speed manual.

The power figures seemed low, but all were net horsepower, so for performance freaks things were not as bad as they appeared: a Formula 455, for instance, could still run the quarter-mile in 14 seconds, so it was no slower than its predecessors. All well and good, but less than 1,300 Trans Ams trickled off the production line (a result in part of labour

OPPOSITE
1992 twin-turbo record-breaking Firebird/
Trans Am.

BELOW
1996 Firebird/Trans Am convertible.

had more cubic inches than any rival, and for some people these things still counted. In the Trans Am, the SD-455 came with beefed-up three-speed Hydra-Matic (with the shift point raised to 5,400rpm), a heavy duty radiator and uprated suspension. Oddly enough, having produced a hot car in a cold era, Pontiac seemed a little shy of the fact. One Trans Am 455 buyer recalled that he 'had to beg' for his car, and wait five months for delivery. And he also had to

pay $675 extra for the privilege, which was quite a chunk of money in 1973. Pontiac's reticence was at odds with the hottest Trans Am yet, especially with its new for 1973 big bird decal, which now covered the entire hood.

Originally, the SD-455 was to have been a Trans Am option only, but Pontiac decided to offer it on the Firebird Formula as well, which continued with the standard 455, 400 and 350 V8s. As ever, the Formula

offered a good-value performance package: for only $27 more than the Esprit, buyers got a twin-scoop hood, heavy-duty suspension, dual exhausts and several other bits and pieces. But as if to atone for the SD, other Firebird powerplants were derated in that year, with lower compressions: the base 250-cu in six was down to 100hp (74.5kW), and only 10 per cent of base Firebird customers chose it. Most went for the torquier 350 V8. In fact, the best-seller in 1973 was not that one, nor the sporty Formula, still less the flamboyant Trans Am, but the luxury Esprit. All told, Pontiac produced just over 46,000 Firebirds and Trans Ams for 1973, so the SD had not reversed the decline.

In fact, 1974 would be the SD's second and final year. Although applauded by the performance freaks, it really was swimming against the tide: gas was getting expensive, and it almost seemed unpatriotic to waste the stuff. Less than 1,000 Trans Am SDs were sold in 1974, and a mere 58 Formula SDs (evidently there were not enough performance freaks around). But sales of less macho Firebird/Trans Ams actually rose that year, to well over 70,000. Once again, the luxury Esprit was the best-seller, followed by the base Firebird, the Formula and, bringing up the rear, the Trans Am. The Trans Am package had become comprehensive, and was no rebadged Firebird: power steering, front discs, limited-slip differential, Rally gauges, Rally II wheels, sport suspension and many other parts were all standard. Even with the milder-sloping front end fitted to all Firebird/Trans Ams in that year, it looked the part.

There are two ways of looking at the Firebird/Trans Am in the mid-1970s. Enthusiasts would bemoan the dropping of first the SD-455, then the basic 455 (though

it would return in derated form), with ever lower compression ratios and power outputs for the other engines. On the other hand, Pontiac were selling more Firebird/Trans Ams than ever before. In 1974, the Trans Am became the best-seller, with over 27,000 sold, while the following year combined sales exceeded 110,000, a significant milestone. There were few

important changes to the actual cars, more a juggling of engine options to give more choice to base and Esprit buyers, and more emphasis on the Formula's appearance than its quarter-mile times. The base Firebird, for example, actually got a slight power boost in 1976, to 110hp (82kW), the choice of 160- or 175-hp (119- or 130.5-kW) 350 V8s and, for the first time, the 185-hp (138-

kW) 400. Meanwhile, the Trans Am was still the best-selling model, with over 46,000 finding homes. Even more significant for Pontiac's sibling rivalry with Chevrolet, the Trans Am was now outselling the Corvette. In short, it had become a muscle car model in its own right, and from now on, 'Trans Am' would be just as recognizable as 'Firebird'.

BELOW
The 1996 Firebird, smoothed out and aerodynamic.

OPPOSITE
1997 Hurst-tuned Firebird.

Boom and Bust

In the late 1970s both the Trans Am and Firebird enjoyed a sales boom, with over 150,000 cars (almost 70,000 of them Trans Ams) sold in 1977 alone. Well over 200,000 found homes in 1979. It is hard to say why this happened. With the 455 V8 finally gone, the Pontiac pony was following all the other muscle cars down the road of lower compressions and fewer cubic inches, though looks must have had a lot to do with the car's success. Pontiac's pony still looked the part of a true muscle car, especially in Trans Am form or as the Formula with its optional W50 body package. Trans Am special editions in black and gold, or Firebird Esprits in bright blue or red, all with loud decals and stripes, were also popular.

Recognized by its four rectangular headlamps, Trans Am/Firebirds of this era also saw some significant engine changes. The faithful straight six was replaced by a 231-cu in (3.785-litre) V6, sourced from Buick, in two- or four-barrel forms. Meanwhile, a small-block V8 of 305 cu in (5.0 litres) was brought in from Chevrolet, offering 145hp (108kW). The familiar 400 continued, but was topped by a 403-cu in (6.6-litre) V8 with 220hp (164kW): it was not a 455, but certainly on the way there.

To celebrate its tenth birthday in 1979, the Trans Am enjoyed its best sales figure yet, at 117,000. On the tenth anniversary special edition, there was a bigger bird on the bonnet, silver leather bucket seats and a silver-tinted hatch roof. The pure convertible had long since gone, replaced by an optional T-roof. The special edition also celebrated the fact that, once again, the Trans Am had been chosen as the official pace car for the Daytona 500; this always impressed the buying public, and Pontiac made the most of the fact with pace car replicas.

In the following year, however, both Trans Am and Firebird sales slumped. Was it because the big 400 and 403 V8s had been dropped? Possibly it was, though the 301-cu in (4.93-litre) turbo V8 which replaced them was almost as powerful, at 210hp (156.5kW). That 301 had become the standard powerplant, available in 140- and 155-hp (104- and 115.5-kW) forms alongside a single V6, and of course, the 210-hp turbo. Once again, there was a Daytona pace car replica, and over 5,000 of

these were sold. But maybe the Trans Am/Firebird was simply looking old: after all, the basic design stretched back over a decade, and in 1981 sales had slumped again. Pontiac needed a new one.

It arrived in the following year, with a sleeker, cleaner all-new body shape that nevertheless managed to retain a family resemblance to the old Firebird. With more attention given to aerodynamics, there was a steeply raked windscreen and squared-off tail, while the new car weighed 2,800lb

(1270kg), significantly lighter than the old one. Pontiac was following Ford's example with the new Mustang: shaving off weight to keep up performance with less power and better economy than the old-style muscle cars. Like the Mustang, the base power unit was a four-cylinder 153-cu in (2.5-litre) motor, the 'Iron Duke' with a mid-range 171-cu in (2.8-litre) V6 and, for the Trans Am, a 150-hp (112-kW) 305-cu in (5.0-litre) V8. For 1983, a V6 HO was added, with 135hp (100.5kW), while the

RIGHT
2001 Firebird Raptor convertible.

OPPOSITE
Standard 2001 Firebird convertible.

V8 came with a choice of carburettor or fuel injection. There was a special edition too, the 25th Anniversary Daytona 500 Pace Car, plus the black-and-gold Recaro Trans Am with special interior and an extra $3,610 on the dealer's bill.

By and large, buyers liked the new cars, though sales did fluctuate through the 1980s. They soared the first year, dipped in 1983 then soared again to nearly 130,000. In 1985 they were down again, falling to less than 100,000.

There were just three models: base Firebird, S/E and Trans Am, the last of which remained the best-seller, making up nearly half of all sales. The two top models were facelifted for 1985, with new front and rear ends, with the new look especially dramatic on the Trans Am with its optional W62 ground effects package. This was clearly inspired by racing, with aerodynamic 'skirts' as well as the usual front and rear spoilers. They might have reduced ground clearance, but who cared? Perhaps more significant was the rebirth of performance.

Along with other muscle cars of the mid- and late-1980s, the Trans Am began once again to offer big horsepower figures. The 305-cu in (5.0-litre) V8 now came in three versions: base, HO and TPI (Tuned Port Injection) with 155hp (115.5kW), 190hp (141.5kW) and 205hp (153kW) respectively. Performance, it seemed, was back in fashion. Even cubic inches were

making a comeback, and for 1987 Pontiac fitted a 350-cu in (5.735-litre) V8 with 210hp (156.5kW). The engine was from Chevrolet, but Pontiac needed it to counter the new 5.0-litre V8 Mustang. It was hardly surprising to learn that the 2.5-litre four-cylinder Firebird had been dropped.

There was a multiplicity of options to go with the new-found performance. The Y99 suspension package, for example (front and rear stabilizer bars with custom shocks), and a whole range of rear axle ratios. For 1988, the 350-cu in TPI V8 was up to 235hp (175kW), available both in Trans Am and a reborn Formula, while there was a new GTA, which slotted in midway between those two. This was a sort of performance Firebird, with a whole range of options like all-wheel disc brakes and performance suspension to turn it into a budget Trans Am. It was a popular car, with over 20,000 built. Once again, the Trans Am enjoyed pace car status in 1989, though the replica, of which more than 5,700 were sold, used a turbo V6 rather than one of the big-cube V8s. In actual fact, it was more powerful than any of them, with 245hp (183kW).

On the face of it, the Trans Am and Firebird seemed to have moved with the times. Lighter and more efficient than the old-school muscle cars, but now with big performance once again, from a choice of V8s offering 200hp (149kW) or more. They looked the part too, muscular, but aerodynamic and clean. And yet the honeymoon was over. From 1987, sales fell year on year, plumbing even greater depths than the dark days of the early 1970s. Pontiac sold over 110,000 pony cars in 1986, little more than half that in 1989 and a little over 20,000 in 1990. Nor was the Trans Am the tower of strength it once had been: it became a minority seller in the

range, with less than 2,500 sold in 1990. Sales did recover slightly in 1991, thanks to a complete restyle front and rear, and a new convertible option across the range, while the 5.7-litre TPI V8 came in 205-, 230- and 240-hp (153-, 171.5- and 179-kW) forms. For economy-minded buyers, there was still a 3.1-litre injected V6. But it was a temporary blip, and sales slumped again in 1992, despite a 25th Anniversary Trans Am and the special Firehawk. The latter was a hot, high-priced rival to the ZR1 Corvette, with 350hp (261kW) and 390lb ft (528.8Nm) from its tuned 5.7-litre V8. Add in competition options like Recaro seats and a Simpson five-point harness, and the Firehawk could cost as much as $50,000.

Fifth and Final
The fifth-generation Firebird/Trans Am appeared in 1993. Now with rounded 1990s styling, to the casual observer it was little different from any other sports 2+2 of the time. And as ever, Pontiac's pony was little more than a restyled Chevrolet Camaro. It shared the new body and its 350 V8 with that eternal arch-rival, the only styling differences being below the waistline. Still, there was no denying that it was substantially new, with only 10 per cent of its parts carried over from the old car. The 1990s Firebird was still a rear-wheel-drive V8-powered 2+2, and in that at least little had changed.

Under the skin, a whole range of safety equipment included ABS brakes, plus driver and safety airbags. There were just two basic engines, a 160-hp (119-kW) 207-cu in (3.4-litre) V6 and a 280-hp (209-kW) 5.7-litre V8. But the high-performance Firehawk had proved so popular that this returned, now with a fuel-injected LT1 power unit of 300hp (224kW) and the choice of six-speed manual or four-speed

automatic transmission. Customers could expect a 13.5-second quarter-mile, so if there had been any doubt that performance was back in fashion, here was the proof.

As ever, there were both Firebirds and Trans Ams; for 1994 the former came with the V6 or a 275-hp (205-kW) version of the LT1, as base or Formula. Both Trans Ams (base and GT) were fitted with the 275-hp LT1 and six-speed manual transmission. The long tradition of performance options was upheld by the WS6 package: this tag had first appeared back in 1978 as a handling package, and it offered the same option in the mid-1990s, with larger wheels and tyres, stiffer suspension, larger stabilizer bars and four-wheel disc brakes. By 1996, the LT1 V8 had been boosted to 305hp (227.5kW) at 5,400rpm, which according to *Motor Trend* allowed the WS6-equipped Trans Am to accelerate to 60mph (96.5km/h) in 5.7 seconds and make the quarter-mile in 14 seconds dead. In short, the latest Trans Am was just as quick as the old ones, and complaints that the glory days of performance were over were simply wrong. That was underlined in 1998, when the LT1 was uprated again, this time to 320hp (238.5kW) and 345lb ft (467.8Nm), enough for a 0–60mph time of 5.1 seconds.

The following year was the Trans Am's 30th anniversary, and once again Pontiac made the most of its heritage. A limited run of both coupés and convertibles left the production line in white, with two blue racing stripes, just like the 1969 original. There were white leather seats and blue-tinted 17-in (3.2-cm) wheels. Meanwhile, the Firehawk remained the performance flagship. It was still built by SLP Engineering (which had produced the original Firehawk a decade earlier). By 2002, this was offering 345hp (257kW) and

350lb ft (474.6Nm) from its LS1 V8, 17-in Firestone low-profile tyres, spoilers and 9-in (22.86-cm) aluminium wheels. The Firehawk was not actually a model in its own right, but an option package that could be applied to a Firebird Formula, or the Trans Am coupé or convertible.

In 2002, the Firebird, Trans Am and Firehawk were all still in production, though there was talk of Pontiac dropping all three later that year. That would have finally closed a 30-year run of the longest-lived muscle car of them all – the great survivor. What was certain was that an all-new Pontiac GTO was on the way, due to be launched in late 2003. Whatever happened to the Firebird, this would be Pontiac's new performance flagship for the 21st century.

OPPOSITE
The legend lives on: the 2003 Firebird.

Chapter Seven
THEY ALSO SERVED:
Other Muscle Cars

GTO, Mustang, Hemi, Trans Am, Firebird: these are the muscle cars everyone knows, but there are plenty of others. The 'Big Three', plus American Motors, all produced a great deal of muscular metal in the 1960s and 1970s. Some were hardly worthy of the name, and most were mildly pepped-up versions of existing cars; but all had performance as a primary aim. This chapter does not attempt to cover all of these, for that would fill an entire book; it aims simply to describe a representative selection.

AMERICAN MOTORS: RAMBLER AND AMX

It had never been easy for American Motors to compete with the might of Ford, General Motors and Chrysler, and yet it survived the 1960s and 1970s, only succumbing in the end to a takeover by Chrysler in 1987. It never produced a rip-roaring muscle car in the classic tyre-smoking tradition, but neither was it completely left behind. AMC's first contribution to the muscle era arrived in 1966 with the Rambler Rogue V8. There had been a 270-hp (201-kW) fastback Marlin the year before, but that

was limited by AMC's venerable V8 engine, which could not be stretched beyond 327 cu in (5.36 litres).

The Rogue used the new Typhoon motor, initially as 290 cu in (4.75 litres) in two-barrel 200-hp (149-kW) or four-barrel 225-hp (168-kW) forms. This was far more stretchable, and was eventually expanded right up to 401 cu in (6.57 litres). The Rambler was, of course, a compact by American standards, so the Typhoon gave it respectable if not tarmac-melting performance; in fitting it AMC was following the lead of Ford and Chevrolet, which had both shoehorned V8s into their own compacts.

The Typhoon was also slotted into the bigger Marlin the following year, this time in 280-hp (209-kW) 343-cu in (5.62-litre) guise. But the Marlin was no lightweight, and took nearly 10 seconds to reach 60mph (96.5km/h). Better was to come, however. The attractive fastback AMX, which resembled a 2+2 but was actually a pure two-seater, turned out to be AMC's first true muscle car. The 390-cu in (6.39-litre) Typhoon put out a useful 315hp (235kW), which turned out to be more than useful

when powering the little AMX, which itself weighed only a little over 3,200lb (1452kg). *Car and Driver* recorded a time of 6.6 seconds for 0–60mph (0–96.5km/h) and 14.8 seconds over the quarter-mile, estimating top speed at 122mph (196km/h). AMC had been disadvantaged by a somewhat staid and sensible image, but the AMX marked a complete break with that, and it succeeded. It gave AMC a toehold (albeit a small one) in the youth market, especially after Craig Breedlove established 106 new world records with the AMX early in 1968.

The Javelin, launched in 1968, looked very similar but had a much longer wheelbase, four seats and the Mustang in its sights. Like other pony cars, it came with a wide range of motors, kicking off with a 232-cu in (3.8-litre) six, but the real muscle variant was the SST, with that 390 that worked so well in the lighter AMX. This option was introduced late in the 1968 model year, so late that there was no mention of it in AMC brochures! At first, it was hampered by a wide-ratio three-speed manual gearbox, but a four-speed 343 Javelin was almost as fast. But for 1969, it

came into its own, especially with the loud and proud options aimed directly at the muscle car aficionados. The 'Go-Package' brought heavy-duty suspension and wide wheels, or one could choose from garish new colours: Big Bad Orange and Big Bad Green. If a standard Javelin 390 was not quick enough, there were tuning parts down at the dealers, and a whole variety of rear axle ratios. There could be no doubt about it, AMC was determined to leave its sensible past behind, spurred on by an encouraging start to its racing programme.

It took things one step further in 1969, teaming up with tuning specialist Hurst to produce the hottest Rambler yet. It was actually Hurst which had the idea of combining the lightest 3,000-lb (1361-kg) Rambler with the 390-cu in (6.4-litre) V8 in

OPPOSITE
American Motors' 1969 AMX two-seater was smaller than other muscle cars.

325-hp (242-kW) form. That gave it the terrific power to weight ratio of 10.03lb/hp (6.1kg/kW); according to Road Test magazine, when combined with the four-speed Borg-Warner box, it produced a quarter-mile time of 14.4 seconds at just over 100mph (161km/h). No one could mistake the SC/Rambler for any lesser AMC, with its loud red, white and blue colour scheme, wide wheels and red-stripe Goodyear tyres. Once again the SC proved that the classic muscle formula of big engine in a small light car was a simple way to high performance. The same 325-hp 390 found its way into the AMX and Javelin SST as well, and these too were quick cars. AMC also collaborated with Hurst in 1970 with the 'Rebel Machine', now with 340hp (253.5kW) from the faithful 390, with Ram Air induction and a low back pressure dual exhaust. This too came with an extrovert red, white and blue paint job, but if that was too much, one could go for something more sober. In the event, it was these 390s which proved to be the ultimate AMC muscle cars.

For 1971, the AMX and Javelin benefited from the company's biggest, most powerful engine yet, the 401-cu in (6.57-litre) V8 with 330hp (246kW). The trouble was that they now both shared a bigger, heavier bodyshell, so the power/weight ratio was actually down, though it was still

RIGHT
The 390 engine gave a high power to weight ratio.

OPPOSITE
The AMX interior provided ample space for two.

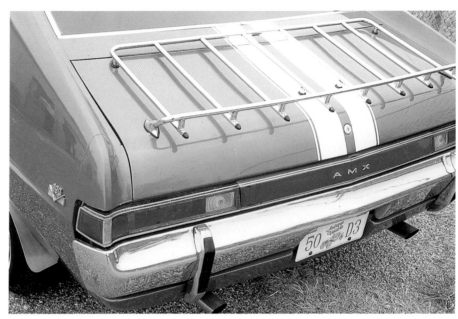

a fast car, at 7.7 seconds to 60mph (96.5km/h) for the AMX, and a 15.5-second standing quarter-mile. By now, muscle cars were attracting high insurance costs, and AMC responded with a mild-muscled version of the compact Hornet, which had replaced the Rambler. The 360-cu in (5.9-litre) V8 was not AMC's biggest or hairiest, but it was enough to propel the lightweight Hornet over the quarter-mile in 14.8 seconds. In a few short years, these modest muscle cars had helped AMC to transform its image.

The AMX was a compact muscle car, though the trunk rack hinted at limited luggage space.

ABOVE
Familiar engine, unfamiliar setting.

RIGHT AND OPPOSITE
The mid-engined AMX/3 of 1970.

OPPOSITE BELOW
1978 AMX.

THIS PAGE and OPPOSITE
From 1971, both AMX and Javelin shared
the same restyled body, now with a
401-cu in (6.6-litre) engine option.

229

BUICK: THE GRAN SPORT

William Mitchell, so the story goes, wanted to create an American Jaguar. As General Motors's head of styling, he liked the way Jaguars combined sportiness with luxury in a sedan package. The new Riviera of 1963 was not that, but the Gran Sport derivative, which appeared a couple of years later, was much closer. In contrast to other Buicks and, for that matter, most other American cars, the Gran Sport came with just one engine and transmission option. But it did not need alternatives as the 425-cu in (6.96-litre) V8, with its 10.25:1 compression, produced 360hp (268.5kW) and a massive 465lb ft (630.5Nm) of torque. According to *Car and Driver*, its three-speed automatic was 'without question, the best automatic transmission in the world'.

Twin four-barrel Carter carburettors and big dual exhausts pointed to the power ambitions of this Detroit Jag. There were suspension changes too: a front anti-roll bar and stiffer springs and shocks all round. All this, and a time of 7.2 seconds for 0–60mph (0.96.5km/h), made the Gran Sport a fully-fledged muscle car.

In that same year of 1965 Buick unveiled the Skylark GS (Gran Sport). This was a direct response to Pontiac's GTO, being smaller than the Riviera. In fact, 'direct response' is quite an appropriate: an early GS advertisement described the car as 'your own personal-type nuclear deterrent!'

RIGHT and OPPOSITE
1968 Buick Gran Sport 430/4.

OVERLEAF
Gran Sport engine.

ABOVE
The Gran Sport name survived into the 1990s. This is a 1991 Skylark GS coupé.

introduced later in the year: even without special tyres and ratios, that could trip the lights at just under 15 seconds. In fact, the muscle trend was spreading right across the division, and in 1966 Buick offered a GS version of the full-sized Wildcat, complete with heavy-duty suspension, Positraction and the 340-hp V8.

Meanwhile, the Skylark GS range was expanded with the cheaper 340, with a 340-cu in (5.57-litre) motor giving 260hp (194kW) at 4,200rpm and a useful 365lb ft (494.9Nm) at 2,800rpm. The engine was a common fitment to mid-sized Buicks at the time, but in the GS 340 came with a four-speed manual gearbox, red stripes, badges and hood scoops to leave no one in any doubt that this was a budget muscle car. In the event, most buyers (4 to 1) went for the GS 400, and the 340 was soon replaced by the slightly beefier GS 350.

For buyers of muscle cars, the 400 was still the Buick to have, especially in 1967, when it received a brand-new 400-cu in (6.555-litre) engine. Of lighter weight and with better breathing than the old Wildcat motor, it was slightly oversquare, though the claimed power was no different from that of the 340-hp Wildcat. To match it, GS 400 buyers (the car was now a model in its own right) could opt for the latest variable-pitch-stator Super Turbine transmission for an extra $237, which until then had only been available on the big Buicks. But the four-speed manual option was still the fastest: it was a full second quicker to 60mph (96.5km/h), for example.

Reflecting these muscular times, the 400 was getting gaudier, with more stripes, side vents and hood scoops, and one could pay $90 extra for chrome-plated wheels. Its performance was getting more serious too. For 1969, there were two optional levels of tune. Stage I was dealer-fitted, a

It was not quite as forceful as the big-engined Riviera, but the 401-cu in (6.57-litre) Wildcat power unit allowed 325hp (242kW) and 0–60mph (0-96.5km/h) in 7.8 seconds. It was also held back by a two-speed automatic and just one four-barrel carburettor.

GS buyers had a choice of six different rear axle ratios, however, and the car could be coaxed into impressive drag strip performance. *Motor Trend* tested one with a 4.3:1 rear end, racing slicks, headers, shimmed front springs and a transmission kick-down switch. It responded with a standing quarter-mile of 14 seconds at 101mph (162.5km/h), reaching 60mph in 5.7 seconds.

Well aware of the growing interest in muscle cars, Buick upped the GS's power with a 340-hp (253.5-kW) option

ABOVE
1995 Buick Regal Gran Sport coupé.

OPPOSITE
1995 Buick Skylark saloon.

comprehensive list of parts that included a high-lift cam, high-output oil pump, heavy-duty valve springs and tubular (thus lighter) pushrods. A large dual exhaust and modified Quadrajet carburettor were part of the package, as was a 5,200rpm governor in the transmission to prevent over-revving, and a choice of 3.64 or 3.42:1 Positraction rear axles. Pay a little more, and one could have heavy-duty suspension and power

front disc brakes as well. Fitted up and ready to go, the GS Stage I produced 345hp (257-kW) at 4,800rpm. Stage II was intended only for racing, and was not recommended for use on the street or for any car with a silencer. The Buick dealer was not even able to fit the parts: they had to be bought over the counter, from which point the buyer was on his own. That year, a GS 400 was the fastest car tested by *Car*

Life magazine, and achieved 0–60mph in 6.1 seconds.

But cubic inches were the final arbiter in the muscle car wars, and Buick obliged in 1970 with the Gran Sport 455. This latest 455-cu in (7.46-litre) V8 was a stretched version of the 430, and produced 350hp (261kW) at 4,600rpm, breaking the 500-lb ft (678-Nm) barrier too, at 510lb ft (691.6Nm) at 2,800rpm. That was in a relatively mild state of tune (single four-barrel carburettor and 10.0:1 compression), but once again Stage I was ready and waiting. For a little under $200, buyers could have extra-large valves, big-port cylinder heads, stronger valve springs, a high-lift cam, modified carburettor and even blue-printed pistons. Rallye Ride stiffer suspension cost just $15.80 extra: Buick seemed determined to give the horsepower fanatics a good deal! They would not have been disappointed either, as the Stage I GS could rocket to 60mph (96.5km/h) in 5.5 seconds and over the quarter-mile in less than 14 seconds. Not surprisingly, these Stage I 455s were popular, making up more than 1 in 4 Buick sales in 1970.

But all of these GS Buicks, however impressive their performance, still looked quite subtle, even understated, compared with the more garish muscle cars, but Buick responded with the GSX; bright yellow with rear spoiler, black hood and rally stripes, this was really a GS (either with the 350-hp/261-kW V8 or Stage I) in a flashy new suit, plus all the performance options: hood-mounted tachometer, power front disc brakes, four-speed manual box, bucket seats, stiffer suspension – the list went on. Less than 700 GSXs were sold in 1970, suggesting that Buick's traditional clientele preferred the classy look, but that did not prevent the company from offering the

ABOVE
1962 Buick Riviera V8.

OPPOSITE
1963 Buick Riviera.

GSX package on any Gran Sport in 1971–72 as well.

The Gran Sports were tamed and detuned in the early 1970s, but 1982 saw a new generation of Buick muscle cars. The Regal Grand National (to commemorate Buick's NASCAR win) was actually built for Buick by Cars & Concepts of Michigan. As standard, it came with a flabby 4.1-litre V6 of 125hp (93kW), but a few cars were fitted with the Regal Sport Coupé's turbocharged 232-cu in (3.8-litre) V6, boasting 175hp (130.5kW). The idea behind the turbo was to provide something closer to V8 power with V6 economy. The figures may have looked pale next to a late 1960s muscle car, though of course they were SAE net rather than gross; but by 1987 the V6 was intercooled and delivering 245hp (183kW) and 355lb ft (481.4Nm), powering a range of all-black Buicks.

LEFT and OPPOSITE
The 1962 Buick Riviera V8 401.

OVERLEAF
A famous name from Buick history: the
Riviera Gran Sport.

OPPOSITE
The Riviera Gran Sport seen from above.

LEFT
1962 Riviera V8 401 engine.

LEFT
The 455 was the biggest Buick engine.

OPPOSITE
For 1971, the GS became the flashier GSX.

PAGE 246
GSX front view.

PAGE 247
*The GSX was very different from Buick's
earlier models and seems to have
abandoned all notions of subtlety.*

OLDSMOBILE: THE 442

If there was one thing that helped to keep General Motors healthy in the 1960s, it was the competition encouraged between its divisions. They shared some components, of course, and that made economic sense for all concerned, but as far as sales went they were left to sink or swim on their own. Apart from the odd directive from top brass (such as the banning of triple carburettors on any GM car except the Corvette) they were left strictly alone.

So as soon as Pontiac launched the GTO package, its sibling rivals lost little time in coming up with GTOs of their own. Buick had the Skylark Gran Sport, so what would Oldsmobile have? The answer was the 442. Those numbers would be as evocative to muscle car fans as GTO or even 409. Officially, they stood for four-barrel carburation, four-on-the-floor and two dual exhausts. At least, they did until the four-speed manual gearbox could be replaced by an optional automatic, and then Oldsmobile claimed that the second '4' represented cubic inches.

Like GTO, the 442 started out as an option package, in this case 'Option B-09 Police Apprehender Pursuit', to give it its full official title. A $285 option on the Oldsmobile Cutlass, this brought 310hp (231kW), an increase of 20hp (14.9kW), as a result of a high-lift cam and high compression, that four-speed manual and dual exhaust. There were also heavy-duty shocks and springs and a rear stabilizer bar. As well as being as fast as a GTO, the 442 rapidly gained the reputation of being the best-handling muscle car of all, an accolade it retained right through the 1960s.

Word soon got round, and the 442 became a popular option, especially from 1965 when Oldsmobile shoehorned in a bigger 400-cu in (6.555-litre) engine: this

was a downsized version of Oldsmobile's new 425-cu in (6.96-litre) motor, and incidentally had the added benefit of more cubic inches than the 389-cu in (6.375-litre) unit in the GTO. In practice, it meant 345hp (257kW) at 4,800rpm and a hefty 440lb ft (596.6Nm) of torque, enough for a 0–60-mph (0-96.5-km/h) time of 5.5 seconds and a standing quarter-mile of exactly 15 seconds. *Car and Driver* loved it ('a very worthwhile balance of all the qualities we'd like to see incorporated in every American car') and so did the buying public: just over

25,000 of them ordered the 442 package that year.

For 1966 the Cutlass was restyled, while the 442 package now included convenience features like two-speed wipers and bucket seats. Another 5hp (3.7kW) was coaxed out of the V8, thanks to a higher compression, but the big performance news was an optional triple two-barrel carburettor set-up, which claimed 360hp (268.5kW). This was Tri-Power, but it was only available for a year before the GM management handed down the banning order. Still, the standard

*ABOVE and OPPOSITE
The Buick-like Cutlass was an unpromising start, but led to the 442.*

It certainly didn't look like a muscle car, but the Cutlass 442 performed like one, especially from 1965 when a bigger 400-ci engine was fitted. The ultimate factory 442 was the lightweight W30, and from specialists, the 455-ci Hurst 442.

Oldsmobile that dealer John Demmer of Michigan was persuaded to build replicas, and being dealer specials, no GM power limitations could apply! This car was the first in a long line of Hurst/Oldsmobiles, which used the standard 442 base with a Force Air 455 supplying 390hp (291kW) and 500lb ft (678Nm). The engine itself was special, based on that of the Tornado but with special crank, high-lift/duration cam, Ram Air cylinder heads and a modified auto transmission: this last was equipped with a Hurst Dual-Gate shifter that could be operated either manually or left to itself. It was quick, according to *Super Stock* magazine, to the tune of a 12.9-second quarter-mile, tripping the lights at 109mph (175km/h).

The hottest factory 442 remained the W30, which had started out as a drag-racing special but was now firmly aimed at the man in the street, though with optional rear axles down to 4.66:1, it is fair to say that many W30s ended up on the strip anyway. Little cosmetic touches underlined the 360-hp (268.5-kW) W30's status: bucket seats, red stripe tyres and hood stripes. There was also a slightly milder W31 package for 1969, with Turbo Hydra-Matic transmission, but this made up only one per cent of Oldsmobile's sales that year though. For

350-hp (261-kW) 442 in 1967 was surely fast enough, especially when it cost a mere $184 extra. As well as the engine, it brought heavy-duty suspension, wheels and engine mounts, wide, low-profile tyres and those desirable little red '442' badges. If one insisted, the bucket seats could be swapped for a good old-fashioned bench seat. That year, the 442 option was available on all Cutlass Supreme two-door cars, which indicated its popularity.

But the 442 had become such a strong badge in its own right that, just like the GTO, it was made a model in its own right. For 1968, the 442 was still a hopped-up Cutlass, but was not badged as such. There were three of them: holiday hardtop, sports coupé and convertible, all with a new 400-cu in (6.555-litre) engine in 325-, 350- and 360-hp (242-, 261- and 268.5-kW) forms. The last gave the same power as the triple-carburettor Tri-Power, but Oldsmobile got

around the ban by finding the extra power in a different way. It was almost as if there was unspoken warfare between the top brass bureaucrats and the designers on the shop floor.

There was another way to avoid GM bans: team up with an outside supplier. That is what Oldsmobile did with famed tuner George Hurst. Hurst had already squeezed Oldsmobile's biggest 455-cu in (7.46-litre) motor into a 442, and this so impressed

1970, the W30 package also included 10.88-in (27.64-cm) front discs, as well as the familiar Ram Air induction system, for which Oldsmobile claimed only an extra 5hp (3.7kW) over the standard 442. What everyone agreed was that the 442 was still the muscle car of choice for handling.

But times were changing, and 1971 was the last year for the 442 as a separate model: just like the GTO, changing times brought a decline in popularity, and the first sign that the manufacturer were aware of this was a reversion of these muscle car models to option packages, rather than being models in their own right.

By the end of the 1970s, the wild times of 360-hp (268.5-kW) 455-cu in (7.46-litre) 442s must have seemed a distant memory

indeed, but in 1979 there was an attempt to inject a little of the old excitement back into the new downsized Cutlass. For around $2,000 (a lot of money on top of a $5,631 base price) buyers received a bigger 350-cu in (5.735-litre) V8 of 170hp (127kW) in place of the standard 130-hp (100-5-kW) 305 unit, with gold paint job, gold aluminium wheels and a Hurst Dual-Gate shifter on the auto transmission. In sanitized form, the Hurst/Oldsmobile lived on. In fact, so strong was the name that it returned for 1984, complete with three-lever Lightning Rod Automatic Shifter, 180-hp (134-kW) 307-cu in (5.03-litre) V8, heavy-duty suspension and fat tyres: it sold 3,500 in that year, and was the most popular Hurst/Oldsmobile ever.

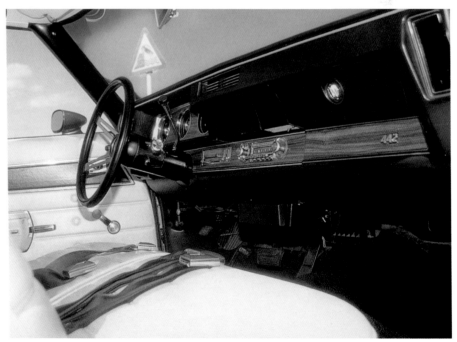

The 442 (W30 apart) was never a stripped-down performance special, as this white-upholstered 1971 holiday hardtop shows. This would be the final year for the 442 as a separate model. Why? Because performance was briefly going out of fashion.

LEFT and OPPOSITE
1970 Cutlass Supreme 442 convertible.

BELOW LEFT
A bold grille and vestigal front fender.

BELOW
The 442 had its moment of glory as an official pace car.

CHEVROLET: THE CHEVELLE

Just as Oldsmobile quickly responded to the GTO threat in 1964, so did Chevrolet, though at first it was turned down by General Motors's top management. The concept of a biggish V8 bolted into a mid-sized car had obviously worked so well for Pontiac that GM's 'cheap car' division wanted to do the same. Oldsmobile had lost no time in turning the Cutlass, with police-specification engine and suspension, into the famed 442. Chevrolet, not unreasonably, decided to fit its small-block 327-cu in (5.36-litre) engine into the Chevelle. Inexplicably, the concept was turned down: the 327 was actually mild by comparison with the 310-hp (231-kW) Oldsmobile unit, let alone the GTO's 325-hp (242-kW) 389-cu in (6.375-litre) motor.

Fortunately for Chevrolet, head office relented, and the Chevelle SS 327 was born. The Chevelle actually made a good base for a muscle car. First of all it was cheap, the lowest priced of GM's four A-body mid-sized cars. There was already a Super Sport (SS) option with bucket seats, console and badging, but with a maximum of 220hp (164kW) from the biggest V8 available it was no GTO scarer. Finally, the small-block 327 would slot straight in, and the engine itself was a proven quantity. So in the middle of that 1964 model year, two new options joined the Chevelle's list: the L30 (250-hp/186.5-kW) and L74 (300-

The 1967 Chevrolet Chevelle SS396 convertible, combining the mid-size Chevy with well over 300hp.

hp/224-kW) versions of the 327, costing $95 and $138 respectively over the base 283-cu in (4.64-litre) V8. In theory, one could even have the Corvette's hot 365-hp (272-kW) version of this engine, the L76, but it is thought that these super-Chevelles went in limited quantities only to drag racers.

So the Chevelle had its muscle derivative at last, but it was not really strong enough to challenge a GTO or 442. For that it needed a big-block motor, and this was not long in coming. Not that it was just a case of slotting Chevrolet's 396-cu in (6.49-litre) engine straight into the Chevelle. In fact, it was so awkward that in

its first year Chevrolet did not even advertise the fact that a 396 Chevelle was available, preferring to sell it in very limited numbers.

The problem was that to fit the big-block was expensive and time-consuming. A convertible frame was used with a coupé body, with two extra body mounts and rear

suspension reinforcements. Special left- and right-hand exhaust manifolds had to be made to squeeze the bigger engine in. Bigger power-assisted brakes (11-in/27.9-cm drums all round) were fitted, as were stiffer springs and shocks, plus stronger hubs and wider wheels. Even the Chevelle's ring-gear had to be swapped for a bigger one, and the engineers also added a bigger 11-in (27.9-cm) clutch and four-speed Muncie gearbox. Just 201 of these Chevelle 'Z16' SS396s were built for 1965, so it was not possible for a prospective purchaser to stroll into his local Chevrolet dealer, order one and expect immediate delivery. No matter, Chevrolet had made its intention clear.

This intention was made clearer still in the following year, when the rebodied Chevelle came as an SS396 from the start. In fact, there were three of them. The base 396 (it was a de-stroked version of the famous 409) produced 325hp (242kW) at 4,800rpm and 410lb ft (556Nm). If that was not enough, one could opt for the 360-hp (268.5-kW) L34. This had lots of internal

OPPOSITE
Not flashy, but fast: the Chevelle SS.

LEFT
The basic 396-cu in engine offered 325hp, but there was a 360-hp option, not to mention the 375-hp dealer tune-up.

PAGE 260
The 1967 Chevrolet Chevelle SS396 Turbo Jet.

PAGE 261
Behind the plumbing, the 396 was a de-stroked version of the original 409.

changes: a higher-lift cam, chrome piston rings, forged alloy crankshaft and dual exhaust, though it was only slightly torquier than the base L35, majoring on that substantial power increase. Still not enough? Then there was the top L78 with hotter-still cam, 11.0:1 compression and other parts to give 375hp (279.5kW) at 5,600rpm. That could reach 60mph (96.5km/h) in an alleged 6.5 seconds, but the L78 was in a very high state of tune, and it is thought that only around 100 Chevelles were equipped with it. The point was that a big-block Chevelle out-cubed the GTO and was now available at any Chevrolet dealer, in four-speed manual or automatic form, sport coupé or convertible. Together, over 72,000 of these were built in 1966, with another 63,000 in the following year.

The engine range was trimmed in 1967,

though. The base engine was still the 325-hp L35, while the L34 was derated to 350hp (261kW) at 5,200rpm. As for the top-powered L78, this 375-hp unit was not available as a factory option any more, but one could buy all the necessary parts at a local dealer. Whatever the engine choice, a Chevelle 396 came with three- or four-speed manual gearbox, or a Powerglide automatic, with no less than nine rear axle ratios available, between 3.07:1 and 4.10:1. With the 350-hp motor and the 4.88:1 axle, one could turn in some impressive performances on the drag strip.

For 1969, the 375-hp option was back, a clear sign of the times that the muscle car war was hotting up: 350hp as top power just was not sufficient any more. The Chevelle had a new body that year, the popular long hood/short deck look, with a fastback on the coupé, though sales slid

again to 57,000. For 1970, the SS396 reverted to option package status rather than being a model in its own right. Normally this is a signifier of low and falling sales, but that year they rocketed right back up to over 86,000, the best yet for the Chevelle SS.

Smart but not flashy, the package brought lots of detail items to differentiate the SS from lesser Chevelles: twin hood bulges, black grille, bright wheel rims and roof drip mouldings, rally stripes and white-letter F70 x 14 tyres with 7-in (17.8-cm) sports wheels. At $440 it was still good value, especially as the heart of the 396 was now the 350-hp engine, with a new 375-hp unit with aluminium heads (and probably more power than was claimed) as the top option.

Or was it? Through GM's infamous Central Office Production Order (COPO)

ABOVE LEFT and *ABOVE*
Subtle badging, though not so subtle naming, for the 'Super Sport Turbo Jet'.

OPPOSITE
The interior reflected the Chevelle's low-budget origins.

system, it was possible to order a Chevelle with even more power, direct from the factory. COPO (as detailed in the Camaro chapter) was intended as a means of satisfying fleet managers who wanted non-standard specification cars; for example, a bench seat in place of standard buckets, or a cheaper three-speed gearbox instead of a four-speeder. But if one knew the system, it could be used to order big-block engines. Chevrolet dealer Don Yenko did just that with the 427-cu in (7.0-litre) big-block V8, and some of these found their way into very special Chevelle SS427s. Yenko even converted 30 lightweight Novas with COPO-procured 427s, and later admitted that the result was 'a beast, almost lethal', capable of reaching 60mph in less than 4 seconds. The insurance companies agreed: they refused to cover the Nova 427, and no more were converted.

Chevrolet's Monte Carlo could not have been more different. Launched in 1970 as a luxury two-door, it was really an extended Chevelle. From the muscle point of view, the Monte Carlo's most significant feature was its SS454 package, which used Chevrolet's new 454-cu in (7.44-litre) version of the Turbo Jet big-block V8. This came in a mild state of tune – a 10.25:1 compression ratio and a single Rochester four-barrel carburettor – but still pushed out 360hp (268.5kW) at a relaxed 4,400rpm, plus 500lb ft (678Nm) at 3,200rpm. Still, the Monte Carlo was not really marketed as a muscle car, and this explain in part at least why only 2.6 per cent of them were ordered with the SS package and big motor.

In that same year, Chevrolet did the obvious thing and slotted the 454 into the Chevelle. It was obvious because the car had built up quite a reputation as one of the leading muscle cars, and even the top 396s were starting to get left behind by the 400-

muscle cars, in combination with new emissions and safety legislation, meant that the days of cars like the SS454 were numbered. For 1971, Chevrolet took the significant step of making the SS package (the stripes, suspension and show-off bits) available on lower-powered 350 and 400 V8s as well as on the 454. It was the right move, as over three-quarters of SS buyers chose the smaller engines that year. By 1972 one could even get a Chevelle SS307, while the 450-hp 454 had gone. The remaining 454 was detuned, with lower compression and 270hp (201kW) net, but Chevrolet sold only 2,500 of this model in 1973. This was no longer what people wanted.

hp (298-kW) opposition. Chevelle SS454 buyers had a choice of two tunes: they could have the motor in its soft Monte Carlo form, nice and lazy, with bags of torque at low revs. But of more interest to the muscle car crowd was the LS6 version, with a higher 11.25:1 compression , bigger 780-cfm

(22.09-m³/minute) Holley four-barrel carburettor, big exhaust valves and solid lifters. All told, it came to 450hp (335.5kW) at 5,600rpm and had the same peak torque as the softer LS5. To cope with the extra power, there were four-bolt main bearings, nodular iron bearing caps, and heavy duty con rods.

Together, they could shift the Chevelle to 60mph (96.5km/h) in just 5.4 seconds, and turn in a quarter-mile in the high 13 seconds. It is little wonder that collectors see this as the ultimate Chevelle muscle car.

But this was the turning point. Insurance problems with high-powered

ABOVE and OPPOSITE
The SS396 was very popular in the late 1960s, but within a few years, high insurance rates (among other things) saw its popularity plummet.

265

In 1969, over 86,000 Chevelles were ordered with the SS package, which included the 396-cu in engine, wide wheels and tyres and all sorts of badges and trim details. As a special COPO order, there was a 427 V8 as well.

The Chevelle was only one Chevy available with the SS package. By 1969 the Impala SS had grown into a big four-seater (now with a 427 V8 only). Maybe more exciting for hot car fans was the smaller, lighter Nova SS, complete with a 396-cu in 375-hp option.

The Chevelle was Chevy's mid-sized SS, sandwiched between Nova and Impala. Meanwhile, Camaro took care of the pony-car market.

THESE PAGES and 274
For 1970, the Chevelle had a mild facelift, but lovers of muscle car could still opt for a 'Turbo Jet 396' option, now actually measuring 402 cu in (6.6 litres).

*THIS PAGE and OVERLEAF
By 1972, the '396' tag had finally gone,
replaced by the SS400. But this wasn't the
Chevelle with the biggest number of cubic
inches any more. Ultimate was the 270-hp
(SAE) 454-ci unit. A four-speed
transmission was standard, and Turbo
Hydra Matic optional.*

275

PLYMOUTH/DODGE: BARRACUDA/DART

Plymouth's Barracuda of the late 1960s and early 1970s, the hell-raising Hemi-powered 'Cuda that was tricky to insure, was a quintessential muscle car. But the original Barracuda was not like that at all. It started out in 1964 as a mild-mannered fastback version of the Valiant sedan. 'We are sure,' said Plymouth's general manager P.N. Buckminster, 'that the Plymouth Barracuda is just right for young, sports-minded Americans who want to enjoy the fun of driving a car that also fulfills their general transportation needs.' And that summed it up. The first Barracuda was a wholesome, sensible, fun car, though its degree of wholesomeness depended on what one got up to on the fold-down rear seat: '7 feet of fully carpeted "anything" space'.

Although it was Plymouth's response to the Mustang, the Barracuda was in no way a hot car. There was just one V8 option, a 273-cu in (4.47-litre) unit with single two-barrel carburettor and mild 180hp (134kW), though a four-speed manual gearbox with Hurst shifter was optional. This was not what mid-1960s America wanted, and sure enough, only 23,000 Barracudas were sold in their first eight months.

But Plymouth realized what was holding back sales and rushed a revamped 'Cuda into production. Now the 273 V8 came with four-barrel carburettor, a 10.5:1 compression ratio and 235hp (175kW). The four-speed box was still an option, but could now make the car sprint to 60mph (96.5km/h) in 8.2 or 9.1 seconds, depending on which magazine was doing the driving. To go with the hotter

1970 Plymouth Barracuda. Not all Barracudas were Hemi-powered – most had milder, more insurable options such as this 383.

In the early 1970s, showing off was definitely in, which would account for the bright orange livery, bold black stripes and wide wheels of this Barracuda.

V8, a Formula S package brought wide wheels and tyres, stiffer suspension and rally stripes. This was more in tune with the market, and over 64,000 were sold.

That success encouraged Plymouth to make the Barracuda a model in its own right for 1967, and introduce a still-more powerful engine, this one a 383-cu in (6.28-litre) V8 pushing out 280hp (209kW) with its Carter four-barrel carburettor and a 10.0:1 compression. Front disc brakes, bucket seats and Sure-Grip differential were among the options, plus of course the inevitable rally stripes. Once again, over 60,000 Barracudas were sold, making these warmed up versions more popular than the hot and hairy 'Cudas ever were.

The Barracuda grew out of the Valiant, Plymouth's compact car. Fellow Chrysler division, Dodge, had its own compact, the Dart, and this became a formidable mini-muscle car for a few years in the late 1960s. Announced in 1968, the Dart GTS (it stood for GT Sport) was Dodge's equivalent of the Plymouth Road Runner, though unlike that mini-muscle, it never received the legendary Hemi power unit. But as it turned out, what it had was quite enough.

OPPOSITE
A U.K.-registered Barracuda 440, in orange with body-coloured bumper and prominent rear spoiler.

RIGHT
There were three two-barrel carburettors on the 440.

GTS buyers had the choice of two V8s. The 340-cu in (5.57-litre) small-block had a bore and stroke of 4.04 x 3.31 in (102.6 x 84.1mm); with 10.5:1 compression and a single four-barrel carburettor it could push out a respectable 275hp (205kW) at 5,000 rpm and 340lb ft (461Nm) at 3,200rpm. Alternatively one could have a 383-cu in (6.28-litre) big-block with 300hp (224kW), which was a lot of power for a compact. To go with the big V8, the GTS brought what Dodge described as Rallye suspension, 14 x 5.5-in wheels and Red Streak tyres; most cars were also ordered with a four-speed manual gearbox with Hurst shifter, or a competition-type TorqueFlite automatic. And being part of the Dodge 'Scat Pack' (applied to the Charger R/T and Coronet R/T as well as the GTS) there were rear-end bumblebee stripes and hood power bulges.

There was little need for the little Dart to persuade anyone it was quick: 6 seconds was claimed for the 0–60-mph (0–96.5-km/h) sprint, and 15.2 seconds for the quarter-mile. If anything, those claims were slightly modest, as *Hot Rod* magazine recorded a 14.38-second quarter-mile in a TorqueFlite GTS. It got even faster in 1969, when the 383 V8 was uprated to 330hp (246kW), though the GTS remained a minority interest, with less than 7,000 (both hardtops and convertibles) sold in that year.

More popular was the Dart Swinger 340. This was an unashamed budget muscle car that gave performance great priority and luxury very little. 'Dart Swinger 340,' went the advertisement, 'Newest member of the Dodge Scat Pack. You get 340 cubes of high-winding, 4-barrel V8. A 4-speed Hurst shifter on the floor to keep things moving. All other credentials are in order.' And they were: the Swinger had just as much power

THESE PAGES and OVERLEAF
The 1968 Dodge Dart GTS was more of a budget muscle car.

The Dart's origins lay in the typical 1950s four-door sedan, a far cry from the Scat Pack of ten years later.

and performance as the GTS, not to mention the Rallye suspension, wide wheels and bumblebee stripes. One could not have a convertible, and full carpeting only came if the four-speed was specified.

But who cared? At less than $3,000 the Swinger gave more performance per dollar than almost anything else, and Dodge sold 20,000 of them in 1969. Nor was a low price the only attraction: the Swinger proved cheaper to insure than other muscle cars with the same performance, as the insurance companies considered it a true compact car, and thus a better risk. Presumably they had not seen the performance figures: 6.5 seconds to 60mph (96.5km/h) and the standing quarter-mile in around 14.5 seconds could be expected. Scat Pack, indeed.

By 1971 the Dart had moved on. The year before, Plymouth had enjoyed great success with the Valiant Duster compact, and now it was Dodge's turn. So the 108-in (2.74-m) wheelbase coupé variant became a new Dodge for 1971, the Demon. Economy-minded motorists could order one of these with a 198-cu in (3.24-litre) six, but of more interest to muscle car fans was the small-block 340 V8, which took on that 275-hp motor that had done such good

289

service in the Dart GTS and Swinger. The add-ons were much the same: standard three-speed manual transmission, with a four-speeder or TorqueFlite auto optional. Heavy-duty suspension, Rallye instrument cluster, E70-14 tyres, stripes and dual exhaust were all part of the package as well. If they did not make a big enough statement, then the optional black hood with two gaping air scoops, a rear spoiler or 'Tuff' steering wheel, surely would.

Motor Trend tested a Demon 340 against a Mercury Comet GT, Chevrolet Nova SS 350 and AMC Hornet SC360. The Demon was the heaviest of the lot, at 3,360lb (1524kg), but also the quickest, with a standing quarter-mile time of 14.49 seconds and a time of 6.5 seconds to 60mph (96.5km/h). For 1972, the 340's compression was lowered to 8.5:1, though the power drop to 240hp (179kW) was not as drastic as it seemed: it was now measured

on the SAE net rating. Whatever, it still made an affordable muscle car, and was certainly easier to insure than its bigger brothers. Interestingly, the car carried on into 1976, but the 'Demon' name did not. Religious groups took exception to it, and from 1973 the Demon was renamed the Dart Sport.

The 1970 Dodge Dart Swinger, a true budget muscle car, with high performance and low price.

FORD: COUGAR & 427S

One would have expected Mercury, maker of luxury, upmarket Fords, to have been above the whole muscle car thing, but not a bit of it: there were performance Mercuries right through the 1960s. They may not have been as flashy as some (all those stripes, wings and spoilers were not really in Mercury's marketplace), but they were there. Take the Comet Cyclone, a powered-up version of the standard Comet. For 1966 the Cyclone GT (based on Ford's Fairlane) was selected as the Indy 500 pace car (a sure sign of performance pretensions). Powered by Ford's 335-hp (250-kW) 390-cu in (6.4-litre) V8, complete with handling package and front disc brakes, it could do the quarter-mile in the high 14 seconds. So it was fast enough, though only around 16,000 were sold.

The Cougar, launched in 1967, promised to have more mass appeal. *Car Life* magazine described it as a 'Mustang with class', and that is exactly what it was. The Cougar was based firmly on the pony car floorpan, but with its own bodyshell and tweaked suspension to provide a more comfortable ride. As far as buyers of muscle cars were concerned, the most serious Cougar was the GT 390. This made use of the same 390-cu in V8 as the Cyclone GT, and in the same relatively mild state of tune with three- or four-speed

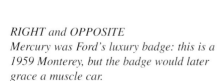

RIGHT and OPPOSITE
Mercury was Ford's luxury badge: this is a 1959 Monterey, but the badge would later grace a muscle car.

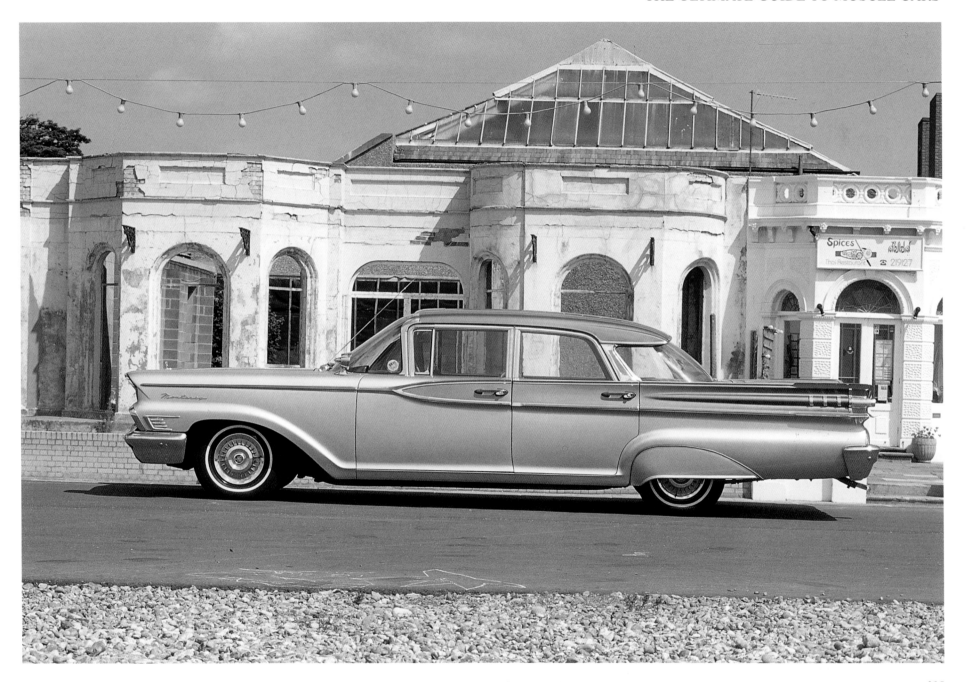

manual gearboxes or a three-speed Merc-O-Matic. Having softened up the suspension for standard Cougars, Mercury firmed it back up for the GT: stiffer springs, beefier shocks and a larger front anti-roll bar, plus power front disc brakes and wider tyres. But the Cougar was not particularly fast (8.1 seconds to 60mph/96.5km/h and 16 seconds for the quarter-mile) and the fact that almost half

were sold with the three-speed manual or auto suggested that many were being bought by non-sporting customers.

Things got more serious in 1968, with the 427-cu in (7.0-litre) GT-E, giving 390hp (291kW) in a fairly mild state of tune, rapidly superseded by the 428 Cobra Jet. Ford actually quoted only 335hp (250kW) for the new engine, but this was probably a ploy to make the performance

Fords and Mercuries cheaper to insure. It is more likely that power was around the same as that of the 427 it replaced. Mercury was now getting serious about racing, and entered the Trans Am series at around this time. One spin-off was the XR-7G : the G stood for Dan Gurney, and in fact 'signature' special editions like this were popular at the time. The XR-7G was really a cosmetic package, and could be

A customized Mercury wagon.

had with any of the Cougar power units.

By 1970, Mercury's slogan for the Cougar and its new Eliminator fastback derivative was 'America's most completely equipped sports car'. In keeping with the Mercury badge, it was marketed as a luxury sports car, which by and large it was. There was more noise insulation than in a Mustang, and a better-equipped interior. Although the engine range was the same as that of the Mustang (including the high-revving Boss 302, the Cleveland 351, 428 CJ and even the 375-hp/279.5-kW Boss 429), the interior was pure Mercury, especially on the XR-7: vinyl high-back bucket seats with leather accents, map pockets on the seat backs, burr walnut effect on the instrument panel, loop yarn

nylon carpeting, electric clock, tachometer, rocker switch display, rear seat armrest, map and courtesy lights – so it went on.

For 1971, Cougar grew bigger and fatter (it was already larger than the original Mustang), and had now abandoned its pony car roots. Available as the base and sporty XR-7, choices of Cougar engine started with a two-barrel 351-cu in (5.75-litre) motor, offering 240hp (179kW). The same engine with a four-barrel carburettor produced 285hp (212.5kW), while the top-range 429-cu in (7.0-litre) motor claimed 370hp (276kW). It was a far cry from the Mustang, or indeed any other muscle car: it was heavier, with as much emphasis on trim and appointments as sheer performance.

That explained why the Cougar was never a major player in the muscle car market, and as the 1960s wore on the same was true for full-sized cars. They were too heavy and unwieldy to compete with a GTO or LS6 Chevelle, the whole basis of the muscle car concept being to squeeze a big engine into a relatively small car. Big engine in big car did not have the same effect.

Throughout the 1960s, however, the bigger Fords were able to turn in fast straight-line speeds as a result of one engine, the 427-cu in 'side oiler'. This had first appeared in 1963, primarily for NASCAR and drag racing, but Ford also built nearly 5,000 big Galaxies that year with 427 power. They came either in 425-hp (317-kW) street-tune form but with dual four-barrel Holley carburettors, or milder 410-hp (307-kW) form with a single carburettor. Whether for weekend racing or pure road use, in the base Galaxie or 500 XL, the new 427 gave a good account of itself. Heavy the Galaxies may have been,

The 1956 Mercury Montclair: pre-1960s Mercuries were not performance machines.

but from the way they scorched off the line many thought that 425hp was a conservative estimate. Ford itself claimed a 14.9-second standing quarter-mile for the 500XL hardtop 427 in 1965. By now the engines had names: Thunderbird High Performance and Thunderbird Super High Performance for the 410- and 425-hp units respectively.

Until 1966, the 427 could be had only in the full-size Galaxie, but for that year the mid-sized Fairlane was redesigned to make room in the engine bay for this big-block. Only about 60 Fairlane 427s were produced in 1966, but unofficial claims of a 14.5-

The Cougar was very much a performance car, an upmarket version of the Mustang, with the same performance options but a more luxurious interior.

second quarter-mile heightened the anticipation. As it happened, even in 1967 the 427 remained a limited-production option on the Fairlane, most GTs and GTAs leaving the line with Ford's familiar 390-cu in (6.4-litre) unit. Meanwhile, the new Galaxie '7 Litre' received Ford's new 428-cu in (7.0-litre) motor in 345- and 360-hp (257- and 268.5-kW) forms, though one could still pay extra and order the hot 427 in 410- or 425-hp (306- and 317-kW) forms.

From the power point of view, that was the high spot: for 1968, the 427 was detuned to 390hp (291kW), and production ended in the middle of that year. The newer Cobra Jet 428 and Thunder Jet 429 were certainly powerful, but could not compare with the original 427. Ford's mid-sized muscle-car flag was taken up by these engines in the Torino, the sporty version of the Fairlane 500. That came in stripped-down budget form for $2,699, and although on paper it produced a relatively paltry 335hp (250kW), Ford still claimed a 14.5-second quarter-mile as a result of the fact that the Torino was lighter than the big Galaxie. The fastback Talladega Torino, unveiled in the following year to bring NASCAR honours, used the same CJ-428 engine. For 1970, the new 429 motor replaced the 428, promising 360 or 370hp (268.5 or 276kW) depending on tune. But the vast majority of buyers went for the cheaper 302-powered car. It was surely a sign of the times.

Pre-Mustang, this was the closest thing Ford had to a sporty car. By no means a muscle car, the Thunderbird did combine V8 power with two seats.

1959 Thunderbird. Ford's two-seater was putting on weight and ornate metalwork, more like a standard sedan with fewer seats. In concept, it was a generation behind the Mustang.

1960 Thunderbird.

*The 1960 Thunderbird, showing the
column-mounted shifter (right) – a muscle
car no-no.*

Chapter Eight

REVIVAL:
The 1990s Muscle Cars

For ten years, from the early 1970s to the early 1980s, many people regarded the muscle car era as a thing of the past, and it looked as though they were right. Two global oil crises had brought North America's total dependence on oil into question, while queues at gas stations and a nationwide 55-mph (88.5-km/h) speed limit emphasized the fact, especially when President Jimmy Carter castigated the 'gas-guzzlers' for squandering a precious resource. A whole new raft of emissions and safety legislation was already in train, and in the wake of Ralph Nader there was a growing feeling that power without restraint may not have been a good idea after all.

The 'Big Three' responded as one might expect: engines were derated and advertising copy soft-pedalled on performance: now the emphasis was on safety, luxury and 'responsibility'. Given this new climate, how could the traditional muscle car survive?

But these things go in cycles, and from the early 1980s onwards there were signs of a muscle-car comeback. Those four-cylinder options, which had found their way into base-model muscle cars, were quietly

generation of muscle cars, making some of them even faster than any Boss Mustang, Trans Am or Street Hemi. It goes without saying that they stopped better and were tidier around corners as well. In short, the muscle car was back, and in no uncertain terms.

MUSCLE TRUCKS

Remember Little Red Wagon, the Hemi-engined Dodge A-100 pick-up that Chrysler built in the 1960s? That was a one-off, a novelty vehicle to entertain crowds at the drag strip. But 30 years later, pick-ups made up a significant sector of the road-going muscle car market, some of them as fast and fearsome as so-called 'sports cars'.

Pick-ups have long had pride of place in American hearts, matched only by the popularity of the ubiquitous 'ute' in Australia. For decades, they were the workhorse of farmers and tradesmen. But times change, and they have gradually

ABOVE
A 1954 Chevrolet hot-rod pick-up. This is powered by a 350 Chevrolet V8 and has a 1974 Camaro suspension set-up at the front and a Camaro rear axle at the rear. The wheels are from a Corvette and the truck is finished in two shades of green.

LEFT
1930 Model A Ford street-rod.

OPPOSITE
1935 Ford street-rod pick-up. This rod was built from scratch using the vintage truck and chassis but with the installation of a Heidt front-end kit to fit Mustang parts, a Maverick rear axle and a 302 Ford V8. The truck rolls on Budnik alloy wheels and is finished in Porsche red.

dropped; V6s gained turbochargers, and the V8s got bigger and more powerful by the year. For better or worse, it really was business as usual.

Of course, some things had changed. Since the days when that heavy, brutish muscle ruled the highways in the late 1960s, technology had moved on. Cars were now

lighter and more efficient, their engines designed by computer and controlled by microchip. Six-speed transmissions and all-wheel ABS disc brakes featured: brake fade, floppy handling and mushy auto transmissions were no longer facts of life. Moreover, the technology would be enthusiastically embraced by the new

It had to happen: the Viper's V-10 engine was shoehorned into the Dodge Ram pick-up, and the SRT-10 was the result.

acquired a kind of highway chic: pick-ups, like four-wheel drives, have become something of a fashion accessory. Just as the well-heeled urbanite with a 4x4 would never dream of actually driving off-road, his neighbour will rarely fill his pick-up's load bed with anything heavier than the weekly groceries. But he loves the image it conveys, linking him to America's past.

This pick-up revival was given a boost by CAFE, the early fuel consumption regulations introduced by the U.S. government. Classified as light trucks, the pick-ups were therefore exempt, and their popularity soared. Pick-ups are now subject to a gas-guzzler tax, but they are still very popular, and by the late 1990s made up half of new car sales, with Ford's F-150 the best-selling vehicle of any type.

So maybe it was only a matter of time

before someone applied muscle car technology to pick-ups. This was the Chevrolet 454SS of 1990, though it was not especially high-tech. To build it, Chevrolet took a regular C1500 pick-up, added a 230-hp (171.5-kW) 452-cu in (7.4-litre) V8 truck engine, 15-in (38.1-cm) chrome wheels with radial tyres, and a suitable interior. A performance suspension package reduced the payload capacity by half but gave the 454SS a chassis better able to cope with 230hp. The SS looked what it was: heavy, chunky and basic, and weighed in at over 4,700lb (2,132kg). Nor was it especially fast: *Motor Trend* recorded a time of 7.8 seconds for 0–60mph and 16 seconds for the quarter-mile. But buyers loved it, snapping up nearly 14,000 in the first year. Maybe it was the name, a cunning re-use by Chevrolet of its 454SS

Chevelle of the 1960s. This SS for the 1990s did not last, however, as more compact performance pick-ups came on the scene, but it was really what started it all.

Chevrolet's next muscle truck could not have been more different. The SS was basically a re-engined and tweaked version of a commercial vehicle. The Syclone, introduced the year after, may have resembled the S15, on which it was based, but under the skin it was very special indeed. It was, in the words of authors Patrick Paternie and Dan Lyons, 'trying to be a Porsche 959 with a cargo bed'. The 262-cu in (4.3-litre) Vortec V6 could be found under the bonnets of workaday GMC pick-ups, but this one was equipped with a turbocharger, intercooler and electronic multi-port fuel injection. That meant 280hp (209kW) at 4,400rpm and 350lb ft

(474.6Nm) at 3,600rpm. GM's four-speed automatic from the Corvette was recalibrated to suit, and there was full-time four-wheel-drive. One problem with high-powered two-wheel-drive pick-ups is that their lightly laden rear ends are prone to wheel spin and axle tramp, but this was not the case with this machine. There was ABS as well, with 16 x 8-in wheels with 245/50 VR16 performance tyres. Like the 454SS, the Syclone came in black only, with a suitably sporty interior. The result was 4.9 seconds to 60mph (96.5km/h), according to *Motor Trend*, with a 13.6-second quarter-mile. Top speed was limited to 126mph (203km/h), and the load capacity was a mere 500lb (227kg). At over $25,000, the Syclone proved that all this technology did not come cheap, but like the SS, it helped to kickstart the concept of a performance

pick-up, direct from the factory.

Ford entered the fray a couple of years after GM with a hopped-up version of its own F-150 pick-up, the SVT Lightning.

Like the Chevrolet SS, this was a fairly crude device compared with later muscle pick-ups, retaining twin I-beam front suspension and adding the simple 351-cu in

(5.75-litre) cast-iron V8. But the addition of GT40-style cylinder heads and multi-port fuel injection, among other things, boosted output to 240hp (179kW) at 4,200rpm, plus

340lb ft (461Nm). Ford claimed a 0–60-mph (96.5-km/h) time of 7.6 seconds, which was respectably fast, but took the precaution of electronically limiting the top speed to 110mph (177km/h), given the workaday suspension.

Produced up to 1995, the first Lightning launched Ford into the sports pick-up market, but its second-generation successor, announced four years later, was a far more sophisticated animal, showing just how far the breed had developed in a short space of time. The old 354-cu in (5.8-litre) V8 was gone, replaced by a supercharged 331-cu in (5.42-litre) Triton V8 pushing out a massive 380hp (283kW), with 450lb ft (610.2Nm) at 3,250rpm. These are serious figures, belonging to true muscle car territory: here they just happened to be pushing a truck body. All that power came courtesy of an Eaton Gen supercharger with water-to-air intercooler, electronic fuel injection and aluminium alloy heads. The standard transmission was a four-speed automatic, driving through a 4.5-in (11.4-cm) aluminium drive shaft and limited-slip differential. To keep control, there were vented discs all round, with ABS, and

The SRT-10 wasn't intended for hauling –
this was a serious performance machine.

In fact, Dodge had been in on the sports pick-up concept before anyone else. As well as Little Red Wagon, that one-off drag racer, 1977 saw Li'l Red Express, a D150 full-sized pick-up with police specification 360-cu in (5.9-litre) V8 and over 200hp (149kW). Classed as a truck, it therefore dodged the emission laws of the time (no catalyst or air pump), and Chrysler underlined the truck image with tall chrome exhaust stacks each side of the cab. Over 7,000 were sold.

Twenty years later, the Dakota R/T placed even more power in a lighter, more compact package. Order the R/T Sport Group option, and one had 17-in (43.2-cm) aluminium wheels, wide tyres, lowered sport suspension and various cosmetic bits and pieces. But with that came the mandatory options of an electronic four-speed auto transmission and 360-cu in Magnum V8 with 250hp (186.5kW) and 345lb ft (467.8Nm). This was not bad for a truck that weighed less than 4,000lb (1814kg), and owners had to be careful when flooring the throttle or that lightly laden rear end was liable to step sideways. Not that anyone complained: antics like this have always been part of the muscle car fantasy, even if they weren't an everyday experience. If this was not enough, one could fit an aftermarket supercharger, which according to *Motor Trend* resulted in 7 seconds to 60mph and 15.4 at 89mph (143km/h) over the standing quarter-mile,

super-wide 18 x 9.5-in alloy wheels. The original Lightning's I-beam suspension was ditched in favour of a short/long-arm system with coil springs and Bilstein gas shocks. Nor was this a stripped-down performance special: the cab had a power-adjusted driver's seat, CD player, power windows, locks and mirrors. But the

Lightning remained a specialist muscle car: Ford sold only 2,500 of them in its debut year, and only through SVT-certified Ford dealers.

By the time the first of those 1999 Lightnings were sitting in dealer showrooms, Dodge was already selling the Dakota R/T. Based on the compact Dakota

pick-up, this used another evocative muscle car nametag from the 1960s: R/T (for Road & Track) had originally been used on the flanks of those the rip-snorting Charger and Challenger R/Ts, 30 years earlier. In the early 1990s it reappeared on the outrageous Viper two-seater, a good enough inheritance for a muscular truck.

ABOVE
The SRT-10's imposing grille.

OPPOSITE
It was a tight fit to get the Viper's long 10-cylinder engine into that truck bay.

RIGHT
Alongside muscle trucks, Ford went on building conventional ones, intended as workhorses rather than playthings. This is an F-750 Super Duty XL.

OPPOSITE
An F-350 Super Duty with double cab.

which was certainly not bad for a truck.

But like the other muscle pick-ups, the R/T was not cheap. Although the least expensive Dakota started at just over $13,000, one could not simply order one of these with a Magnum V8. As well as the special transmission and R/T package, buyers generally opted for some of the luxuries of life, such as air conditioning and a top-specification sound system. The final bill could be nearly twice that of the basic Dakota, but Dodge still managed to sell 2,000 R/Ts in 1998 and 1999.

The R/T's Magnum V8 was also available in the bigger Ram pick-up, as the Ram SS/T, though in 245-hp (183kW) form. Like the Dakota, to order one meant

Later, Ford did a deal with Harley-Davidson, which allowed the hallowed motorbike badge to be fixed to Ford pick-ups.

trawling through the Ram options list, as officially it was not an actual model. It was just like the old days: Pontiac's GTO had started out in a similar way as a package of options which added up to a model in its own right. This was much the same. That Magnum V8 cost an extra $860 over a standard Ram, while a heavy-duty four-speed overdrive automatic came in at $960. Finally, the SS/T package itself would leave one $1,360 lighter, which brought stiffer shocks and springs (though the ride height was unchanged), wide low-profile tyres and big alloy wheels, plus a special paint job which featured Viper-style racing stripes. The impetus for the SS/T had come in 1996, when Dodge offered a striped replica of its Indy 500 support truck, the Indy Ram. The SS/T turned that special edition into a regular option package. By 1999 it had disappeared from the lists, but it was still possible to order a Ram to the same sort of specification, if one was diligent enough to search through the options.

323

For 2004, the Pontiac GTO was back, still with rear-wheel-drive and still powered by a V8, though there the resemblance with older GTOs ended.

The original GTO was a hopped-up sedan, but for the 21st century it was transformed into a 2+2 coupé.

OPPOSITE
Firebird, in Stealth Bomber guise

LEFT
Pontiac Firebird Rytek.

BELOW LEFT
Johnson Goodwrench racing Firebird.

BELOW
A Firebird pace car: it was still an honour to be chosen.

LEFT
Recognize the family resemblance? Ford's concept Mustang of 2003.

OPPOSITE
And for paying customers, the 2004 Mustang GTO. It would be interesting to know what General Motors thought of that!

VIPER & PROWLER: LATERAL THINKING

Chrysler was not having a very happy time of it in the 1970s and 1980s. The Corporation was fighting for its very existence, so making limited-edition muscle cars to please enthusiasts came way down the priority list. The company survived by concentrating on everyday cars like the minivan, which was cheap to make, easy to sell and hugely popular. By the late 1980s, however, Chrysler could afford to relax a little and devote some time to its image. Better still, it had a new president, Bob Lutz, who sparked a talented design team, led by Tom Gale, into some lateral thinking.

Only a combination of events like this could have brought about the Viper. By 1989, Chrysler needed to make a bold statement, to show the world that it had more to offer than minivans. And what a statement it turned out to be. The Viper RT/10 was unveiled at the Detroit motor show in January 1889 to an astonished world. No one had seen anything quite like it before, and certainly not from one of the 'Big Three', not always known for daring innovation. It was not only the Viper's ground-hugging stance, muscular flanks and sheer presence. There were also ten cylinders, and a 488-cu in (8.0-litre) V10 truck engine that outsized and outpowered almost any previous muscle car. There was

Dodge's Viper wowing the world in 1996: the unashamed muscle car was back!

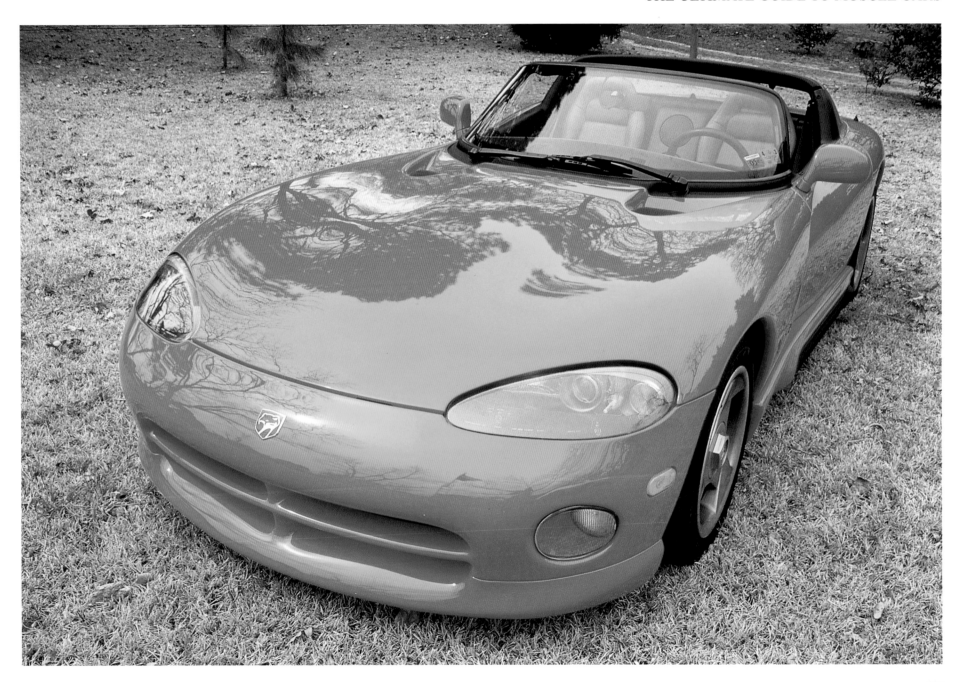

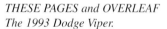

*THESE PAGES and OVERLEAF
The 1993 Dodge Viper.*

something inherently American about the Viper, in the way it emphasized raw power, torque and cubic inches over sophistication. In doing so, it spoke to generations of U.S. drivers, and was a true inheritor of the muscle car tradition. It was no wonder that the vehicle made an impact.

Chrysler may even have been surprised by the public's response. The first Viper was a concept car, intended to do little more than attract people to the Chrysler show stand, generate some press coverage and boost the corporate image. But by the end of the show, there was a list of people ready to buy, even though they would have to wait three years. A team of 100 engineers, designers and managers was rapidly assembled, and the car was approved for production six months after that show debut. Twelve months later, it

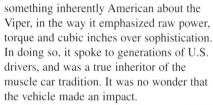

reappeared as an official pace car for the Indy 500 (a real muscle car seal of approval); in December 1991 the first batch of customer Vipers finally left the assembly line. It may have taken three years to bring a one-off concept to production stage, but this was good going.

Those early buyers would not have been disappointed; the new Vipers remained true to the back-to-basics concept of the original. There were few concessions to comfort, and driver and passenger were crammed into a narrow space between door and centre tunnel. 'Weather protection' consisted of a flimsy folding top with crude plastic side curtains that zipped on. But none of that mattered.

What did matter was what happened when buyers put their foot down. As launched, the 488-cu in V10 produced 400hp (298kW) at 4,600rpm, plus a monstrous 465lb ft (630.5Nm) of torque, which given a sufficiently brave and skilful driver, could rocket the Viper up to 60mph in just 4.6 seconds, and cover the standing quarter-mile in 12.9 seconds (113.8mph/183km/h). Now that was faster than any other muscle car, faster even than the legendary AC Cobra, which had combined a big Ford V8 with the lightweight AC two-seater in the 1960s. Despite massive 335/55 rear tyres on 13-in (33-cm) wide aluminium wheels, however, wheel spin was something of a problem.

But that was part of the Viper's appeal. At the time, there was nothing else like it, and over the next decade it came to rival the legendary status of the Cobra, another muscle sports car of its time that had placed sheer power above all else. Back to basics it might have been, but the Viper was not cheap: it shared few components with any other Chrysler, and production was limited, so it would not be undercutting minivans

RIGHT and OPPOSITE
The 1996 Dodge Viper RT/10.

on the dealer's forecourt. On top of the basic $50,000 there were delivery charges, $2,600 of gas-guzzler tax and $2,280 of luxury car tax. The Viper was, and remains, a very expensive car.

The first major change came in 1996, with the hardtop GTS, though it had actually been shown at the Los Angeles motor show three years earlier. This was a step up from the open-top Viper's basic appeal, and was far more than a mere RT/10 with a hardtop bolted on. In fact, so different was the GTS that Chrysler claimed over 90 per cent of it to be new. The new bodyshell was of transfer-moulded resin composite, with two major advantages over the open-top RT. It was far more aerodynamic (with a drag coefficient of 0.39 instead of 0.50) and offered the promise of greater comfort. A taller windshield and twin-bubble roof allowed more headroom, while Chrysler engineers had taken the opportunity to increase seat travel and introduce an adjustable pedal cluster. At the back, a one-piece glass hatch covered a luggage area big enough to take a full-sized wheel and tyre, while bigger doors could now accommodate glass power windows and exterior door handles, which the original Viper did not have.

So a GTS Viper seemed far easier to live with than the original (one could even take it out in the rain without getting wet!), but it was also more potent. Despite standard air conditioning, it weighed nearly

100lb (45kg) less than the RT/10, due partly to all-aluminium suspension (which reduced unsprung weight) and to careful development work on the engine and cooling system, which alone saved 80lb (36kg). But this would not have been a muscle car without a corresponding increase in power. Thanks to a higher compression and hotter camshaft, the latest V10 produced 450hp (335.5kW) plus nearly 500lb ft (678Nm). The transmission was still a six-speed manual with a highly necessary limited-slip differential, and the whole caboodle tipped the scales at a relatively light 3,460lb (1569kg). According to *Motor Trend*, acceleration was 0–60mph in 4.1 seconds, with a 12.2-second quarter-mile.

That was not the end of Viper development. By 2000, the RT/10 had the 450-hp motor and lightweight suspension, and it had abandoned its back-to-basics roots, with air conditioning and a 200-watt stereo standard, while a Connolly leather

ABOVE and OPPOSITE
1996 Dodge Viper RT/10.

interior was optional. If that was too sybaritic, purists could opt for the ACR from 1999. ACR stood for American Club Racer, and the idea (or at least, the dream) was for a Viper that one could take racing at weekends. To save weight, the air conditioning, stereo and driving lamps were

omitted, and the ACR came with a 460-hp (343-kW) version of the now-familiar V10, plus a five-point safety harness. Reflecting the Viper's racing success (it won its class in the Le Mans 24 Hours in 1998, 1999 and 2000) a GT2, in white with blue stripes, was another limited edition.

Not that any of the Vipers could be described as mass-production cars: between 1992 and late 2000, Chrysler built 7,191 RT/10s, and 4,484 coupés. But the impact it had was out of all proportion to these numbers. It may not have been affordable in the muscle car tradition, but it was an

embodiment of the same philosophy: cubic inches, power, torque. Period.

The Prowler was not a muscle car in the same mould, though by the time production ended in December 2001, it had been powered up to over 250hp (186.5kW). Instead, it paid homage to American hot-rods of the 1950s: it was one of the first retro cars, and certainly one of the most radical. Like the Viper, it was a Chrysler concept car that was inspired by designer Tom Gale and given the green light by president Bob Lutz. And also like the Viper, once the public had caught a glimpse of this 'one-off', Chrysler had no choice but to build it.

The idea was to recreate the look of a Southern California hot-rod, complete with exposed front wheels and open-top boat-tail body. Tom Gale proved to be a particularly enthusiastic supporter of this concept, which had revealed itself at a brain-storming session: he happened to be building a hot-rod in his garage at the time! Named the Prowler, and finished in a suitably sinister metallic purple, Chrysler's new retro-mobile was shown at the Detroit Motor Show in January 1993, and within a year Chrysler had received around 130,000 enquiries. It looked like a difficult car to bring to production, but even the concept Prowler had been designed with production in mind, so it already had practical details like front bumpers and cycle fenders.

For production, the hollow aluminium bumpers had to be enlarged and shifted forward slightly, while the headlights had to be redesigned. The body was made 3-in (7.62-cm) wider to make room for side-impact protection, while the wheelbase was lengthened a little to keep the car in proportion. (Whatever else the Prowler was or pretended to be, it had to look right.) Otherwise, the Prowler that was available

from a Plymouth dealer from 1997 looked much the same as the Detroit original. Another factor that speeded the production process was the number of components poached from existing Chrysler parts bins: namely the engine, steering gear, suspension and interior details, which all came from existing models.

Interest in the car was intense, so despite a $40,000 price tag, all the early

production was soon spoken for. In fact, demand was so strong that speculators were soon selling almost-new Prowlers for up to double the list price, having effectively sold their place in the queue. There was not much room under the narrow bonnet, and the biggest engine Chrysler could squeeze beneath it was a 215-cu in (3.52-litre) V6 from the LH sedan. A V8 would have been historically correct, and given the Prowler

ABOVE, OPPOSITE and OVERLEAF Plymouth's Prowler was a show car that actually made it into production.

some muscle car credibility, but it simply would not fit. As it was, the V6 produced 214hp (159.5kW), which was not enough to smoke the massive rear tyres but could push the Prowler to 60mph (96.5km/h) in 7 seconds. Performance was helped along by the car's low kerb weight of 2,850lb (1293kg), resulting from the use of aluminium to a larger extent than was common on American cars of the time.

Despite the huge interest it had generated when launched, the Prowler was not in fact the huge seller that many had expected it to be, and in four and a half years only 11,000 were sold. Quite apart from the lack of a V8, the Prowler had other, more practical drawbacks, most notably the fact that it was really a car for sunny Sundays. There were only two seats, no hardtop option (Tom Gale insisted that no bona-fide hot-rod had one) and luggage space was so limited that a stylish little trailer was one of the official options. Performance had been improved, with the

V6 boosted to 253hp (188.5kW) for a 0–60mph time of 6.3 seconds, and there was even a choice of colours. With the early Prowlers, it was any colour one liked as long as it was metallic purple. Sadly, Chrysler's retro hot-rod just didn't have the long-term appeal of the Viper, which was still going strong in 2003. Prowler production ceased in December 2001.

TWO-SEAT MUSCLE? – THE CORVETTE

Can the Corvette really be classed as a muscle car? Conventional wisdom includes V8-powered mid-sized sedans and compacts, or 2+2 pony cars, but not two-seater sports cars. Well, the Corvette was a V8 too, and it always concentrated on delivering a high performance per dollar rating, a key factor in the muscle car concept. And over a production life of 40 years it remained faithful to the front engine/rear drive layout, despite endless speculation about mid-engined prototypes. Straight-line performance via American V8 power was always part of that Corvette story: this, more than anything else, makes it a muscle car.

Like the four-seat muscle cars, the Corvette had its performance heyday in the 1960s, and each of its five generations featured a performance flagship. So a 327-hp (244-kW) fuel-injected small-block motor was offered as early as 1962. Then came the dramatic-looking Sting Ray of 1963, in open-top or twin-window convertible form. That car, with the ultimate L84 V8 with Ram Jet fuel injection, offered 375hp (279.5kW) at 6,200rpm, and 350lb ft (474.6Nm) of torque. Big-block Corvettes, the 396 and 427, soon followed, the latter in 390- and 425-hp (291- and 317-kW) forms, allowing 14-second quarter-miles and

0–60mph in less than 6 seconds. Most awesome of all was the special all-aluminium 427 fitted to just two Corvettes in 1969. This was the ZL-1, complete with ultra-high 12.5:1 compression, big valves and 850-cfm (24.07-m³/minute) Holley four-barrel carburettor. For 1970, there was the biggest-yet 454-cu in (7.44-litre) V8 and high-compression, high-tune, high-

revving 350 small-block at 390 and 370hp (291 and 276kW) respectively. Then came the 1970s and, like every other muscle car, the Corvette was forced to retrench and peg back its power to suit the less hedonistic times. But after a while, power outputs began to creep back up again, as performance came back into fashion and new technology allowed the combination

ABOVE and OPPOSITE
The Corvette was a two-seat muscle car: a 1962 racing version is shown here.

THIS PAGE and OPPOSITE
The classic Corvette, the Sting Ray was
available with fuel injection and over
400hp.

THIS PAGE and OPPOSITE
By 1967, the Corvette could be had with
big-block power in 396 or 427 forms. This
is a coupé from that year.

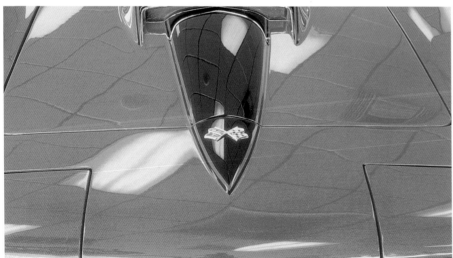

LEFT and OPPOSITE
Another 1967 Corvette, this one showing
the double-bend rear window (left).

launch of the ZR-1, but when it finally came, it fulfilled all expectations, with 375hp (279.5kW) at 6,000rpm and 370lb ft (501.7Nm) at 4,800rpm. According to *Motor Trend*, that was enough for 0–60mph (0-96.5km/h) in 4.4 seconds, 12.8 seconds for the quarter-mile and a flat-out speed of 180mph (290km/h). Supporting the exotic engine was a six-speed manual gearbox, adjustable dampers (Performance, Sport or Touring) and a luxurious interior specification. The Z51 package (an option on other Corvettes but standard on the ZR-1) brought stiffer springs and stabilizer bars, while the ZR-1 added ultra-low profile Goodyear Eagle unidirectional tyres: 275/40 ZR17 front and 315/35 ZR17 rear.

Cheaper than a Ferrari it may have been and just as fast, but the ZR-1 remained a limited-production Corvette. Only 18 LT5 engines per day were produced for Chevrolet by marine engine specialists Mercury (chosen for their long experience of building aluminium engines), and less than 7,000 ZR-1s rolled off the line over five years. Most of these were built in 1990–91, with orders trickling in

of high power and lower emissions. Between 1987 and 1991 GM offered a 345-hp (257-kW) twin-turbo Corvette, the actual conversion completed by Callaway Engineering.

But it was 1990 when Chevrolet finally announced a spiritual successor to the all-aluminium ZL-1 V8 in the form of the ZR-1. This was soon nicknamed 'King of the Hill', and for good reason: Chevrolet wanted it to be the world's fastest

production car. Whether it was or not, the ZR-1 was certainly far cheaper than any exotic supercar from Germany or Italy. It was top-dollar by GM standards, however, costing about twice as much as a standard Corvette. Most of the dollars went on an all-new small-block V8. Designed and developed in England by Lotus Engineering (now a GM subsidiary), it fairly bristled with technology. All-aluminium, it had twin overhead cams per bank and four valves per

cylinder, sequential fuel injection and a high 11.0:1 compression ratio. Named LT5, the new engine had a clever induction system with three valves in the throttle body (a small one to give good response at low power, twin big ones for full) and twin injectors per cylinder. The full-power valves could be 'locked out' in the unlikely event of a ZR-1 being loaned to junior for the weekend.

Valve-train problems delayed the

355

THIS PAGE and OPPOSITE
For 1968, the Sting Ray coupé gained that
split rear window (left).

LEFT and OPPOSITE
In the 1970s, the Corvette became wider,
fatter and heavier.

1996 flagship came in Admiral Blue with Artic White racing stripes, a reference to the original 1963 Grand Sport Corvettes that raced successfully that year. All this added $3,250 to the price of a standard Corvette coupé, and $2,880 to the convertible: it may not have been quite as quick as a ZR-1 (Chevrolet claimed 4.7 seconds to 60mph/96.5km/h and 13.3 seconds for the quarter-mile), but it was certainly better value.

The Grand Sport turned out to be the swansong for the Corvette C4, the fourth-generation car since the 1953 original. There was fevered speculation that the 1997 replacement, the C5, would be mid-engined, or not built of glassfibre (so far, every Corvette had been), or might come with a new, exotic specification that would put it in contention with European imports. It was a tough call: with over a million Corvettes built over 45 years, the car had a very loyal following. But to succeed, C5 had to attract drivers who might otherwise have bought a Honda or Porsche.

In the event, the design team, headed by Dave Hill and John Cafaro, came up with something to please everyone. The C5 was rear-wheel-drive, powered by a front-mounted pushrod V8, and it was still built

between 1992 and 1995. Production ceased altogether in April 1995, but the ZR-1's job had been done. It had put the Corvette back onto the performance map.

With the ZR-1 gone, the Corvette performance flagship for 1996 was the Grand Sport. On paper, this did not seem a patch on its exotic predecessor: no aluminium block, good old-fashioned pushrods in place of overhead cams, and just two valves per cylinder, while its engine made a 'mere' 330hp (246kW)! In practice, it was almost as fast as the ZR-1 and little more than half the price. The LT4 engine was a highly-developed version of the existing small-block V8, with high 10.8:1 compression aluminium heads, Crane roller rockers, reprofiled camshaft, stronger crank and new fuel injectors.

As part of the Grand Sport package, buyers received 17-in (43.2-cm) aluminium wheels, ultra-wide tyres and a six-speed transmission. In place of the ZR-1's manually adjustable dampers, those on the Grand Sport used high-tech wheel travel sensors to adjust each shock individually, many times a second. To finish it off, the

of glassfibre. On the other hand, the engine was all-aluminium, stronger and breathed more freely than the old one: it was more powerful than the LS1, but used less fuel. The transmission was rear-mounted, giving a 50/50 weight distribution and freeing interior space. The chassis was stiffer and lighter, while the C5's new shape (a cunning combination of 21st-century sleekness and recognizable nods to the Corvette's past) slipped through the air with a drag coefficient of just 0.29.

Even with the standard motor it was fast, able to reach 60mph in 4.7 seconds, but inevitably, there had to be a performance flagship, and this was launched in 2001 as the Z06. Once again, the name was part of Corvette history: the original Z06 was a race-ready option package offered in 1963. Chevrolet had the same in mind for this one, or at least some of that race-ready aura. For example, by

2001 Corvettes now had traction control, but skilled drivers can use wheel spin to good effect when racing, so on the Z06 it could be locked out. The car was 36-lb (16-kg) lighter than standard, thanks to a titanium exhaust system, lighter wheels/tyres and thinner glass. The suspension was retuned and the big fat Goodyears built especially for the car.

As for the engine, this LS6 was a development of the all-aluminium LS1. New pistons, bigger injectors, higher-lift cam, stronger valve springs and reshaped combustion chambers combined to produce 385hp (287kW) at 6,000rpm, with 385lb ft (522.1Nm) at 4,800rpm. Make good use of the six-speed gearbox, and the Z06 could sprint to 60mph in exactly 4 seconds, if one believed Chevrolet's own figures, and achieve a top speed of 171mph (275km/h). High-tech yet traditional, the Z06 carried the Corvette genes, and was very fast.

There is a footnote to the Corvette muscle car story, and one pleasing to those who believe that the only real muscle cars have four seats, and were never originally intended to run as fast as they could. Chevrolet had learned to resurrect old and evocative names: its own history was thick with them, and so was born the 1994 Impala SS. The original Impala SS had been a legend in its own time as a result of its high-compression 409 V8 that claimed over 400hp (298kW). It was the one the Beach Boys wrote a song about, and in 1964, one could not get much more street 'cred' than that. Standing quarter-mile times in the high 12 seconds were possible. In 1964, cars like that had produced lustful cravings in boys in short trousers: maybe their father, or an uncle or a neighbour actually owned one. Thirty years later, these same boys had the income to indulge that dream, so along came Chevrolet with

an Impala for the 1990s generation.

It was based on the quite ordinary Caprice Classic sedan, but with police-specification engine and suspension which propelled the performance into the extraordinary. The Caprice had already proved a hit with customizers, its big smooth shape responding well to lowering. So an all-black version with polished aluminium wheels, straight from the factory, did not look like mutton dressed as lamb. The interior was a little underwhelming (no tachometer, and one was stuck with a column shifter until 1996), but what counted was under the bonnet. In

THIS PAGE and OPPOSITE
A Corvette convertible for California cruising.

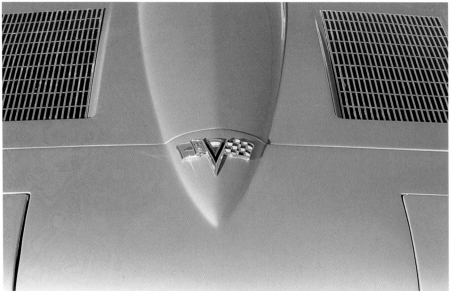

Caprice option-speak, the V8 was part of the Law Enforcement Package, which really meant the 260-hp (193.5-kW) LT1 motor that also saw service in the Corvette and Camaro Z28, complete with sequential fuel injection and 10.5:1 compression. Mated to an electronically-controlled four-speed automatic, it could rocket the big Impala over the quarter-mile in 15.4 seconds, which was not bad for a 4,200-lb (1905-kg) car. Wider wheels and tyres, plus beefed-up police-specification suspension, were all part of the package, as were all-wheel disc brakes with ABS and a limited-slip differential.

It was only offered for three years, but the 1990s Impala SS sold nearly 42,000, proof that the muscle car concept was far from dead. And just to underline the value of old names, in late 2003 Pontiac was preparing to launch a new V8-powered rear-wheel-drive coupé: the GTO. That seems to be where we came in!

THIS PAGE, OPPOSITE and OVERLEAF The 1967 Corvette Sting Ray: these too were raced on both circuit and drag strip.

THIS PAGE and OPPOSITE.
Subtle restyling, less power from lower
compression engines, and a T-roof: that
was how the Corvette met the early 1970s.

RIGHT, OPPOSITE and *OVERLEAF*
Late-model road-going Corvettes were fast
enough to take to the drag strip at
weekends, and not be disgraced.

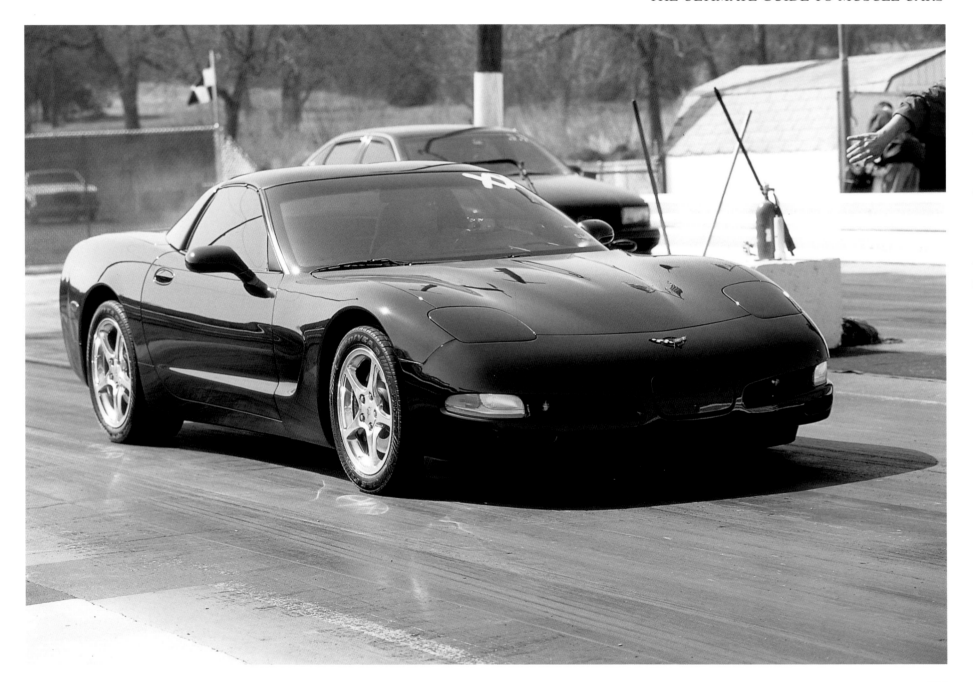

LEFT
The 21st-century Corvette came in convertible form or as a coupé.

BELOW LEFT: 2008 Corvette convertible.

OPPOSITE: 2009 Corvette Stingray concept at Chicago Motor Show.

Chapter Nine
QUARTER-MILE MONKEYS:
The Drag-Racing Muscle Cars

Drag racing lay at the core of the muscle car concept. That is, the biggest possible engine in the lightest possible bodyshell, with brakes and cornering ability a secondary consideration. Later muscle cars could corner and stop as well, but the seeds of their development sprang from drag racing.

The sport itself was invented in the U.S.A. The first organized drag race took place in 1948, and from there races of the same format spread rapidly across the country – two cars, side-by-side, timed over a standing quarter-mile. This both encouraged, and in turn was encouraged by, street racing; kids in tuned hot-rods would burn rubber between red lights on Saturday nights. So through the 1950s, drag racing (whether on street or strip) became an integral part of American car culture.

Not everyone was pleased. Magazines

RIGHT
The supercharger on a Camaro SS396.

OPPOSITE
Chevrolet Camaro SS396.

RIGHT
Camaro SS350.

OPPOSITE
A Chevrolet Camaro of the 1990s.

such as *Life*, having been suitably horrified
by 'motorcycle gangs' in the late 1940s and
early '50s, now found new terror lurking in
Middle America. 'Safety groups and some
police officers,' went a *Life* cover story in
April 1957, 'feel that the glorification of
speed on the strips infects teenagers with a
fatal spirit of derring-do on the highways.'
It was an age-old debate. Were young
Americans encouraged to behave badly by
drag racing, or rock 'n' roll or motorcycles
or movies? Or would they have done 'bad'
things anyway?

In the end, the debate resolved itself (or
moved onto something else), as drag racing
gradually became more organized and
'respectable' as the 1950s progressed.
Wally Parks, editor of *Hot Rod* magazine,
was instrumental in setting up the National
Hot Rod Association (NHRA) in 1951,
which set up rules and regulations
governing safety and competition classes.
And as the sport gained in respectability
and its following grew year by year, the Big
Three – Ford, GM and Chrysler – gradually
realized that there was potential profit in it
for them. But despite all this, and the best
efforts of the NHRA, drag racing was still
getting a bad press.

The mainstream manufacturers could
never be seen to be involved in anything
irresponsible, and in 1957 the Automobile
Manufacturers Association imposed a ban
on factory-sponsored racing. But winning at
the strip also brought tremendous prestige
and street credibility, so none of the Big
Three actually complied, and from the late
1950s onwards offered a whole range of

special parts aimed at success on the strip,
but which could be bought over the counter
or even ordered as a regular option on a
new car. Giveways such as low-ratio rear
axles or high-cube, high-compression V8s
were listed, innocently enough, alongside
all the other options, but everyone knew
what their purpose really was.

Some of these, like the original 421-cu
in (6.7-litre) Super Duty Pontiac engines,
weren't sold through dealers at all, simply
passed on to racers favoured by the factory.

In the early 1960s the standard form was to
buy special parts over the counter and fit
them yourself. But manufacturers soon
realized that the best way to control the
process was to offer drag-ready cars, brand-
new and ready to go, with most of them
available in their local showroom. Take the
Oldsmobile W30, a new option package
offered from 1966 on the 442. Ostensibly, it
was just another option, but choosing a
W30 brought heavy-duty pistons, high-lift
cam, a stronger valve train and high-

capacity air intake: according to Olds, that
added just 10hp to the standard 350hp,
which was a modest underestimate.
Fibreglass inner wings shed some weight
(and this was a real indication of the car's
intended purpose), while the battery was
remounted in the boot, to give better
traction from a standing start. Did anyone
buy a W30 for trundling down to the
stores? Unlikely, and in any case the option
did its job, bringing C/Stock victories to
Olds. By 1970, in 455-cu in (7.4-litre)

form, the W30 could reach 60mph in less than six seconds, with a mid-14 standing quarter at over 100mph (161km/h).

Olds, of course, wasn't alone in doing this. In 1966 and '67 Chevrolet offered a very special Chevy II, combining this compact and relatively light car with a well-tuned small-block 327, producing 350hp. Wild street car? Perhaps, but one had to be a particularly thick-skinned performance freak to order a road car in stripped-bare form, without heater or radio. As author Steve Statham later wrote in his book, *Maximum Muscle*: 'It was hard to picture any other function for the car but racing, despite official protestation otherwise.'

As the 1960s wore on, specials like this became more difficult to pass off as road cars, but for the devious there were ways around the system. Chevrolet dealers who were able and willing, for example, could

THIS PAGE and OPPOSITE BELOW
Chevrolet Camaro SS.

OPPOSITE ABOVE
A 1967 Chevrolet Camaro pace car for the Indianapolis 500.

established dealer in hot Chevys. He also replaced the standard exhaust manifolds on those 500 specials with headers, and rated the 427 at 450hp, 25hp above Chevrolet's official claim. The cars were sold through a small selection of dealers across the country, badged as 'Yenko/SC' Camaros. Two other Chevy dealers – Fred Gibb and Berger Chevrolet – were instrumental in getting the even more rarified ZL-1 Camaro through COPO. This used an aluminium version of the 427, with a true power rating of close to 500hp: the engine alone cost over $4,000 and all 69 ZL-1 Camaros were sold to racers.

Something to Sing About

In fact, Chevrolet was in right at the beginning. Its high-revving small-block V8 gave it an immediate advantage in mid-1950s drag racing, pushed along by Chief

Engineer Ed Cole, who understood that race victories on Sunday helped to sell cars on Monday. The small-block was rapidly upgraded, first to the 265-cu in (4.3-litre) Power Pack of 1955: a four-barrel carburettor and dual exhaust helped produce 180hp, and the following year a twin four-barrel option boosted that to 225hp. In 1957, boring the motor out to 283 cu in (4.6 litres) allowed 245hp, or 283hp with Rochester fuel injection, which incidentally reached the magic one horsepower per cubic inch rating.

But the 283 wasn't Chevrolet's hottest offering for long, being overshadowed by the 'big-block' 348-cu in (5.7-litre) in 1958. In standard form, this 'W-head', as it was also known, produced 250hp, but of more interest to drag racers was the top 315-hp option: three two-barrel carbs, mechanical valvetrain and an 11.0:1 compression ratio did the business. The following year it was

take advantage of something called a Central Office Production Order, or COPO. This was basically a back-door route to getting GM to build a car/engine combination that wasn't available to the man in the street. COPO wasn't designed to help drag merchants. Instead it was a means of encouraging fleet orders by adding special requests like a non-standard colour or different transmission. Enterprising dealers soon discovered that the COPO route could also be used to order big, hot engines to put in smaller cars, for example the top-rated 427-cu in (7.0-litre) in a Camaro or Chevelle.

The drawback was that it wasn't possible to order just one. Don Yenko, of Yenko Chevrolet in Cannonsburg, Pennsylvania, had to order 500 427 Camaros for 1969, and convince the top brass that he could sell them all. He did, but not everyone could stroll in and take advantage of COPO: Yenko could, because he was a well-

THIS PAGE and OPPOSITE
Chevrolet Camaro Z28s.

PAGES 384 and 385
A 1967 Corvette: these too were raced on
both circuit and drag strip.

up to 335hp, thanks to even higher compression, with 350hp by 1961. By then, it had been overtaken by bigger engines from Chrysler and Ford, so for that year Chevrolet unveiled a bored and stroked 409-cu in (6.7-litre) version, which even in mild, single four-barrel form produced 360hp and 409lb ft. Fitted to the relatively small Impala, it became a legend – the Beach Boys even wrote a song about the 409, considered in 1961/62 to be the engine to have. 'She's so fine my 409,' they harmonized, 'Gonna save my pennies and save my dimes. Gonna buy me a 409, 409, 409.'

And here again we see the origins of the muscle car. The Impala wasn't a full-sized American behemoth, but a car that was downsized. GM recognized its sporting potential by offering more powerful V8 options: the Turbo-Thrust 340- and 350-hp versions, or the Turbo-Fire 409 itself, with 360-hp (single four-barrel), 380-hp (three two-barrel) or 409-hp (twin four-barrel). To underline that, one chose the SS package, available on Impala sedans and hardtops. Dealer-installed, this brought power steering and brakes, heavy-duty suspension, sintered metal brake linings, floor-mounted shifter, tachometer and various other bits and pieces – not bad for $54, though a close-ratio transmission cost nearly $200 extra.

All this was ostensibly aimed at road-going hot-car freaks; in standard form, a 409 could manage a mid-14-second quarter. But it was the drag racers who really benefited, and suitably modified Impala 409s in SuperStock were running mid-13s that same year. In 1962, engine changes brought yet more power and quarter-mile times in the high 12s. For the time being, the Impala 409 was the car to beat.

LEFT
There are extra-wide tyres on this Corvette,
set up for drag racing.

OPPOSITE
A 1965 Sting Ray, about to leave the line.

and various parts for Pontiac's new 389-ci (6.3-litre) V8 were available. Special heads, high compression pistons, header exhaust manifolds, aluminium intake, high-lift cam – with all these fitted, a 1961 389 produced 368hp. The men behind it were Semon E. 'Bunkie' Knudsen, Pete Estes and John DeLorean, all of whom were to play key roles in the muscle car story: all were hot-car enthusiasts, and all were in a position to turn concepts like Super Duty into reality.

Super Duty Pontiacs were soon winning on the strip, or at least winning anything the 409 Chevy hadn't already walked away with, but a change of strategy came in 1962, when the NHRA ruled that any parts sold for racing had to be available on production cars. The idea was to prevent extra-special parts from finding their way into Super Stock. Pontiac's response was simple: make the Super Duty a production car! It simply put everything together in one option package, albeit a very special one. So the 421 Super Duty package of

It was, however, a road car being modified for drag use, and the Z11 Impala of 1963 was a race car pure and simple, though it was built by the factory. Compared to the original 409, this was much more radical. Weight was stripped out by adding an aluminium front end, and by ditching the heater, radio and sound insulation. The 409 power unit was race-tuned, stroked to 427 cu in (7.0 litres), with special cylinder heads, 12.5:1 compression

ratio and twin four-barrel carburettors. Result? 430hp in a 3,350-lb (1523-kg) car.

The Z11 was a formidable weapon, and only 57 were made, reflecting its special race-only status. But it was short-lived. The NHRA had lost patience with these ever more exotic cars, which were undermining the ethos of SuperStocks. A new class, FX (Factory Experimental) was inaugurated the same year that the Z11 was introduced, and the hottest Impala of all became the

first entrant in FX. In any case, Chevrolet's domination of the drag strips was about to draw to a close, Z11 or not. In the later 1960s, modified versions of the 396 Chevelle or Camaro were waving the Chevy flag.

While Chevrolet had the 409, its GM compatriot Pontiac sold Super Duty parts, available for Catalina hardtops, sedans and the Grand Prix coupé. Initially, they were available only across the spares counter,

ABOVE and OPPOSITE
1971 Corvette Sting Ray 350.

for such purposes.' You couldn't get much clearer than that.

Meanwhile, for 1963 the Super Duty 421, now with 13.0:1 compression and aluminium exhaust manifold, was up to 410hp. That was the official figure, the actual output of that final 1963 Super Duty 421 was more like 540–550hp. They also lost an extra 100lb that year, thanks to Plexiglass, aluminium trunk lids, plus more aluminium substitutes for the splash pan, radiator core supports and bumper brackets. Sub-14 second quarters were possible in Super Duty Pontiac Catalinas. But although the Super Dutys were very fast, and in theory anyone could walk into a showroom and buy one, in practice they were made in tiny numbers: 162 complete cars in 1962, 88 in '63.

Then everything changed. Later that year, General Motors imposed its 'no racing' edict, which spelled the end of the Super Duty Pontiacs. But in a way, they'd done their job. Pontiac's dowdy image had been turned around in a few short years, and a Pontiac was no longer a poor man's Cadillac, but one of the hottest cars money could buy. That left the way open for Estes and DeLorean to develop a Pontiac that would begin the muscle car era proper: the GTO.

Get the Max!

So Super Duty and 409 were among the hottest names in early muscle car drag racing, but the most enduring of all (as it's still out there, and winning) was the Chrysler Hemi. The Hemi (see Chapter Four) became a legend in its own time, from the 300-hp 331 of 1955 to the 500-hp+ 426 Race Hemi of the early 1960s. But it wasn't Chrysler's only drag-race weapon. In fact, for several years it didn't build it at all, concentrating on the conventional Max

1962 included a 405-hp version of the V8, with 11.0:1 compression, twin four-barrel carburettors and big valves with heavy-duty dual springs. There were forged aluminium pistons and an aluminium intake manifold, plus header-type exhaust and solid lifter cam. Designed specifically for racing, the 421 came with a forged-steel crankshaft, lightened flywheel, bigger main bearings than standard, and large six-quart oil sump. To cut weight, there were aluminium wings, bonnet and bumper. Some cars actually had holes drilled in the chassis to save weight (the famous 'Swiss cheese' cars) and Plexiglass windows (lighter than real glass). If there was any doubt that the Super Duty Pontiacs were intended for racing, rather than fast road cars, the 1962 manual attempted to make things clear: 'Super Duty Pontiacs are not intended for highway or general passenger car use and they are not supplied by the Pontiac Motor Division

389

ABOVE and OPPOSITE
The outwardly-standard 1964 Pontiac
LeMans lays down some rubber.

full race-kit version of the 413 Max Wedge, known as either the Dodge Ramcharger or Plymouth Super Stock, depending on which car it was powering. Either way, they claimed 410hp with an 11.0:1 compression, or 420hp with the optional 13.5:1. In either state of tune, the 413 came with twin four-barrel carburettors mounted on an aluminium short-ram intake; a streamlined exhaust manifold with 3-inch outlet; forged aluminium pistons; magnafluxed connecting-rods; heavy-duty valve springs and retainers; and a deep, baffled sump.

Offically, of course (to keep within NHRA rules), the latest Max Wedge was for fast road use. 'The engine is designed for maximum acceleration from a standing start,' said Dodge's chief engineer George Gibson, 'and should be excellently suited for special police pursuit work.' One didn't have to search between the lines too carefully to work out what George was trying to say – that the Ramcharger was built for standing quarters, pure and simple! Bona-fide racers also had access to special lightweight panels: aluminium wings, bonnets, bumper brackets and splash pans. And if anyone was in doubt, a boot-mounted battery was optional – there was no reason for that other than to maximize rear-end traction for a scorch down the strip.

But in drag racing, it was necessary to run to stand still, and for 1963 the RB (raised block) engine enabled a capacity boost to 426 cu in (7.0 litres), taking power up to 425hp with that optional 13.5:1 compression. In fact, there were three power options for racing. The base 400-hp engine was intended for stock-car circuit events, with a single four-barrel carburettor; next up were twin four-barrels on a cross-ram manifold with 11.0:1 compression, giving 415hp at 5,500rpm and 470lb ft at

Wedge. The major difference between the two is hinted at in the names: Hemi was shorthand for a hemispherical combustion chamber, which gave the engine its deep-breathing characteristics and allowed space for big valves. The Max Wedge name stemmed from its wedge-shaped combustion chambers, though rated power

was very similar to that of the Hemi.

Launched in 1959 to replace the original Hemi, the Max Wedge first came as 383 cu in (6.2 litres) in a Dodge, or a big 413-cu in (6.7-litre) Chrysler. These of course, were pure street engines, but in 1962 Chrysler responded to the drag dominance of Chevrolet by announcing a

RIGHT and OPPOSITE
A 1967 Firebird, highly modified for drag racing.

4,400rpm. Finally, that high-compression, ultimate Max Wedge: 13.5 compression, twin four-barrel carbs, 425hp at 5,600rpm and 480lb ft at 4,400rpm. The basis for all of these 426 Max Wedges was a new road-going Chrysler unit from 1962, but the Stage II of the following year was intended purely for racing. Although only a modest capacity boost, those extra 13 cubic inches necessitated a new block, new nodular iron crankshaft and bigger oil sump, but were necessary for drag strip wins, as the NHRA had instituted a 427-cu in (7.0-litre) capacity limit on Super Stock for that year.

The Dodges and Plymouths were certainly competitive, and many drivers flocked to use them. Bill 'Maverick' Golden and Roger Lindamood scored notable successes with Max Wedge-powered drag cars. There was even a semi-factory team in the guise of the Ramchargers, which started out as a group of enthusiastic Dodge engineers, who campaigned red-and-white Max Wedge cars to great effect.

The Max Wedge's prodigious power was given an easier time by the fact that Plymouths and Dodges had downsized in 1962, so they were starting from a smaller, lighter base. In the 1950s, Chryslers had been held back from drag-strip success by building the first Hemis into big heavy sedans like the C300, but now the tables had been turned. The logic went further. If a racing Max Wedge (denoted 426R) could be fitted to any Chrysler, it should be to the

Max Wedge had become a Stage III, now in 415- and 425-hp forms only, but both designated 426R (racing only) as a $500 option. Just like the cars, badge engineering was in evidence for otherwise identical Plymouth and Dodge versions. For the record, a Plymouth 426R came with a black radiator fan, where the Dodge's was chromed. Also new for 1964 was the 426S ('Street') with lower-compression (10.3:1) single four-barrel carb, standard exhaust and 365hp, according to Chrysler, though once again they were playing safe – 410hp is thought to be nearer to the mark. Better still, it could be ordered in any Plymouth from the Savoy to the Sport Fury hardtop or convertible, and could still dash to 60mph in less than 7 seconds. Unlike the 426R, it came with a full warranty. For 1965, a new sporting sedan based on the Belvedere, the Satellite, was launched, smaller than the Sport Fury (which was edged upmarket) and effectively Plymouth's new muscle car. There were four street V8s, of 230hp to the 426S 'Street Wedge', but the 426R was still there for drivers serious about drag-strip performance, though as ever it carried no

smallest, lightest bodyshell on the production line. So most racing Max Wedges ended up in the Savoy two-door sedan, the lightest full-sized cars built by Plymouth, or the 330, its Dodge equivalent.

Although a modest car by road standards, with a 426R under its bonnet, the Savoy was formidable, especially when lightened further with aluminium front end and aggressive hood scoops. Chrysler also cut weight by removing non-essentials like the rear seat, arm rests and sun visors, none of which would be of much use on the average drag strip, but made up a considerable amount of dead weight. By 1964, when the Savoy was available, the

THIS PAGE and OPPOSITE
1967 Firebirds, highly modified for drag racing.

warranty. Now with compression slightly reduced to 12.5:1, it was still rated at 425hp, with a NASCAR 'Tri-Y' exhaust system, long-duration cam (320 degrees of overlap) and notched valves.

Take a Deep Breath …
But as Chrysler's ultimate drag motor, that was the swansong for the Max Wedge. Its role was taken over by the latest 426 Hemi, which combined the 1950s Hemi's good breathing with the cubic capacity of the

biggest Max Wedge. Details are in Chapter Four, but it's worth recounting that Chrysler was up to its under-rating tricks again: the new racing Hemi was rated at an ultra-conservative 425hp, the same as the old 426R. The real figure was at least 500hp. But maybe that's the fundamental difference between road and race engines: battling for sales on the high street, road power was constantly talked up (in the days before standardized forms of rating) but in competition, it doesn't do to let the

opposition know exactly how much you're making: best to keep them guessing.

In fact, drag racers had NASCAR racing to thank for making a race-tuned Hemi accessible to them; to be legal for racing, Chrysler had to make several thousand of them, and in 1964 over 6,000 Hemis and Wedges were used in Plymouths and Dodges. They still weren't cheap, at $2,000 for the 425-hp Hemi, or $200 less for the 415-hp motor, but they were state-of-the-art. The engines were also available

over the counter. They justified their price not only by their performance, but also by an exotic specification: compared to the later street Hemis, these had a magnesium inlet manifold for twin four-barrel carburettors; aluminium cylinder-heads and a header-type exhaust system; bigger valves with heavy-duty springs; a 328-degree cam and 12.5:1 compression. Many of these went into the base Plymouth Belvedere coupé. As ever, the drag car of choice for the hottest engine was the lightest available. Despite being temporarily banned from both NASCAR and Super Stock, the Hemi had made its mark, and was here to stay. That was underlined in no uncertain terms by 'Hemi Under Glass', a 1965 special built by Hurst Performance Research Co. as an exhibition car. And exhibition was right. Although based on a 1965 Plymouth Barracuda, its 426 Hemi was mid-mounted, and clearly visible through the Barracuda's large rear window. So when it reared up on the strip, everyone could see what was doing the work, not to mention the 'Bear of a 'Cuda' script painted on its belly pan. A similar mid-engined Hemi, the 'Little Red

RIGHT and OPPOSITE
Drag racers soon became aware of the potential of the GTO. (This is a car from 1965.)

Wagon' was built, based on a Dodge A-100 compact pick-up. Both played their part in making a Hemi the V8 of choice for drag racing.

In 1964 and '65, Chrysler's drag-racing muscle cars became ever more radical, more removed from their production-line siblings. By this time, Chrysler was fighting it out with Ford alone, General Motors having withdrawn from official (and unofficial) support of racing of any kind. That was reflected in the A-990, Chrysler's Super Stock drag weapon of the mid-1960s. The A-990 was either a Plymouth Belvedere or Dodge Coronet, and both had more detail changes than any previous production drag racer from Chrysler.

Under the bonnet was the now-familiar Race Hemi, in its 12.5:1 guise, with magnesium intake manifold. But it was the Belvedere/Coronet body that received most attention. To get the big Hemi to fit, the passenger side shock tower had to be modified, but attempts to slash weight were far more involved. Here Chrysler had a problem, as the NHRA had decreed that steel body panels could no longer be swapped for glassfibre, the quick and easy way to slash weight from heavy steel-bodied cars.

So it kept the sheet metal, but made it as thin as possible: all the body panels were about half the standard thickness, and even the bumper was of thinner steel. Nothing in the rules said they couldn't do that, neither did the rules mention windows, so all of those on the A-990 (apart from the windshield itself) were of acrylic. The quarter windows didn't open, which saved a few ounces, while the door hinges were made of aluminium which saved a few more. As for the body itself, Chrysler didn't only omit the sound insulation, but also the seam filler as well. Inside, two bucket seats were fitted from the Dodge A-100 pick-up. They were small, basic and didn't adjust; they also weighed a mere 22lb (10kg) apiece, so in they went. Mounted on lightened brackets, they sat on carpet with

ABOVE and OPPOSITE
A Pontiac LeMans coupé, plus a Trans Am
tuned engine and lots of extra goodies,
equals Can Am.

no backing or insulation. There was no point in earmarking an A-990 for family outings, as there was no rear seat – the space was covered by a large piece of cardboard, though obviously not the thick and weighty type. Nor were there any door panels, radio, heater, sun visors, coat hooks or interior light. And finally, there was just one windshield wiper, on the driver's side.

Surprisingly, given this austere specification, buyers could still specify an automatic transmission in place of the heavy-duty four-speed manual, though Chrysler's TorqueFlite auto had actually

been used in competition for years. The shift pattern was changed though, to make quarter-miles easier and prevent accidental shifting into revese. NHRA rules specified a silencer, so the A-990 had one, but it was mounted as far back as possible, transversely under the rear bumper, to maximize its weight benefit for rear-wheel traction. For the same reason, a very large battery was mounted in the boot. Although the A-990 resembled a standard Coronet or Belvedere, the wheelbase was actually an inch shorter in either case. The heavy-duty rear springs were mounted so as to move

the rear axle forward an inch, which again put more weight over the rear wheels and maximized traction.

Hood scoop aside, there was nothing else to show that the A-990 was anything out of the ordinary, at least to the casual observer. No 426 badging, no stripes nor fancy wheels, just a car built to do a job. Despite all the changes, they were still eligible for Super Stock, and tremendously successful: at the 1965 NHRA Winternationals, they made up almost the entire class. Bill Jenkins was the quickest on the day, with an 11.39-second time at 126.05mph (203km/h). It goes to show what attention to detail can do.

But impressive though it was, Super Stock wasn't the top class any more. The NHRA had initiated Factory Experimental (FX) as an anything-goes class, in an attempt to keep Super Stocks closer to standard production cars, at least in appearance. There were three sub-classes: A/FX, B/FX and C/FX, allowing for different power to weight ratios, and here again Chrysler made a determined effort to come out on top. FX was to become today's Funny Car class, and allowed chassis as well as engine modifications. Getting as much weight as possible over the rear wheels is crucial in drag racing, and one way to do this is to move the rear axle forward. Chrysler had already done this with the A-990, but took the technique to its logical conclusion in 1965. That year, a few Coronets and Belvederes were built with the rear axle 15 in (38cm) ahead of the standard position, and the front axle 10 inches ahead. These AWB (altered wheelbase) cars were otherwise similar to the A-990. Unfortunately, the NHRA took them to be a step too far, and the AWBs were refused entry. Not that it mattered very much. The NHRA now had a rival, the

Hemi's grand finale came fitted to the smaller Dodge Dart and Plymouth Barracuda. Hotter than the 1967 super stocks, they were built by Hurst Performance, with fibreglass wings and hood, acid-dipped doors and lightweight Chemcor glass in the side windows. Well-known Mopar drivers Ronnie Sox and Buddy Martin ran them in 1968.

Start ing from the Back …

In muscle-car drag racing, Ford was a late developer. It seems odd now, given the company's impressive sporting record later in the 1960s, that for the first few years of the decade, it was simply outclassed. The blame for this is usually laid at the door of divisional general manager, Robert McNamara, who later became more of a household name as President Kennedy's secretary of defence. McNamara wasn't a car enthusiast like Estes or DeLorean, he was a businessman who saw cars as simple, basic transportation, no more, no less. In that respect, he had much in common with the original Henry Ford, and indeed his view has more resonance in the early-21st century, in a world troubled by finite resources, than it ever did in the 1960s.

So under his leadership, Ford took the AMA's 1957 ban on factory involvement in racing very seriously and allowed no factory support for the drag strips or circuits. GM and Chrysler, of course, found various back-door routes to get around the ban (they cheated, in other words), while Ford got left behind.

That all changed after McNamara left to join Kennedy, and was replaced by Lee Iacocca. Iacocca loved hot cars, and his legacy to Ford was the astonishingly successful Mustang. He also approved a new programme of race support. Unfortunately, Ford was having to start

ABOVE
A pre-muscle muscle car: the 1964 Plymouth Fury.

OPPOSITE
A mid-1970s Trans Am with the big 455-cu in (7.5-litre) V8.

American Hot Rod Association (AHRA) which had no such qualms. In AHRA events, the AWBs soon proved the fastest stock-bodied drag racers of all. At their debut at the AHRA Winternationals in Arizona, the winning AWB of Bud Faubel posted a 10.9-second time. In April, Ronnie Sox in an AWB was the first to take a stock-bodied unblown car under 10 seconds, with a 9.98 at York, Pennsylvania. By August, Jim Thornton of the Ramchargers was using Hilborn injection, nitromethane fuel and radically high intake

risers. The result was an 8.91-second quarter-mile.

Less radical were the super stock Coronets and Belvederes built in 1967. Instead of the pure race engine, they used a modified version of the street Hemi, with lower compression; all the panels were of standard thickness. In fact, they were tractable enough to be bought as road cars, albeit with street racing firmly in mind. Nor were they cheap at $3,875 for both WO23 (Coronet) and RO23 (Belvedere), though still affordable. The following year, the

impact-extruded pistons and reinforced connecting rods. There were solid lifters for the high-lift cam, header-style exhaust manifold and aluminium intake, a choice of single or twin four-barrel carbs, with a claimed 425hp at 6,000rpm for the latter, and 480lb ft at 3,700rpm.

But promising as the 427 was, it was still hampered by the Galaxie's avoirdupois. The latest lightweight Fords had all the usual fibreglass panels, and ditched non-essentials like the heater, carpets, spare tyre and so on. Despite all of this, and aluminium bumpers and brackets, the Galaxies were still 150–200-lb (68–90-kg) heavier than the opposition, and the results were disappointing.

It wasn't until 1964, when Ford finally abandoned the Galaxie and fitted the 427 to the smaller, lighter Fairlane, that light began to dawn at the end of Ford's long dark tunnel. With fibreglass body parts, the intermediate Fairlane weighed only 3,225lb (1463kg), which put it into more serious contention; with a 427 under the bonnet it became the drag-racing Thunderbolt, capable of sub-12-second quarter-mile times. Finally, Fords began winning at the strip once again, coming with a Borg-Warner four-speed manual gearbox or beefed-up Lincoln automatic, and once the first few T-Bolts showed their speed, orders flowed in for more; in 1964, Ford built 100 of them. But the Fairlane Thunderbolt's moment of glory didn't last long, for by 1965 the Mustang was common currency, a better proposition for drag racing than the sedan-based T-Bolt. From then on, most of Ford's drag efforts were concentrated on its successful coupé.

But Ford wasn't out of the woods yet. The 427 was a good unit, but Chrysler was busy developing the Hemi, which remained the engine to beat. Ford's answer was an

from the back of the grid, and it was several years before it became a front-runner in drag racing. Its standard big-block V8s, the 332-cu in (5.4-litre) and 352-cu in (5.7-litre) were down on power, though Ford did introduce a tuned 352 Special in 1960. Carburation was limited to one small Holley four-barrel, and despite solid lifters, high compression and special manifolds, Ford's claim of 360hp is thought to be optimistic. As rival engines got larger, so

did Ford's, opening the 352 up to 390 cu in (6.3 litres) in 1961, with up to 375hp, then to 401hp with a triple two-barrel carb set-up. The following year, it was up to 406 cu in (6.6 litres) and 405hp.

Impressive on paper, but the car Ford chose to campaign on the drag strip was the gargantuan Galaxie. This was a heavy, full-sized car, whose sheer weight would put Ford at a constant disadvantage. Dearborn Steel Tubing was commissioned to built 11

lightweight Galaxies for A/FX in 1962, with fibreglass wings, hoods and trunk-lids to shed the pounds.

The first signs of life came with the new 427-cu in (7.0-litre) V8 in 1963. Although it would power thousands of Ford road cars, the 427 was also designed with racing in mind. It fitted neatly under the 7.0-litre limit imposed by the NHRA and NASCAR. It was also immensely strong, with cross-bolted main bearing caps,

THIS PAGE and OPPOSITE
An E-body Plymouth Barracuda, in an
almost fluorescent colour.

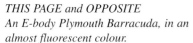

exotic overhead-cam version of the 427. Now this really was a racing special, and it is probable that no 'Cammer' 427 ever found its way into a road car, and most were sold over the counter to established race teams. The Cammer was based on a standard FE 427 block, but with new cylinder heads with one overhead-cam per bank. These were driven by an immensely long timing chain (it measured 6ft/1.8m) and the new heads had hemispherical combustion chambers. It did the trick, producing almost 600hp with a single four-barrel carburettor.

The engine was actually banned by NASCAR, but that didn't stop it from competing in A/FX drag racing; 11 Cammer Mustangs were built. To a casual observer, they looked similar to any other drag-racing Mustang, but the Cammers were very different under the skin. Holman-Moody,

which built the cars, found that the Cammer V8 was much larger and taller than the standard 427, so fitting it was a tight squeeze. (The first Mustang, of course, had been designed to accept nothing larger than a small-block V8.) The front shock towers were cut out altogether and leaf-spring suspension substituted. The rear axle was moved forward 3in/8cm (allowed under A/FX rules) and the entire front end was fibreglass, as were the doors. Deceptively different, the Cammer Mustangs could post 10.6–10.7-second elapsed times. They weren't sweeping the board, but they were fast enough.

But the Cammer Mustang was a horrendously expensive device that bore very little relation to the Mustang one could walk into a Ford dealer and actually buy. The 428 Cobra Jet Mustang was different. In fact, a Ford dealer (Tasca of Providence,

Rhode Island) was the power behind this one; they had squeezed a 428 police interceptor V8 into a standard Mustang to create something that would compete with its muscle-car rivals, something the standard 390GT couldn't. Ford was so impressed, it launched its own 428 Mustang that same year. Fifty of these were built for Super Stock, with some mild weight-shedding measures. No aluminium or glassfibre, but the heater, radio and sound insulation were all omitted. Drum brakes substituted for the road car's discs (they were lighter) and the battery was moved to the trunk. It worked: the Mustang was finally capable of competitive 13-second times, as delivered by Ford, and the Cobra Jet won at its debut event, the 1968 Winternationals.

But like its rivals, Ford began to wind down its drag racing support in the early 1970s. Drag Pack options were offered on

405

the top-range 429 Mustangs and Torinos, bringing oil coolers and suitable gearing. But the days of the exotic factory-built drag racer, with aluminium panels and overhead cams, were finally over.

In at the Finish …

Ford wasn't the only late developer in 1960s drag racing. AMC took the plunge almost as the golden era was coming to an end. Until 1968, AMC officially disapproved of racing and steered well clear of any involvement, but that all changed with the launch of the Javelin and AMX pony cars that year. Aimed at younger drivers, the under-25s, these needed a performance image to have any sort of street credibility, and the answer was to take them drag racing. Before the launch, AMC recruited land speed record holder Craig Breedlove to come up with some suitably impressive figures; he did, taking the 390-cu in (6.3-litre) AMX to 175mph (282km/h) at Goodyear's Texas proving ground.

But drag racing allowed potential buyers to watch AMCs in action, maybe even humiliating the Mustangs and Camaros out on the strip. Hurst Performance Research actually approached AMC with the idea, and helped the company build a series of AMXs for Super Stock. AMC had little experience of tuning for this sort of competition, so many of the parts were bought in. The standard 390-cu in (6.3-litre) V8 used an Edelbrock intake manifold, and 12.3:1 heads modified by Crane Cams. There were Doug headers and the four-speed transmission had a Lakewood bellhousing. Shirley Shahan (the famous 'Drag-On-Lady') campaigned one of these cars.

Alongside the AMXs was the less special SC/Rambler, designed to be a cheap

entry-level muscle car that could run in Super Stock. For just under $3,000, buyers got the top 315-hp 390-cu in V8 in the Rogue two-door sedan, decked out with flashy red, white and blue, plus a massive hood scoop. Again, it was a Hurst collaboration, so there was a Hurst shifter and several other street muscle parts like power front disc brakes, a Sun tachometer and heavy-duty suspension. 'With this car,' went the ad, 'you could make life miserable for any GTO, Roadrunner, Cobra Jet or Mach 1.' Well, perhaps. The first 500 SC/Ramblers sold quickly, so AMC built another batch, then another; in the end just

over 1,500 were made, not enough to worry Ford, but they did a great deal for AMC's image.

But even as SC/Ramblers were rolling off the production line, the era of factory-sponsored drag racing was drawing to a close. For a decade, it had inspired a whole range of muscle cars, some hyper-specials distributed to favoured racing teams, others that anyone could buy from their local showroom. There's no doubt that drag racing and the classic muscle car era fed off each other in the 1960s. But it couldn't last. As the 1970s dawned, it was clear that the Big Three (not to mention AMC) would

have other priorities. There was a new generation of emissions and safety legislation to cope with, the public was questioning limitless power and the 1973 oil crisis put the seal on it. It was the end of an era – but drag racing goes on.

ABOVE
Drag racing improved the performance breed, whatever the car.

OPPOSITE
A 1970 Mustang Mach 1: it took Ford a while to catch up, but it did.

Chapter Ten

SLICING THE AIR:
NASCAR and Trans Am

Drag racing, as we've seen, had a profound effect on muscle-car development, but the same was true of the great American circuit race series of the 1960s, NASCAR and Trans Am. However, the effect was different. Drag-inspired muscle cars sprouted multiple carburettors and lightweight panels, in a sport where brute horsepower was king and weight the ultimate enemy.

In NASCAR, sustained high speed was the key to winning, so more durable motors were needed, and for the first time serious attention was paid to aerodynamics. This led to the most outrageous-looking muscle cars of all time, the Dodge Charger Daytona and the Pontiac Firebird. But comical as they seemed to some, these cars were born of a deadly serious bid for racing success, and were only built in numbers for the street because NASCAR rules said that they had to be.

NASCAR itself changed over the 1960s. At the beginning of the decade, the race cars were little different from those on sale in the showroom. By the end, they were very different indeed; the term 'stock car' was only a nominal one. Dodge had to

OPPOSITE
The good old days at Daytona in 1957, with Fairlane 500s making speed runs on the famous beach.

RIGHT
Daytona 1966. Richard Petty in the Plymouth (43) and Cale Yarborough in the Ford (27) lead the field into Turn One.

BELOW
Chevrolet's Impala was an early 1960s NASCAR contender. Here is Junior Johnson driving a 1966 example, pictured at Goodwood.

build 2,000 Charger Daytonas for general sale, so it did. But they were so expensive and impractical that many sat around on dealers lots unsold. NASCAR's real legacy to street muscle cars was a series of powerful, durable V8s, and new popularity for the fastback style, a spin-off of those all-important aerodynamics.

At the beginning of the decade, Pontiac was the make to beat in NASCAR. Chevrolet had a good couple of years as well, winning 14 Grand National races in 1962 and running Pontiac second, helped by a sloping coupé roofline, more aerodynamic than the average sedan. But really it was Pontiac, with its famed Super Duty performance parts, which made the running. Both GM marques virtually ignored the 1957 AMA ban on factory-sponsored racing, and Pontiac general manager Bunkie Knudsen set up the Super

Duty department specifically to support racers with factory-designed parts. At first, these had to be bought over the counter, but NASCAR rules stipulated that complete engines had to be on sale, so for 1962 Pontiac brought all the special parts together as production-line options, offering the 421 Super Duty V8 on Catalina and Grand Prix cars that year. It all paid off: Pontiac won 30 races in 1961 and 22 in '62, leading the field for two years running.

Ford wasn't about to take this lying down, and was desperately trying to upgrade its FE big-block series into winning form. The 352 Special of 1960, 390 of '61 and 406 V8 of '62 just didn't have the power and durability of the Super Duty Pontiac or Max Wedge Mopars. The

406 in particular had difficulty staying together during an entire NASCAR race. Gus Scussel, one of Ford's race engineers, later recalled the engine's debut at Daytona in 1962: 'Everything broke. Primarily we were losing cylinder blocks…We fixed a lot of things, but it was just a hopeless case.'

So Scussel and several colleagues were put to work on yet another variation of the big-block FE. With this one, the 1963 427 (7.0 litres) they got it right; it was powerful, strong and reliable, moreover it just slotted in under the NASCAR capacity limit. Scussel maintained that much of the extra strength lay in cross-bolted main bearing caps, an idea he first saw in an International Harvester diesel engine. With extruded pistons and forged steel connecting rods,

LEFT
The Bristol 250, 1968. David Pearson, driving the Ford (17), leads Richard Petty in the Plymouth.

BELOW
Daytona 1968: David Pearson trying hard in the Torino.

OPPOSITE
Mario Andretti in his pre-Formula One days, racing in the Yankee 300.

the 427 finally gave Ford a 410-hp motor that stayed together. The big Galaxie may have been too heavy for drag racing, but it was fine at NASCAR, where its fastback body style cut a cleaner hole in the air; the similar Mercury Marauder had the same advantage. With 427s under the bonnet, five Galaxies filled the first five places at Daytona in 1963. Not surprisingly, Ford also won the NASCAR manufacturers' championship that year.

In fact, 1963 was a time of change in the race series. While Ford was coming up to speed, GM was about to instigate its racing ban. To make up for six years of flouting the spirit of that AMA ban, this time GM was serious – no more racing support, back door or otherwise. But in the few months before then, Chevrolet managed a last hurrah with the Mark II big-block V8. It had always been held back in

OPPOSITE
Daytona 1969: David Pearson in a Torino.

RIGHT
*The Riverside 300, Darlington, in 1965,
with Junior Johnson at the wheel.*

NASCAR by the 409 V8. While fine for street or strip, the W-head 409 was hampered by poor breathing at high speeds. The Mark II cured that by moving the combustion chamber from the piston bowl to the cylinder head, and by adding a lightweight valve train, header-style exhaust manifold and bumping capacity up to the NASCAR maximum of 427 cu in (7.0 litres). It won first time out at the Daytona qualifying races, but caused a great deal of controversy. No one knew what was inside this new 'mystery motor', as the press had dubbed it, and tight security at the Chevrolet pit heightened suspicions. The Mark II did actually break the letter of the rules, as it wasn't a production engine. Chevy argued that it would soon be, and won, though they had to sell Ford a couple of Mark IIs to prove it wasn't a one-off special.

In the event, this was all irrelevant anyway. Chevy may have won that qualifier, but top driver Junior Johnson retired from the actual race, and GM's race ban soon followed.

It must have been frustrating for those GM engineers, the ones who had developed the Mark II into race-winning form, but there was nothing they could do. Meanwhile, with General Motors out of the picture, the NASCAR battle was between Ford and Chrysler. AMC, of course, had no official involvement, and no imported car was suitable for full-size NASCAR racing. NASCAR was a uniquely American event, in all senses of the word. Ford was freshly reinvigorated by the strong FE 427 and relatively aerodynamic Galaxie, but what would be Chrysler's reply?

Chrysler's Turn

Chrysler was no stranger to NASCAR success, having scored 27 Grand National wins in 1955, and 22 in '56. The secret of that success was the original Hemi, the deep-breathing V8 with hemispherical combustion chambers that provided space for big valves and copious airflow. Even in the big, heavy 300-series sedans, the 331-cu in (5.4-litre) V8 gave impressive performance, but was dropped in 1959 to make way for the big 413-cu in (6.7-litre) Max Wedge, with its wedge-shaped combustion chambers.

When it became obvious that the Max Wedge was getting left behind at NASCAR, Chrysler engineers were told to produce a new Hemi. Just in time for the 1964 Daytona, they came up with a unit that combined the 426-cu in (7.0-litre) capacity of the Max Wedge with the hemispherical chambers of the original Hemi. It was an instant success, with Richard Petty leading three Hemis home in the first three places, not to mention winning the 1964 championship. Both Plymouth and Dodge used the new Hemi that year, and between them won 26 races.

The trouble was, it was hardly a production engine, although a well-established racer, on good terms with Chrysler, could have one. But if the man in the street thought he could stroll into his Plymouth or Dodge dealer, sign a cheque, and drive out in a Hemi-powered car, he would be sadly disappointed. So NASCAR banned the Hemi from racing for 1965. No one could accuse it of bias; Ford's overhead-cam 427 had been banned as well, and of course the infamous Chevy 'mystery motor' had come under heavy scrutiny. The effect for 1965, without factory involvement from either GM or Chrysler, was that Ford walked away with the manufacturer's championship, taking 48 wins of 55 Grand National races.

This would never do; Chrysler men knew their Hemi had the potential to dominate NASCAR circuit racing, just as it was beginning to do on the drag strips. So they bit the bullet and developed a detuned Hemi for the street. This one really was available as a production option, on the Dodge Charger and Coronet, and the Plymouth Belvedere and Satellite. All one had to do was to tick the right box and shell out another few hundred dollars. Despite the Hemi's fast-growing reputation, there weren't that many takers, mainly because of the high cost of the Hemi option for only a marginal performance benefit over an equivalent big-cube wedge-head.

But as far as Chrysler was concerned, this was incidental. What really mattered was that this esoteric option made the Hemi race-legal again, and in 1966 it roared straight back to the top of NASCAR; Hemi-powered Plymouths won 16 Grand Nationals, Dodges grabbed 18, while David Pearson (Dodge) took the driver's title. But

ABOVE
David Pearson, NASCAR Grand Champion, at the Darlington 400.

RIGHT
Wendell Scot was the only black driver ever to race in the Grand National Championship; he is seen here at the Darlington 400.

OPPOSITE
LEFT
Rebel 300, Darlington, in 1965. Marvin Panch (right) and Junior Johnson (left) battle it out.

RIGHT
Cale Yarborough, after winning the Firecracker 400 at Daytona in 1967.

OPPOSITE
Ned Jarrett (Ford number 11) leads Jack
Bowsher (Ford number 33) out of Turn
Four at the Rockingham 500 in 1966.

LEFT
Nelson Stacy and the Ford he drove at
Daytona in 1963. By that time he had been
racing for 11 years.

it wasn't only down to the Hemi. The Dodge Charger also had a fastback shape that gave it superior aerodynamics, though there was a tendency towards rear-end lift at speed. Chrysler solved the problem with a spoiler option the following year, and being an option on production cars, it was eligible for racing. Ever greater velocities were making high-speed lift a problem, and the age of the spoiler was about to dawn. With spoilers sprouting and the race Hemi still the engine to beat, Chrysler could hardly help but dominate NASCAR in 1967. Add to that the driving talent of Richard Petty, and even his incredible 27 race wins that year (including ten in a row) become understandable. He also bagged the driver's championship along the way.

That was all well and good, but the race wins weren't doing much for Dodge in the showroom; Charger sales actually halved in 1968, and it was thought that the extreme fastback was simply proving impractical for everyday use. It may have looked good, was winning races and slipping through the air cleanly at 160mph (257km/h), but it didn't help visibility or ease of parking. Despite the hype that carefree young drivers and hot-car freaks bought muscle cars, they still had to be practical in order to sell. So for 1968 the

up, and when his contract came up for renewal, decided to talk to Ford.

For 1969, both sides raised the aerodynamic stakes yet again. (NASCAR, by the way, was still a two-horse factory race between Ford and Chrysler; GM was still sitting out, and little AMC's first forays into competition that year concentrated on drag racing and Trans Am). Until then, stock-car racers literally used stock-car bodies; the engines and running gear may have borne little relation to what could be bought in the showroom, but the bodies certainly did. That changed in 1969, when Dodge unveiled the Charger 500. For the first time, a specially-tweaked body style was produced specifically for racing. Five

LEFT
The popularity of pace car replicas reflected the status of NASCAR in muscle-car circles. Here, 1964 and 1994 Mustang pace cars pose on the grid.

BELOW
A three-way battle at the Daytona Firecracker 400 in 1963: Fireball Roberts (Ford number 22), Junior Roberts (Chevrolet number 3) and Tiny Lund (Ford, zero).

OPPOSITE
Richard Petty's Dodge Charger (left) and Buddy Baker's bewinged Dodge Daytona (right) flank Casey Attwood's 21st-century Intrepid R/T.

Charger was toned down, with recessed grille, 'tunnel-back' rear window and coke-bottle flanks. The public liked it, aerodynamicists did not.

Meanwhile, Ford had realized that aerodynamics was the key to beating Chrysler, especially now that the FE 427 was fully-developed and bug-free. So for 1968 the Torino and Mercury Cyclone were restyled with a true fastback, or 'SportsRoof', as they liked to call it. With one smooth curving line from the top of the windshield backwards, the new Torino/Cyclones looked good and cut through the air cleanly. They also provided the magic ingredient to get Ford back into the winner's circle. That same year, the Torino won not only the NASCAR stock-car championship, but the USAC and ARCA series as well, thanks to drivers like David Pearson and Cale and LeeRoy Yarborough. In his autobiography (modestly named, *King Richard I: The Autobiography of America's Greatest Auto Racer*), Chrysler driver Richard Petty admitted that Ford had managed to catch

hundred had to be built (hence the name) to make it race-legal, which would cost Dodge a lot of money. But what the hell, if it beat Ford on the race track, it was worth it. As it happened, Dodge needn't have worried about sales, as the Charger 500's svelte looks ensured that all of them found new owners very quickly. Maybe it even had a beneficial effect on Chargers in general, as nearly 100,000 were sold that same year.

The actual development of the Charger 500 was accomplished by Creative Industries, whose work underlined the fact that aerodynamics depends as much on detail as on a good basic shape. Creative Industries smoothed out the Charger's contours, and replaced the tunnel-back rear window with a flush one. The grille was now flush too, with exposed headlamps, in place of the standard recessed grille and hidden lamps. The result was a far cleaner shape than the standard Charger, and if the trunk opening was restricted by the smooth, clean roofline, well, one couldn't have everything.

Ford, of course, had not been idle while all this was going on, and for the same season unveiled its Torino Talladega. Like the Charger 500, this used detail changes to clean up the airflow; the Torino could already be had with a fastback SportsRoof. The nose was extended a little, curving down to meet a new flush grille. Under the nose, the sheet metal extended beneath the car, cleaning up the airflow. As a final touch, a smaller, slimmer front fender was fitted, actually a modified Torino rear fender. These were not major changes, but the Talladega ended up six inches longer and one inch lower than the standard SportsRoof. The name, incidentally, came from the new NASCAR speedway in Alabama, which would host the first round of the 1969 season. In case anyone was still

wondering what the smoothed-out Torino was actually for, there was a Mercury equivalent, the Cyclone Spoiler II, again with a reworked nose, but with the addition of a rear spoiler and a standard 351-cu in (5.7-litre) Windsor V8. In the Mercury tradition, it was sold with more luxury trim than the relatively spartan Talladega.

Ford built 750 or so Talladegas, for which the standard power unit was Ford's 428-cu in (7.0-litre) Cobra Jet. None of the customer cars was fitted with the new Boss 429-cu in unit, as this was homologated for racing in the Mustang. Racing Talladegas also got the 429 early in the season, but although it had been designed from scratch for racing, there were doubts concerning its durability. Many racers actually stuck with the FE 427, ageing though it might have been, but it was a proven, strong performer that won races.

So of these 1969 aerodynes, which proved best on the banking? Well it was bad news for Chrysler, after all that painstaking work cleaning up the Charger. The 500 proved better than its predecessor, but was not fast enough to catch the Talladegas, and Ford took the title again that year.

Drastic action was needed, especially as Ford had the new 429 race engine, as well as the fast, sleek Talladegas. While the 1969 season was running its course, Dodge had been working hard on another

LEFT
Richard Petty.

OPPOSITE
In November 2000, Dodge announced a return to NASCAR, with the Intrepid R/T.

LEFT
Muscle cars were raced in England, too. At a wet Brands Hatch in 1963, Dan Gurney's Galaxie leads the Jaguars.

OPPOSITE
History repeats itself: in 2000, Elliot Sadler's Taurus ran in the same colours used by Tiny Lund in 1963.

aerodynamic racer, but this one was more extreme and more outrageous than anything seen before (or since, if truth be told). It was the Charger Daytona, first of the 'Winged Warriors.' With its race debut at Talladega in September 1969, the new car made a huge impact. One could hardly miss its long, drooping, pointed nose and sky-high rear spoiler. Eighteen inches longer than the standard Charger, its weird looks did serve a purpose, as the Daytona was capable of 200mph (320km/h), and the two-foot-high spoiler made a good job of keeping the car on the ground. It also won that debut race at Talladega; as ever, the race power unit of choice was the faithful Hemi.

Just over 500 Daytona Chargers were delivered to dealers between June and September 1969, making it race-legal. In theory, it could be used for the school run or for shopping, but a very thick skin was needed. This was the age of flamboyant muscle cars that came in bright colours, but for most people the Daytona was just too far out, whatever its success on the race track. That was underlined in 1970 when

LEFT
Muscle cars racing in Canada. Here is the eventual winner, Eppie Wietzes (94), in his Camstock Mustang GT350, at St. Jovite.

OPPOSITE
Darrell Waltrip drives a demonstration lap at Talladega in this Mercury in the October 2000 event. It was the same car used for his first Talladega race in 1972, and which Mario Andretti won with at Daytona back in 1967.

did their job. Bobby Isaac won the 1970 championship in a Daytona, while Plymouth tempted Richard Petty back from Ford with the promise of a Superbird drive; he won 18 races for them that year. But Chrysler's winged beasts failed to herald a new era of ever more outlandish NASCAR racers. Ford tested a radically restyled Torino, the King Cobra, but decided it could not justify the cost of building 2,000 of them, some of which (as Chrysler knew only too well) were liable to linger embarrassingly on dealer forecourts for a very long time. The truth was that the major manufacturers now had other things to worry about besides racing: keeping up with the new legislation on emissions and safety needed money and manpower, resources that could no longer be devoted to NASCAR or indeed any other sort of racing. Still, the Winged Warriors were quite a finale.

TRANS AM
Trans Am – the Trans-American Sedan Championship – kicked off in 1966, as a means of giving pony cars a chance at

NASCAR ruled that 500 cars weren't enough any more: to homologate a design, it was necessary to produce one for every dealer in the network. For Dodge, that meant 2,000 Daytonas had to leave the production line, and they did.

By then, the Daytona had been joined by a very similar-looking Plymouth Superbird, though this was based on a Road Runner rather than the Charger. If one looked closely, one could see that the rear

wing was even taller and at a more extreme angle. However, it didn't help sell cars. News was now coming through from people who had bought Daytonas in previous years. Extrovert drivers may have been able to cope with the stares, and guffaws of disbelief, but the Daytona still ran hot in traffic (the cooling was fine at 200mph, however) and was a little tricky to park, if one couldn't find a big enough space), none of which was cured in the

1970 versions, which still commanded a premium price; at $4,298, a Superbird cost $1,000 more than the Road Runner convertible. Some Daytonas or Superbirds were still sitting on dealers' lots, and some were actually converted back to standard spec, the freaky nose and rear spoiler removed before anyone would buy.

But on the racetrack, which as far as Chrysler was concerned was the whole point of the exercise, the Winged Warriors

circuit racing. The early Mustangs and Barracudas had their following, but they were outclassed by the NASCAR heavyweights; they needed a race series of their own.

Trans Am became exactly that, and for a few short years in the late 1960s was a fierce battleground where factory-backed Z28s, Cougars and Javelins fought it out. Factory-supported cars became ever more exotic as the rules were bent ever tighter. Just like NASCAR and NHRA Super Stock at the time, Trans Am became a symbolic battle for muscle car precedence between the Big Three, plus AMC. But, again just like its sibling series, Trans Am rapidly lost its factory backing in the early 1970s, reflecting the fortunes of the muscle cars themselves.

The story begins in the mid-1960s, when some folk began to circuit-race the new pony cars. The Sports Car Club of America (SCCA) was already running amateur events, chiefly for imported sports cars at the twistier circuits rather than the ovals. For 1966, the new Trans Am series ran two classes: under 2 litres for the BMWs, Alfa Romeos and MGs; over 2 litres for Mustangs, Barracudas, Darts and Corvairs.

As with the early NASCAR, these had to be production cars that were on sale to the general public, though here again, Trans Am mirrored NASCAR and Super Stock as the most competitive cars rapidly became exotic one-offs, far removed from what actually available in the showroom. There was also a 305-cu in (5.0-litre) capacity limit, which suited Ford fine (its 289-cu in (4.7-litre) V8 could have been designed for Trans Am), as well as Pontiac (273-cu in (4.4-litre). GM was less well prepared, as the smallest V8s from Pontiac and Chevrolet (326 and 327 cu in/ 5.3 litres)

were too big. However, all four marques, not to mention AMC, were soon producing engines especially for Trans Am, to slot in just under that 305-cu in limit. That alone showed just how important the series had become in a few short years.

Early on in Trans Am, the pony cars did not make a dramatic showing. Alfa Romeo won the inaugural 1966 overall championship, with Ford second. Of those early pony-car racers, there's no doubt that the Mustang was king. Carroll Shelby had realized early that Lee Iacocca's baby had racing potential, and one of his GT350R Mustang's won the SCCA's B-Production Class Championship in 1965.

In those early days, before the Big Three woke up to Trans Am's potential, it was a largely amateur affair. Drivers were mainly enthusiasts with day jobs, who would work late into the night peparing their own cars. Sponsorship, if there was any, came from local dealers and clubs. Mustang driver Jim Whelan worked for a Ford dealer, so was able to buy his car at cost, but he couldn't make any big changes. 'It was basically strip the interior out,' he

OPPOSITE
Celebrating the Hemi: Chrysler CEO and
Group President Dieter Zetsche, and
NASCAR's great Richard Petty, flank a
Hemi V8 at the Chrysler museum.

RIGHT
The 1967 Daytona 500, and Mario Andretti
enjoys the victor's spoils. That year, he
drove a Holman-Moody Ford.

later recalled, 'put a roll bar in – you didn't have to have a full cage – and go racing…The privateers could afford to compete with the factories, because the rules were so limiting.'

Everything changed in 1967. Interest in Trans Am increased rapidly as new pony cars came on to the market – the Camaro, Firebird and Cougar in that year alone. Crowds increased, and the number of races went to 12 from just seven the previous year. Trans-Am's high-profile era was about to begin.

GM was first to take advantage of the situation; despite its self-imposed ban on official support for any sort of racing and the SCCA's ban on factory-backed teams, GM was first with a pony car designed to contest Trans Am. Even before the new Camaro had been publicly launched, Chevrolet had been working on a Trans Am-friendly version. It combined a 327 block with a 283 crankshaft to produce a capacity of 302 cu in (4.9litres). Tuned to the eyeballs, the Z28 (the name came from its option package designation) came with a high 11.0:1 compresson, solid lifters, big valves, high-flow Holley carburettor and

aluminium intake manifold, enough for 290hp at 5,800rpm. To complement the motor, there was a close-ratio four-speed transmission, heavy-duty suspension, Quick Ratio steering and better brakes. Everything in fact, to make a standard Camaro competitive on track. Of course, it still wasn't race-ready, but the basis was there. A mere 602 Z28s were sold that first year, but it went on to win two Trans Am championships, and the badge itself gained

sufficient cachet to sell over 20,000 cars in 1969 alone.

Roger Penske's team recognized how hard GM had worked on the Z28, and campaigned two of them in that 1967 season. Mark Donohue and Craig Fisher scored its first win, at the Marlboro Speedway in August. But by season's end, the Z28s had been bested by the unlikely Mercury Cougar. Unlikely, because the Cougar was basically a plusher, more

upmarket brother to the Mustang – heavier and less aerodynamic. However, it also had the same strong, well-developed 289-cu in (4.7-litre) V8; moreover, Mercury had put a great deal of effort into Trans Am that year; Bud Moore's shop ran the factory cars, with drivers like Dan Gurney and Peter Revson.

The effort paid off with several wins (including Gurney's at Green Valley Raceway, where he took the chequered flag just three feet ahead of Parnelli Jones) and

427

OPPOSITE
The Shelby GT350 Mustang of Roger West and Richard Macon, at the 1966 Daytona 24 hours.

RIGHT
The St. Jovite Trans Am, 1969. George Follmer (16), and his Bud Moore Mustang, with Mark Donohue (Penske Sunoco Camaro).

BELOW
Parnelli Jones drove a Mercury at the 1964 Grand National.

only lost the overall championship by two points. And the winner that year? Jerry Titus in a Shelby Mustang; the Shelbys had had an extra season's experience in Trans-Am, and it showed. In any case, 1967 was Mercury's brief moment of glory. Parent company Ford decided to concentrate its corporate funding on racing Mustangs, rather than allow this in-house rivalry. Still, Mercury was able to capitalize on its racing glory with the road-going XR-7G. The 'G' stood for 'Gurney', and the XR-7 came with fake hood scoops, fog lamps and racing mirrors.

The Z28 Camaros may have finished third in the 1967 championship, but swept all before them in '68. Mark Donohue won ten of the 13 races, scoring twice as many points as his nearest rival. One of those was new to Trans Am, indeed to racing, that year; AMC. American Motors had been

OPPOSITE
The Bridgehampton Trans Am c.1970.
George Follmer (16) and his Bud Moore
Mustang.

ABOVE
Kent Trans Am 1969. George Follmer (16)
and Parnelli Jones (15) in their Mustangs.

forced to take racing seriously after launching its own Mustang rival, the four-seat Javelin and two-seater AMX. For true muscle-car credibility, that meant taking part in Trans Am. Knowing that only a determined assault would have any hope of success, AMC splashed out a big budget on boring out its 290-cu in (4.7-litre) V8 to 304 cu in (5.0 litres) and enlisting top drivers George Follmer and Peter Revson.

They didn't win a single race, but did secure six second placings, which was not bad for a first season; in any case, AMC's glory days were to come.

By 1969, competition in Trans Am was reaching fever pitch, with the Ford, Chevy and AMC-sponsored teams willing to bend the rules (actually to break them) in order to win. Here are just a couple of examples. Penske hit on the idea of squeezing more

fuel into his Camaros by packing it in dry ice. Freezing the gas (which made it shrink) enabled 23 gallons to be fitted into a 22-gallon tank. No rule said that it was forbidden, but it wasn't the sort of thing a privateer team could afford to contemplate.

Then there were parts that kept to the letter of the rules, but not the spirit. These called for doors that opened; on at least one Mustang, the door would indeed open, but

only if one loosened off the bolts holding it closed. 'It was a gutted shell. But it would open, to meet the rules,' recalled its owner/driver Jim Whelan. Then there was rule-breaking, pure and simple; some of the quickest Mustangs were actually 7/8 scale models of the real thing, with acid-dipped body and chassis to shave the weight. 'The

cars didn't look quite right,' said Jim Whelan, 'but the tech inspectors could not figure out why. You had to put a substantial roll cage in to keep the car together.'

Ford were certainly taking Trans Am success seriously. Following the 302-cu in Z28 Camaro, the company came up with its own Boss 302 motor. It was more hard-

edged than the Chevy, with very high lift cams that needed careful running in, huge valves and ports and a reported rev ceiling of 10,500rpm on the works cars. There were exotic touches like a hybrid wet/dry oil system and stainless steel O-rings instead of conventional head gaskets. Hardly road cars, but Ford duly built 1,000

ABOVE
Parnelli Jones, shown here driving a Mustang Boss 302, stayed with Ford until 1970.
OPPOSITE
The Kent Trans Am c.1967, with Dan Gurney in the Bud Moore-prepared Mercury Cougar.

432

Boss 302s to qualify them for Trans Am. There was more new metal from Pontiac, with the Firebird facing its first full Trans Am season in 1969. The division was developing its own 303-cu in (4.9-litre) engine, but in the meantime fitted Chevy Z28 units, which helped it grab third place in the manufacturer's championship, while

Firebird-driving Jerry Titus was third-placed driver. To celebrate its Trans Am entry, Pontiac announced a special Firebird, the striped and spoilered Trans Am, but ironically this car, the longest-lived muscle-mobile of them all, was not a Trans Am race special like the Z28 or Boss 302. Not until 1982 did a car with the Trans Am

badge win the championship whose name it bore; by then, it was a very different car, and a very different series.

Despite all this effort by Ford and Pontiac, Mark Donohue won the championship in his Z28 for the second year running in 1969. He had much tougher opposition this time, notably from Parnelli

Jones in the Bud Moore Boss Mustang, who won two races that year – but Donohue still scored six wins. The Firebird (as we've seen) was third, but AMC was dogged by reliability problems and could manage only fourth.

So far, one of the Big Three had been conspicuous by its absence – Chrysler. But

ABOVE
Parnelli Jones driving one of the effective Bud Moore Mustangs, at Watkins Glen in 1969.

OPPOSITE
Frantic activity in the pits at Kent in 1967.

for 1970 there was a rebodied Barracuda and Dodge Challenger, which seemed like the ideal time to go racing to promote them. The signs looked good, with Dan Gurney and Swede Savage signed up to drive, and a new 304-cu in (5.0-litre) V8, (basically a destroked version of the existing 340-cu in (5.5-litre) unit.

In the meantime, there had been a relaxation of the rules; Trans Am racing engines no longer had to be exactly the same as the road units from which they were derived. So the homologation cars – the Plymouth AAR 'Cuda and Dodge Challenger T/A, used the original 340-cu in (5.5-litre) V8 in place of the special 304,

though it still came with high-performance heads and a strengthened block, just like the racers', plus 'Six-Pack', three two-barrel carburettors. Complete with all the usual additions, like front and rear stabilizer bars, wide wheels and tyres, spoilers and stripes, over 2,700 AAR 'Cudas were built in 1969. 'AAR', incidentally, came from

But that was the high point of the Trans Am glory days. Within a couple of seasons, all the big factories had pulled out, leaving the series much as it had started, relying on privateer teams, and making up more affordable racing. In November 1970, Ford U.S.A. announced that it was bringing its involvement with all types of motor racing to a close. Latecomer Chrysler planned to run 'Cudas and Challengers in 1971, but eventually it too decided to pull out.

That left the field pretty well clear for AMC in 1971, with Firebirds as the only other factory-backed cars. Mark Donohue duly won seven of the ten races that year, taking the championship easily, with Javelin driver George Follmer doing the same in 1972. AMC made the most of these wins, offering production Javelins in the same red, white and blue stripes of the race cars, and a series of high-profile ads. But after its two championships, even AMC decided to pull out of Trans Am, and that really was the end of an era for this showcase of muscle-bound pony cars.

'All American Racers', the name of Dan Gurney's team. For Dodge dealers, there was a similarly engined and equipped Challenger T/A.

It all looked very promising, but in practice the 'Cuda/Challenger proved a little too large to be competitive in Trans Am. They needed to be big, to cope with a wide range up engines up to the substantial 426 Hemi, but chassis development wasn't the best either. They finished the season fourth (Sam Posey) and fifth (Savage) in the driver ratings. AMC had a happier 1970, with Mark Donohue in the Javelin (he'd finally defected from that Z28), losing the championship by just one point to Parnelli Jones in the Boss Mustang. The AMC cars were now reliable as well as fast, and with the experienced, talented Donohue at the helm, made a very strong combination.

ABOVE
A Camaro Indy pace car.

OPPOSITE
Ronnie Bucknum makes a pit stop at the Kent Trans Am, c.1967.

INDEX

Photographic Acknowledgements

All photographs supplied by Garry Stuart, other than the following:

Chrysler: pages 6, 18, 19 all, 186, 187 all, 188, 189, 190, 191, 192, 193, 314, 315, 316, 317, 318, 319, 324, 325, 326, 327, 328, 329 all, 344, 345, 346 all, 347
Ford Motor Company: pages 9 below, 20 both, 21 all, 78, 79 both, 87 all, 88, 89, 90, 91, 92, 93 all, 320, 321, 322, 323 both, 330, 331
General Motors: pages 94, 106, 107 all, 112, 114 both, 115, 116, 118, 119, 120, 121, 212, 213, 214, 215, 216, 217, 219
Mike Key: pages 10 all, 11 all, 24, 25, 28, 29 all, 50, 51, 240, 241, 242, 243, 278 all, 279, 280, 281, 282, 283, 288, 289, 290, 291, 294, 295, 296, 297, 298, 299 all, 300, 301, 302, 303, 304 all, 305, 306 all, 307, 308 both, 309, 310, 311 all
The Ludsvigsen Library: pages 68 all, 69 all, 195, 202, 203, 211, 226 both, 227 all, 233, 234, 235, 236, 374 all, 375, 209
Andrew Morland: page 16